D1311381

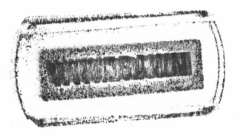

Strategic Defense and the Western Alliance

Strategic Defense and the Western Alliance

Edited by

Sanford Lakoff
Randy Willoughby

Institute on Global Conflict
and Cooperation,
University of California

 Lexington Books
D.C. Heath and Company/Lexington, Massachusetts/Toronto

 Institute on Global Conflict and Cooperation
University of California

Library of Congress Cataloging-in-Publication Data
    Strategic defense and the western alliance.

        Papers were presented at a conference cosponsored
by the Friedrich Ebert Foundation of the Federal
Republic of Germany and the Institute on Global Conflict
and Cooperation of the University of California in May
1986.
        Includes index.
            1. Strategic Defense Initiative—Congresses.
2. Ballistic missile defenses—Europe—Congresses.
3. North Atlantic Treaty Organization—Congresses.
I. Lakoff, Sanford A.   II. Willoughby, Randy.
III. Friedrich-Ebert Stiftung.   IV. University of
California Institute on Global Conflict and Cooperation.
UG743.S75   1987   358'.1754   86-46358
ISBN 0-669-15839-9 (alk. paper)

Published simultaneously in Canada
Printed in the United States of America
Casebound International Standard Book Number: 0-669-15839-9
Library of Congress Catalog Card Number: 86-46358

The paper used in this publication meets the minimum requirements of
American National Standard for Information Sciences—Permanence of
Paper for Printed Library Materials, ANSI Z39.48-1984.
    ∞ ™

87   88   89   90   8   7   6   5   4   3   2   1

Contents

Preface and Acknowledgments

With the exception of the introduction and the contribution by Nathan Rosenberg, the papers assembled for this book were presented at a conference on "The Strategic Defense Initiative and West Europe" held in San Diego and cosponsored by the Friedrich Ebert Foundation of the Federal Republic of Germany and the Institute on Global Conflict and Cooperation (IGCC) of the University of California in May 1986. In the planning of the conference, Peter Schulze represented the Ebert Foundation and Sanford Lakoff the IGCC; Randy Willoughby served as conference coordinator. The IGCC's contribution was comprised of funds provided by the Carnegie Corporation of New York to Lakoff and Herbert F. York for a three-year study of the implications of the deployment of weapons in space. The assistance of the corporation (and of Fritz Mosher in particular) is gratefully acknowledged, as is that of various individuals who also helped make the conference manageable: M. Larry Lawrence, president of the Del Coronado Hotel, where the conference took place; the staff of the Del Coronado Hotel; Arlene Winer and Sue Greer of the IGCC office; and Kelly Charter, who typed the book manuscript.

The paper by Herbert F. York was commissioned as the Corliss Lamont Lecture for 1986 at Harvard University; it is being used here by kind permission of those in charge of this lecture. Nathan Rosenberg's paper was presented in an earlier version at a conference in Lucca, Italy, and has been recast for this book. All presentations at the conference in San Diego were revised to take account of the stimulating comments and criticisms made by other participants, who are listed at the end of the book.

The essays in this book reflect a variety of opinions. A deliberate effort was made to solicit contributions that would reflect diverse viewpoints. The aim was to encourage independent exploration, not to achieve consensus. The introductory essay attempts to provide a synoptic view and to highlight some of the contentious issues that emerged in the give-and-take of the conference. These issues are likely to become even more salient when and if decisions must be made to deploy some of the technologies now being developed. The purpose of this book is to probe the possible consequences before fateful decisions must be made.

Abbreviations

ABM	antiballistic missile
ACCS	Air Command and Control System
AEC	Atomic Energy Commission
A/C	aircraft
ALCM	air-launched cruise missile
ANZUS	Australia-New Zealand-United States
ARPA	Advanced Research Projects Agency
ASAT	antisatellite
ASMP	Air-Sol Moyenne Portée (air-to-surface medium-range missile)
ASW	antisubmarine warfare
ATBM	antitactical ballistic missile
ATM	antitactical missile
AWACS	Airborne Warning and Control System
BAOR	British Army of the Rhine
BM	battle management
BMD	ballistic missile defense
C²	command and control
C³	command, control, and communication
C³I	command, control, communication, and intelligence
CDE	Conference on Disarmament in Europe
CDU	Christian Democratic Union
CIA	Central Intelligence Agency
CSCE	Conference on Security and Cooperation in Europe
CSU	Christian Social Union
CTB	Comprehensive Test Ban

DARPA	Defense Advanced Research Projects Agency
DEW	directed-energy weapons
DEW	distant early warning
DIVAD	Division Air Defense Gun System
DT&E	development, test, and evaluation
EAD	extended air defense
EAR	Export Administration Regulations
EC	European community
ECM	electronic countermeasure
EDI	European Defense Initiative
EMP	electromagnetic pulse
ERIS	Exoatmospheric Reentry Intercept System
Eureka	European Research Coordination Agency
EVI	Europaische Verteidigungsinitiative (*see* EDI)
FAA	Federal Aviation Administration
FBS	forward-based systems
FDP	Free Democratic Party
FOFA	Follow-On Forces Attack
FNS	Force Nucléaire Stratégique
F.R.G.	Federal Republic of Germany
FY	fiscal year
G.D.R.	German Democratic Republic
GDP	gross domestic product
GLCM	ground-launched cruise missile
GNP	gross national product
Hawk	Homing All-the-Way Killer
HEDI	High Endoatmospheric Defense Interceptor
HEDS	High Endoatmospheric Defense System
HOE	Homing Overlay Experiment
ICBM	intercontinental ballistic missile
IEPG	Independent European Program Group
IFF	Identify Friend or Foe
IFRI	Institut Français des Relations Internationales (French Institute of International Relations)
IHEDN	Institut des Hautes Etudes de Défense Nationale

IRBM	intermediate-range ballistic missile
IISS	International Institute for Strategic Studies
INF	intermediate-range nuclear forces
IOC	Initial Operational Capability
ITAR	International Traffic in Arms Regulations
LEDI	Low Endoatmospheric Defense Interceptor
LEDS	Low Endoatmospheric Defense System
LPAR	Large Phased-Array Radar
LRTNF	long-range theater nuclear forces
MAD	mutual assured destruction
MARV	maneuverable reentry vehicle
M(B)FR	mutual (and balanced) force reduction
MFS	Mittleres Fla-Rak-System (medium-range SAM)
MIRV	multiple independently targetable reentry vehicle
MJ	megajoule
MT	megaton
NADGE	NATO Air Defense Ground Environment
NASA	National Aeronautics and Space Administration
NATO	North Atlantic Treaty Organization
NNK	nonnuclear kill
NPT	Nonproliferation Treaty
NSF	National Science Foundation
NST	Nuclear and Space Talks
OECD	Organization for Economic Cooperation and Development
R&D	research and development
RITA	Réseau Intégré de Transmissions Automatiques (Integrated Network of Automated Transmissions)
RPR	Rassemblement Pour la Republique (Rally for the Republic)
RV	reentry vehicle
SAGE	Semi-Automatic Ground Environment
SABM	Systems Analysis and Battle Management
SALT	Strategic Arms Limitation Talks
SAM	surface-to-air missile

SATKA	Surveillance, Acquisition, Tracking, and Kill Assessment
SCC	Standing Consultative Commission
SDI	Strategic Defense Initiative
SDIO	Strategic Defense Initiative Organization
SDP	Social Democratic Party (U.K.)
SEWS	Satellite Early Warning System
SLBM	submarine-launched ballistic missile
SLCM	sea-launched cruise missile
SNDV	strategic nuclear delivery vehicle
SNF	short-range nuclear forces
SPD	Social Democratic Party (F.R.G.)
SRAM	short-range attack missile
SRINF	short-range intermediate nuclear forces
SSAF	Surface/Sol Air Futur (future surface-to-air missile)
SSBN	ballistic missile submarine, nuclear-powered
SST	Supersonic Transport
START	Strategic Arms Reduction Talks
SUAWACS	Soviet Union Airborne Warning and Control System
TABM	theater antiballistic missile
TACMS	Tactical Missile System
TBM	theater ballistic missile
TNF	theater nuclear forces
UDF	Union Pour la Democratic Française (Union for French Democracy)
UNCD	United Nations Committee on Disarmament
USAF	United States Air Force
USDR&E	Undersecretary of Defense for Research and Engineering
VHSIC	Very High Speed Integrated Circuit

Strategic Defense and the Western Alliance

1

Strategic Defense on the Alliance Agenda

Sanford Lakoff
Randy Willoughby

After it seemed to have been removed from the military equation by the ABM Treaty of 1972, strategic defense has again become a major item on the agenda of the Western Alliance. Revived by President Ronald Reagan in his "Star Wars" speech of March 1983, and implemented in his Strategic Defense Initiative, it has achieved renewed emphasis in military spending, in alliance research efforts, and in arms control negotiations. SDI is packaged in a way that makes it the largest single item in the Department of Defense's annual budget.[1] It engages researchers in industrial and military laboratories on both sides of the Atlantic as well as in Japan and Israel. In the arms control negotiations now under way between the United States and the USSR, the conduct of this research and its implications for the strategic balance and for the reduction of offensive weapons are critical considerations. The implications of this largely unexpected development are the subject of the chapters in this book.

That strategic defense would acquire such prominence on the agenda of the alliance was not obvious even for some time after SDI was launched. In 1983 and 1984, the European allies of the United States were far more concerned with such issues as the need to improve conventional forces; proposals for a nuclear-weapons-free zone and for a policy of no first use of such weapons; and, in particular, the Euromissile controversy. In keeping with its previously adopted "dual track" decision, NATO was proceeding with deployment of intermediate missiles while simultaneously expressing a willingness to negotiate the removal or reduction of intermediate missiles on both sides. The Soviet withdrawal from the negotiations in 1983 effectively reduced the decision to the single track of deployment, and a strong campaign of opposition was mounted by groups pressing for disarmament. In this context, many Europeans found President Reagan's call for a defensive shield at best wishful thinking that could only divert attention from the far more pressing problem of controlling the threat of offensive weapons. Even Prime Minister Margaret Thatcher, often bitterly criticized at home for her partiality toward the Reagan administration, has lately been blunt enough to refer to the hope that space-based defenses would eliminate nuclear weapons as "pie in the sky."[2]

In 1985, however, SDI quickly became the leading item on the alliance agenda. As John Newhouse reported in a summer issue of the *New Yorker,* "Obsessive is a fair description of the state of mind into which the Star Wars project . . . has maneuvered European governments."[3] The change of attitude had several sources. As the Euromissiles were successfully deployed and the effort to overturn the dual-track decision failed at the polls, European governments could afford to be less preoccupied with lingering protests. The reelection of President Reagan guaranteed that his skills in public persuasion and legislative arm-twisting would be exercised to assure that SDI became a well-entrenched program while he was still in the White House. An office had been created within the Defense Department to oversee the program, with a budget that was scheduled to expand dramatically, and would almost double between FY 1985 and FY 1986. Several well-publicized experiments seemed to show that the aims of the project were not altogether wishful. The Reagan administration, having neglected to consult its allies in advance of the decision, now became anxious to obtain their endorsement—if only to prove to domestic critics that the program would not disrupt or destroy the alliance.

For their part, the governments of Western Europe had to decide whether to oppose the U.S. initiative and thus risk antagonizing the Reagan administration, or accede to it, even if they could not endorse its aims with enthusiasm, in order to preserve good relations with the United States and avoid being shut out of the technological progress the program might stimulate. Several considerations were paramount in persuading them to join the program. Because the goals were ambiguous, a decision to accede meant only to express a willingness to cooperate in a research program that might or might not have radical consequences. Some European politicians hoped, as Ernst-Otto Czempiel points out in chapter 8 of this book, that the technological challenges would expose the futility of the project and spare them the need to break openly with the United States. They knew that a positive decision might also encourage the Soviets to return to the bargaining table, and that SDI could be a useful bargaining chip in the negotiations. As Pierre Lellouche notes in chapter 7, the governments of the U.K., France, and the Federal Republic of Germany (F.R.G.) are all on record as favoring a deal on SDI in exchange for deep cuts in offensive weapons. They also calculated that European adhesion to the program would help steer it toward the objective of defending vital NATO military assets rather than toward the more ambitious goal of defending populations, on which President Reagan and his spokesmen had been insisting.

These and related considerations produced similar responses from all the major Western European governments, with variations reflecting national styles and concerns. In the U.K., Foreign Secretary Sir Geoffrey Howe questioned the program thoroughly and incisively, but the government then reverted to the usual pattern of its special relationship with the United States by negotiating a memorandum of understanding.[4] Although this conciliatory attitude failed to win a guarantee of a fixed share of research contracts, the Thatcher government was reassured that British industries would be fairly treated. Officials of the French government have explicitly criticized the strategic rationale of the program, and President François Mitterrand launched his European Research Coordination Agency (Eureka) program to promote European collaboration in civil technologies. At the same time, however, the French government quietly encouraged its leading high-technology firms to take part in the SDI program. In West Germany, Defense Minister Manfred Wörner endorsed a European Defense Initiative but sharply distinguished its aims from those of SDI. Because of its special sensitivity to East-West relations, the Bonn government remains particularly anxious about the impact of SDI on the prospects for détente. Following assurances from Washington that deployments would not take place without further discussions with the allies and with the Soviets, the F.R.G. dispatched its economics minister, Martin Bangemann, to sign a memorandum of cooperation with the United States, and leading German high-technology firms have become SDI contractors.[5] Although Norway, Holland, and Denmark have decided not to take part officially, Italy and Israel have agreed, and Japan has also indicated that it will participate in the program. The net result is that at least to some extent SDI has become an alliance project and not simply a U.S. initiative.

This is not to say, however, that strategic defense has yet been truly assimilated by the alliance. As the program becomes better defined and requires more of a share of defense budgets, and especially if deployment decisions must be faced, it will become an increasing source of concern in Europe. Whether NATO can manage all the ramifications SDI may unleash as it has managed other challenges remains to be seen. Already, SDI has revived long-standing European anxieties. Among these is the fear that the United States will retreat from Europe into Fortress America—this time behind a space shield. Alternatively, if the United States does not disengage itself from Europe, a robust defense capabilty could increase its willingness to risk "limited" or conventional wars that could embroil its European allies. Far from trusting the U.S. invitation to share in research on SDI on an equal footing, many Europeans fear that the United States will treat European companies as subcontractors. In all these respects, as a British observer has correctly noted, "Star Wars, like a rubber hammer, has revealed that the old reflexes are still very much alive and kicking."[6]

It is conceivable, nevertheless, that a somewhat successful SDI could reenforce the cohesiveness of the alliance. After Sputnik, a determined U.S.

effort to overcome a perceived Soviet lead was needed to overcome a crisis in European confidence in the ability of the United States to defend Europe. Similarly, a U.S.-led initiative in defensive technologies could be reassuring to some Europeans who fear that the United States will not respond to a continuing Soviet military buildup. If SDI enhances the European effort to develop extended air defenses, and if it leads to deployments of ballistic missile defenses aimed at protecting vital NATO assets—as the Hoffman Report envisaged as the first step in a "defense transition"—the result might be to "recouple" Europe and America.[7] At a minimum, further industrial cooperation would assuage European fears that SDI is intended to give the United States a competitive economic edge over Europe.

These issues are addressed in detail in the chapters of this book. While there is inevitably some redundancy among them, they may conveniently be grouped into five overlapping perspectives:

1. *The impact of SDI on superpower relations.* In the next chapter, Herbert F. York's analysis of the competition between the United States and the USSR in the development and deployment of defensive technologies since World War II considers the lessons to be drawn from past experience and the novel problems posed by the effort to build space-based defenses. In chapter 10, John P. Holdren considers the consequences of a renewed offensive and defensive arms race for strategic and crisis stability and for arms control.

2. *Conceivable deployments of defense technologies designed for the European theater.* In chapter 3, Gregory H. Canavan offers a detailed technical review of the technologies that could be deployed in Europe or with effects on European defense, with special emphasis on the defense of military targets against short-range nuclear and conventional attacks. François Heisbourg, in chapter 4, examines the European effort to achieve the more limited goal of extended air defense—or defense against conventional missile attack.

3. *The impact of SDI on alliance strategy.* David S. Yost, in chapter 5, and Pierre Lellouche, in chapter 7, examine the likely impact of superpower competition with regard to defensive technologies on such key strategic issues as the credibility of extended deterrence, flexible response, and the role of arms control. Their contrasting views highlight the very different evaluations that can be made concerning the impact of the revival of strategic defense on Western strategic thinking.

4. *The political and strategic impact of SDI on the major Western European powers.* In chapter 6, Trevor Taylor examines the possible consequences for the independent deterrents of the U.K. and France, while Ernst-Otto Czempiel, in chapter 8, emphasizes the impact of SDI on the German role in NATO and on German attitudes toward the alliance with the United States.

5. *The economic consequences.* In chapter 9, Nathan Rosenberg examines in detail the question of civil economic benefits and costs by considering

SDI in the light of previous experience, while Heisbourg and others discuss the possible consequences of SDI research, positive and negative, for the economies of the alliance.

The Global Perspective

The question of the likely effects of SDI must be posed first in the context of the global competition between East and West as it has been affected by the advent of nuclear weapons. Since World War II, international relations have been conditioned by the rivalry between the two superpowers and the blocs they have built up through incorporation and alliance. Nuclear weapons began to influence the superpower conflict almost immediately after the weapons were developed. Once they were available to both sides, these weapons began to transform the character of warfare, as Bernard Brodie was among the first to recognize. In 1946, Brodie argued that nuclear weapons were "absolute weapons" designed not for use but for deterrence.[8] In the United States, Brodie's contention that military strategy should be designed to achieve deterrence, not to confer capability for winning wars, was shared by some military leaders but rejected by others, who continued to regard atomic weapons as simply the latest technology for fighting wars. This belief persists among some strategists, who remain convinced that even if deterrence fails, the better-prepared side can still "prevail" in a nuclear war; but in general U.S. military and civilian strategists emphasize reliance on deterrence by threat of nuclear retaliation. Like most Americans, Western Europeans have tended to embrace this belief as the only sensible rationale for the possession of nuclear arsenals. In the USSR, by contrast, military planners persisted in the belief that the military ability to resist aggression was the best means to deter an attack and that such military means should be designed in the expectation that they would confer victory.

It was only after U.S. Secretary of Defense Robert McNamara sought to persuade Premier Kosygin to abandon the view that defense is good because it does not kill that the Soviets agreed to enter into negotiations to ban the deployment of ABM weapons above a certain minimal limit. The Soviets may well have done so out of fear that the United States would develop a superior system, but whatever the motive, the result was that both sides accepted a situation of mutual vulnerability to attack in the event that deterrence failed. Because of the ABM Treaty, however, each side knows it can count on its offensive forces to dissuade the other from attacking, and both sides can consider scaling down those offensive forces, or at least not increasing them, as would have been necessary if defenses had been deployed.

The ABM Treaty, however, does not rule out research by both sides or the upgrading of existing systems. As York points out, both the United States and the USSR have pursued efforts of research in defensive systems since World War II. One difference is that the Soviet effort has been continuous, while the U.S. effort has come in spurts. Another is that the Soviets have actually deployed an extensive system of defenses, mainly against air attack. These defenses are significant, as York observes, because the forces they are directed against carry more than half the megatonnage in the U.S. arsenal. Their effect has been to stimulate American weapons designers to develop penetration aids, including stealth technology, standoff weapons, and cruise missiles. Another indirect result has been the reduction in the megatonnage the U.S. bomber fleet can deliver.

The net result is that defenses have not served their intended purpose of negating or diminishing the effectiveness of the offense. In that sense, the expenditures have been wasteful. An arms race costing $400 billion—measuring only Soviet air defenses and U.S. bomber responses—has not led to any significant change in the strategic relationship of offense to defense.

Will SDI simply repeat the failures of past efforts by stimulating new efforts to overcome defenses? York fears that the effort to build space-based defenses could pose unprecedented issues and raise new operational problems. The extremely short operational time—milliseconds in the counterdefensive mode—necessarily takes "man out of the loop," thus removing the possibility of human intervention to distinguish accidents from attacks or to resolve crises before they escalate to full-scale conflict. The commingling of the systems could result in their mutual destruction, and the placement of these systems in low earth orbits over the airspace of the adversary might be considered unacceptably intrusive, thus provoking political tensions and possibly a preemptive attack. In addition, the reopening of the defensive arms race in full form would stimulate a possibly still more expensive effort on the part of both sides to perfect offensive weapons capable of overwhelming and penetrating any defense and antisatellite weapons whose specific function it would be to disable the space-based elements of a defense.

The impact on strategic stability is another debatable consequence. Proponents of strategic defense argue that it would be stabilizing, both in crisis and strategic terms, because it would introduce a new calculus of uncertainty into the planning for the use of offensive weapons. Holdren disagrees, arguing that the deployment of even an imperfect defense would have to be construed by an adversary as an offensive rather than a defensive measure. Even an imperfect defense could be used to attack the adversary's defenses and to absorb a ragged retaliatory strike, and would therefore be destabilizing. Holdren notes that "many Soviet leaders and analysts at least genuinely fear—even if they are not completely convinced—that the United States is pursuing superiority and would like a first-strike capability, if not to execute such a strike then at least to intimidate the Soviets with the prospect." In his view, moreover, SDI will not only prevent an agreement to reduce arms but could well result in the collapse of the existing arms control regime.

The potential role of SDI in complicating and possibly preventing progress in arms control was shown dramatically at the Reykjavik talks in October 1986, when the leaders of the superpowers could not agree on a common interpretation of the ABM Treaty limits on development and testing. This disagreement may have been more semantic than fundamental, or even a pretext for blaming the other side for intransigence, but the fact remains that the project has thrown a new bone of contention into arms-control negotiations.

Conceivable Deployments of European Defense Technologies

Within the context of superpower relations, SDI entails certain ramifications for the defense of Europe which are to some extent separable from the larger considerations. Canavan provides a survey of the ways in which defensive technologies can conceivably be configured at the theater level, and notes the numerous improvements in these technologies in recent years. He asserts, for example, that the ability to harden radar systems and make them disposable and mobile has solved the problem of radar vulnerability—the Achilles heel of earlier versions, at least with respect to the low endoatmospheric regime. Theater defenses also appear to pose a less complex problem than building a more comprehensive missile defense. The burnout velocities of short-range missiles are much slower than those of ICBMs, making interception easier in spite of shorter reaction times. Because of their lower apogees, short-range missile warheads also experience greater atmospheric drag, thus facilitating discrimination of warheads from decoys if not precluding the use of decoys altogether. Canavan argues that given the prospects for the survivability of such defensive systems, defensive deployments in the European theater will not promote instability during a crisis or provoke an arms race. He is clearly more optimistic about the survivability of such defenses than are many critics. It is also interesting to note that although SDI has been promoted as a non-nuclear program, Canavan's assessment appears to favor a mixed deployment of conventional and nuclear interceptors.

Although the Reagan administration sees more limited defensive efforts for Europe as part of the larger SDI effort, Europeans see them differently. Heisbourg argues that while the technological and architectural elements have much in common, the missions for which extended air defense (EAD) and SDI are designed are completely different. Extended air defense is necessary to prevent a Soviet attack with highly accurate conventional missiles from destroying vital NATO assets located in rear areas, targets difficult to make survivable by other means. It would not be expected to limit damage from a nuclear attack and will not employ nuclear interceptors. Heisbourg sees the project as an extension upward of tactical air defenses and points out that improvements in the NATO Air Defense Ground Environment (NADGE), Homing All-the-Way Killer (Hawk), and Nike-Hercules systems were envisaged by NATO planning well before SDI was conceived.

European proponents of EAD are often eager to dissociate this project from SDI in order to ward off domestic political criticism. They may also fear the opportunity costs associated with SDI: long-standing NATO programs have been chronically underfunded, and the glamor of SDI could result in their continued neglect.

The Impact on the Alliance

The perceived implications of SDI for the unity of NATO are also worrisome. Mainly for this reason, Lellouche is as categorically critical of the SDI program as Holdren. "Three years after President Reagan's March 23, 1983, speech," he writes, "one has yet to hear a single convincing argument as to why an SDI world would be better for Euopean security and NATO." He argues that the program guarantees a new spiral in the arms race and eliminates the Selective Employment Options strategy upon which extended deterrence depends. Although Lellouche observes that most Europeans would welcome an arrangement combining deep reductions of offensive forces with a reaffirmation of the ABM Treaty, he himself appears to see arms control more in political than in strategic terms. The Soviets represent a formidable threat to the alliance, he contends, less because they could launch a "bolt out of the blue" attack than because they can exploit tensions within the alliance. SDI provides them with another wedge to use against Western unity. The best evidence that they see it in this way, according to Lellouche, is that they have returned to the negotiating table at Geneva after an unusually clumsy performance in attempting to use the intermediate-range nuclear forces (INF) controversy to split the alliance, and have offered a flurry of proposals promising détente and total disarmament in order to promote difficulties among the allies. Paradoxically, however, some Europeans fear that the United States will strike a bargain with the Soviets aimed at eliminating nuclear weapons, regardless of the consequences for the alliance. In Lellouche's perspective, what matters are the political rather than the strategic implications, since he assumes that in the foreseeable future deployments can have no fundamental strategic effect.

Yost offers a very different assessment of the potential value of SDI for NATO, based on the belief that Soviet defenses could well undermine the premises of the ABM Treaty. Like the Reagan administration, he argues that the size and pace of Soviet ballistic missile defense (BMD) activities make it clear that these activities reflect a long-standing commitment with strategic bearing. Independently of SDI, the Soviets have modernized their ABM system around Moscow and have produced large quantities of rapidly deployable radars and surface-to-air missiles (SAMs) with potential BMD capability. A large Soviet advantage in BMD, particularly in view of the important increases in Soviet offensive power over the past two decades, would enhance Soviet control over the escalation process and would increase the chance of a Soviet conventional victory. Yost argues that "the SDI program might deter any Soviet inclination to capitalize on this superior capability to deploy traditional BMD systems." In this light, he argues, "The West should prepare its own BMD deployment options, including ATBM in Europe."

Implications for Europe

More particularly European concerns include the impact of SDI on the independent nuclear forces of France and the U.K. and on the domestic political balances of the various countries, particularly the F.R.G. The independent nuclear forces have themselves been the subject of an important intra-alliance debate. In the early 1960s, the United States disparaged independent forces, although the British force was presumably exempted, in view of the assistance the United States lent to their program. This double standard with respect to U.S. and other national nuclear forces, combined with preferential treatment toward the British, contributed to French alienation from the United States and withdrawal from the military organization of the alliance. During the 1970s, however, the United States formally acknowledged the contribution of these independent forces to NATO deterrence; more recently, it has endorsed their modernization.

Although one would expect that the impact of SDI, or, more to the point, the expansion of Soviet defense, on the viability of these forces would be damaging, it is not clear that the impact would necessarily be very significant. To the extent that French and British targeting policies are primarily countervalue in orientation, limited Soviet defense and antisatellite (ASAT) capabilities should not pose a major threat to the credibility of these independent forces. Taylor points out that the French and British have already been required to design their deterrents to take account of Soviet strategic defenses. Both responded by deemphasizing the air component of their strategic nuclear forces and, later, by upgrading the penetrability of their missiles (Chevaline and M-4). SDI has made the Trident more acceptable in some British circles and has led the French to announce increased funding for penetration aids, but both governments continue to express confidence in the viability of their arsenals for their projected missions. It is possible that SDI will actually facilitate rather than complicate the task of the nuclear forces by diverting Soviet resources into countering rather than matching U.S. defenses. On the other hand, should the independent forces be reoriented toward more flexible and selected targeting objectives, the impact of widespread defenses in the USSR would be much more substantial.

The viability of the alliance's nuclear forces can be threatened not only by Soviet defenses but also by domestic opposition to nuclear deterrence. Public commitment to a national security agenda is an essential, if neglected, element of strategy.[9] Lellouche expresses the concern that the antinuclear, antideterrent rhetoric of the SDI program may undermine this commitment by bolstering the arguments of the European peace movements. Ironically, Holdren expresses the opposite concern that the program has defused the momentum of the freeze campaign and the Catholic bishops' letter.

Actually, these two possibilities are not necessarily incompatible. Certainly, the European movements are much more strongly committed to disarmament (and to neutralism in the Cold War), whereas the U.S. movement is more pragmatically oriented toward traditional arms-control objectives. In the United States, moreover, the president's initiative is credited with having resurrected the Geneva negotiations. The ability of the European disarmament movement to exploit SDI may depend on the degree to which Europeans perceive it as something foisted on them against their will. The absence of any American connection in the development of the *force de frappe* helps explain the absence of a strong peace movement in France. By contrast, U.S. association with the British strategic force and with the INF in Germany has contributed to domestic coalitions in both countries which question the value of the alliance. Czempiel points out that the number of West Germans preferring equidistant relations between the F.R.G. and the United States and the USSR over closer relations with the United States rose by about twenty percentage points between 1982 and 1986—an obvious by-product of the INF controversy. His sketch of the reactions to the SDI program in the various factions of the major parties indicates that this trend may not have reached its limits. As in the U.K., support for SDI is precarious. Only fringe elements of the ruling conservative parties express unequivocal support for the program, while the more moderate elements of the governing coalitions have expressed deep reservations. The opposition leftist parties have voiced strong criticism of the program and contain advocates of an "alternative" defense posture that places less emphasis on the U.S. connection.[10]

Although the alliance has survived challenges from peace movements and the election of leftist parties with ties to these movements in the past, it is far from certain that this pattern will continue to hold. SDI could represent the coup de grace in a setting that seems less threatening to the Western Alliance than the early years of the Cold War. The recent separation of New Zealand from the former ANZUS (Australia-New Zealand-United States) alliance could be a harbinger. Thus far, as Taylor notes, SDI has not had a major impact on public opinion. The ultimate test may come when and if the technologies move from the laboratories and test ranges to real deployments.

Economic Consequences

Another important dimension of the SDI program, particularly for the alliance, is the economic relevance of defense spending. European leaders appear almost unanimous in the judgment that the SDI program, whatever its military merits, will generate a spate of spillovers that will stimulate the American economy at the expense of Europe. Once the United States decides to mobilize its resources around a particular research program, as Lellouche notes, "the alternative for European high-technology firms is either to join in or to be sure to perish at some later stage." Commercial tensions have frequently contributed to alliance acrimony—the nonproliferation and gas pipeline episodes in the past two U.S. administrations are recent cases in point. The preeminence of commercial considerations in the European view of SDI was symbolized by the dispatch of the German economics minister to Washington to negotiate participation in the program. Czempiel suspects that a primary interest of the United States in these negotiations was to enforce stricter German export standards; the Robinson affair in the U.K.—involving an American official who was accused of checking on British firms involved in SDI research—was cited as evidence of Strategic Defense Initiative Organization (SDIO) meddling in foreign commercial affairs. Heisbourg considers the EAD program as a European industrial and technological counterpart to SDI and as an opportunity to increase intra-European industrial collaboration. If successful, such collaboration could have a strong positive impact on the efficiency of NATO defense spending. Unfortunately, the actual record of European cooperation has typically been one of underfulfillment. Discussions between the French and Germans over a Hawk missile replacement have been difficult, even though the modular nature of the project would facilitate a division of labor and procurement of the U.S. Patriot would be extremely expensive. The ambitious Eureka program also looks to be a disappointment.

These European failings might nevertheless look rosy by comparison with the economic consequences of SDI. Rosenberg examines the record of commercial spillovers from military research and development in the postwar American economy and concludes that the SDI program is unlikely to have a positive impact and may even have a negative one. He argues that although there is some evidence of technological spillovers in the aircraft and electronics sectors, the prospect of military procurement played a much more productive role than did research and development funding. Moreover, as Rosenberg points out, military R&D is likely to play an even smaller role in the civilian

economy in the future because of the divergence between the design requirements of the two sectors and the tremendous cost of an increasing number of
military features. (Even Porsche drivers in states that impose hefty fines for
speeding are unlikely to become customers for stealth technologies.) Rosenberg indicates that large-scale military projects may already produce negative
spillovers, such as inefficiency and work-force distortions. The difficulty of
measuring these effects in advance makes a large investment in SDI a high-risk
economic gamble which could result both in a weakened American economy
and in embittered American allies.

Conclusions

The net impact of these considerations of alliance politics, economics, and
strategy is not easy to assess, especially because of the many technological
uncertainties. The destabilizing implications of a long-term shift in strategy
may ultimately be of less concern to most Europeans than the more immediate impact of SDI on political relations with the Soviets. On the strategic
front, however, it is worth remembering that misgivings in Europe over the
adoption of the policy of flexible response did not produce irreparable harm
to the alliance, and, in fact, European governments are now campaigning to
rescue flexible response from the threat of SDI. The importance of the political concern is reflected best in Czempiel's references to the Harmel Report,
emphasizing both defense and dialogue, and to the even more emphatic
reminder of Henry Kissinger that there is no alternative to détente. Even if
Yost is correct in arguing that NATO should prepare to deploy ground-based
defenses as a hedge against Soviet creepout from the ABM Treaty, effective
unilateral abrogation of the treaty by the United States would surely have grave
consequences for the political cohesion of the alliance. Now that strategic
defense has begun to assume such a prominent role on the agenda of the
alliance, whatever is done in its name must take account of all the ramifications as well as of the differing interests and perceptions of the member states.
SDI may be an American initiative, but strategic defense is now a problem for
the entire alliance, as the chapters in this book make abundantly clear.

Notes

1. James Gerstenzang, *Los Angeles Times*, July 13, 1986, page 1, reported that
the FY 1987 request for SDI was $5.4 billion (of which $3.53 billion was approved by
Congress.) The next largest single request was for $2.8 billion for the procurement of
F/A 18 aircraft.
2. *Times* (London), March 28, 1986.

3. John Newhouse, "The Diplomatic Round (Europe and Star Wars)," *New Yorker*, Vol. LXI, No. 22 (July 22, 1985), pp. 37-54.

4. Howe delivered his speech to the Royal United Services Institute in London on March 15, 1985; it was reported in the *Times* (London) on March 22, 1985, according to the *Foreign Bulletin Information Service–West Europe*, March 25, 1985.

5. Manfred Wörner, "A Missile Defense for NATO Europe," *Strategic Review* (Winter 1986), Vol. 14, No. 1, pp. 13-20.

6. Ian Davidson, "A New Jerk in Old Reflexes," *Times* (London), May 28, 1985, p. 17.

7. U.S. Department of Defense, *Defense Against Ballistic Missiles, Assessment of Technologies and Policy Implication* (Washington: D.O.D., April 1984), p. 22.

8. Bernard Brodie, *The Absolute Weapon* (New York: Harcourt, Brace, 1946), *passim*.

9. See Michael Howard, "The Forgotten Dimensions of Strategy," *The Causes of War* (Cambridge, Mass.: Harvard University Press, 1984).

10. See, for example, Andreas von Bülow, "Defensive Entanglement: An Alternative Strategy for NATO," in Andrew J. Pierre, ed., *The Conventional Defense of Europe: New Technologies and New Strategies* (New York: Council on Foreign Relations, 1986).

2

Strategic Defense from World War II to the Present

Herbert F. York

Philosophers have often wondered whether lessons can be drawn from history. Hegel was skeptical, but Santayana warned us, in a famous aphorism, that we ignore such lessons at our peril. Unfortunately, whatever philosophers may say about the virtues of drawing such lessons, it is no easy matter to make use of them. A good example is the effort to develop strategic defenses by the United States and the USSR. In certain respects, there are clear lessons that can be drawn from past experiences—lessons that are not without cautionary value. The difficulty is, of course, that history never repeats itself so exactly that we can be sure these lessons will apply to future situations. Both conclusions apply, as I shall try to show, to the attempt to understand the implications of the current SDI proposal in the light of previous similar efforts.

During the postwar period, each of the superpowers has twice undertaken a major effort to develop and deploy a strategic defense of its homeland. President Reagan's March 1983 speech has set in motion a fifth try.

Each of the two Soviet efforts has been characterized by steadiness in purpose and in spending, and each continues to the present day. Each of the two prior American efforts was characterized by a decade-long burst of activity, followed by a protracted period of neglect.

In this chapter I will present brief "case studies" of each of the four earlier efforts and the reaction of the other superpower to each one. I will then attempt to use this brief historical review to derive lessons that may be of help in predicting the possible strategic effects of the fifth case, President Reagan's SDI. After that I will turn to those particular features of the SDI which are unique to it, or which have no analogue in the prior cases, and will speculate about their potential effects on the future strategic situation.

Four Historical Cases

Case 1: Soviet Air Defense, World War II to the Present

The Soviet attempt to build an effective air defense against the U.S. air offense is by far the largest of its kind ever undertaken. At present, Soviet strategic air defense forces are made up of 635,000 men, a force almost as large as the entire United States Air Force (USAF). They operate approximately ten thousand surface-to-air missiles (SA-1, 2, 3, 5, 10, X-12), some twelve hundred interceptors, ten thousand radars of various sorts, thirteen Airborne Warning and Control System- (AWACS) type aircraft, and a Command, Control, Communications, and Intelligence (C³I) system presumably appropriate to the purpose. These defenses are deployed in locations which make clear that their purpose is to defend the entire country, including population, industry, and general military resources, as well as the strategic offensive forces. Maintaining such an air-defense system and developing new equipment for future systems would cost us, if we were to do the same thing, approximately $24 billion (in 1986 dollars) annually. (I intend to include here all the costs of strategic air defense: operation, maintenance, procurement, and R&D.) Working backwards, it is reasonable to estimate that the Soviets have been spending approximately the same fraction of their GNP on this program element for the last decade or so (see figure 2-1).

Today, as throughout the entire postwar period, the major fraction of U.S. strategic offensive power is deployed on aircraft. This is true whether this power is measured in megatons or by its capacity to kill people and destroy things. The obvious basic purpose of Soviet air defense is to blunt a U.S. air attack to the maximum degree possible. This purpose is not different from the aim of SDI, which focuses its entire attention on the Soviet missile force—the component that carries the major fraction of the USSR's offensive power. (In making this comparison of purposes, I ignore purely utopian or polemical statements about what the ultimate aims may be.)

In the period 1955-65, the United States responded to the Soviet air defense program with special vigor. In order to assure penetration, the United States undertook the simultaneous development of two supersonic aircraft (B-58 and B-70), two intercontinental cruise missiles (Navaho and Snark), several standoff missiles (Skybolt, Hound Dog, and SRAM) and a variety of electronic countermeasure (ECM) devices and techniques. In addition, the Pentagon also carried out the development of five different long-range ballistic missiles, weapons that were seen at the time as the certain and final answer to any Soviet attempt to intercept a U.S. strategic air attack. At its peak, the annual cost of all these programs exceeded $10 billion in 1986 dollars. This was, roughly speaking, about the same as the Soviets were then investing in air defense. (In this case, I intend to include only costs of those actions directly responding to Soviet air defense, not the general expense of maintaining the U.S. offense.)

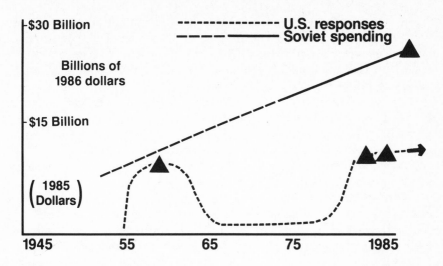

Now consists of:

635,000 men
SAMS: 10,000-SA1, 2, 3, 5, 10, X-12
Interceptors: 1200
Radars: 10,000
SUAWACS: 13 A/C

U.S. responses:

1955-65	1980s
ICBMs	SRAM
B-58	ALCM
B-70	B-1
Navajo	Stealth
Snark	ECM
B-52 + Houndog	
Skybolt	
ECM	

Source: This figure is derived from many different sources. My estimates of Soviet spending are based on data from several editions of *The Military Balance* published by the International Institute for Strategic Studies (IISS); estimates of Soviet procurements presented in the FY 1985 report of the Undersecretary of Defense for Research and Engineering (USDR&E); and in R.M. Gates and L.K. Gershwin, "Soviet Strategic Force Developments," testimony before a Joint Session of the Subcommittee on Strategic and Theater Nuclear Forces of the Senate Armed Services Committee and the Defense Subcommittee of the Senate Appropriations Committee, June 26, 1985. My estimates for the U.S. response are based on various reports to the Congress by the Secretary of Defense and USDR&E, particularly for FY 1981 and FY 1986.

Figure 2-1. Soviet Air Defense

By 1965, the United States had essentially accomplished its basic purposes, and spending on systems specifically designed to enhance penetration dropped to a level between $1 and $2 billion in 1986 dollars per year. Even in 1980, the last Carter year, the United States was still spending only approximately $1.5 billion for this purpose, mostly on long-range standoff missiles—air-launched cruise missiles (ALCMs)—and stealth technology. In the Reagan years, U.S. spending in reaction to Soviet air defenses jumped back up to about $10 billion annually. In the early 1980s, most of this amount went to procure B-1s. In the latter 1980s we can speculate that the purchase of Stealth bombers and other advanced systems will require about the same annual expenditure. The value of the current U.S. inventory of air offense forces is $50 billion.

Throughout the postwar period there has never been a time when the commanders of the U.S strategic forces were not confident they could cope successfully with Soviet air defenses. Twice—once in the late 1950s and then again in the early 1980s—the United States has felt compelled to mount a major effort to ensure continuing penetration, but there has never been any substantial doubt that the warheads in the U.S. arsenal would be delivered successfully.

Case 2: Soviet Missile Defense, 1960 to the Present

The Soviets initiated a program to develop and deploy an antiballistic missile defense (ABM) in the late 1950s, shortly after the United States initiated its intercontinental ballistic missile (ICBM) programs (see figure 2-1). In the 1960s, various systems believed to have this capability were deployed near Tallinn (SA-5), Leningrad (Griffon), and Moscow (Galosh). Of these, the SA-5 is no longer considered to have an ABM capability, the Griffon was abandoned, and only the Moscow system remains deployed today. It originally consisted of an early type of ABM called the Galosh, but these are now being replaced by new silo-based systems known in the West as the SH-04 (an exoatmospheric interceptor) and the SH-08 (a high-acceleration endoatmospheric system). These missiles are supported by a remote early warning system consisting of eleven "hen house" radars and five large phased-array radars (and, perhaps, eventually by the notorious new one at Krasnoyarsk), plus a larger number of locally deployed "dog house," "cat house," and other battle-management radars. In keeping with the 1972 ABM Treaty and its 1974 Protocol, the Soviets have limited the deployment of such missiles to one site at Moscow with no more than a hundred launchers.

In addition to this modest deployment, the Soviets have been conducting a very substantial ABM development program throughout the last twenty-five years. The Sary Shagan test range, located in Central Asia, supports this activity.

The level of effort the Soviets devote to this development program cannot be explained solely by a desire to defend only Moscow with a force limited to no more than a hundred missiles. Its purpose has to be to stay up-to-date in an area of technology the Soviets have always considered, and still do consider, very important. As recently as 1985, when pressed about why the Soviets continue to maintain and improve the Moscow system, a senior Soviet defense official replied to the effect that doing so enabled them to have practical, real-world experience with a very important weapon system. Otherwise, they would have experience with it only under experimental test range conditions, and they wanted more than that. None of the forgoing is evidence that the Soviets are planning to "break out" of the present constraints, but the magnitude of the effort shows clearly that they are keeping all their options open. It is important to note that the Soviets were pursuing these particular options long before the current revival of U.S. interest in strategic defense.

A reasonable estimate of what the Soviet program would cost the United States is several billion 1986 dollars per year, with the cost peaking modestly in the 1960s and now again rising above the average figure (see figure 2-2). These amounts are substantially more than the United States was spending on corresponding programs in the years immediately preceding 1983. If we again set aside utopian statements of purpose, the basic goals of the Soviet ballistic missile defense (BMD) program seem not to be substantially different from those of the SDI program.

The U.S. response to Soviet BMD developments has always emphasized penetration aids. In the early 1960s, multiple independently targetable reentry vehicles (MIRVs) were considered to be the ultimate "pen-aid," and the United States has relied on them for that purpose ever since. In addition, the United States has always maintained modest research programs devoted to the development of penetration technology more generally, including decoys and other countermeasures. U.S. expenditures specifically devoted to overcoming Soviet missile defenses have always been much lower than the cost of the defenses themselves.

It is commonly said that the installation of strategic defenses by one side will lead to an expansion of the strategic offensive forces of the other side. In neither of the two cases discussed so far did this happen. The total number of U.S. strategic delivery vehicles—aircraft plus intercontinental ballistic missiles (ICBMs) plus submarine-launched ballistic missiles (SLBMs)—has remained essentially constant since 1955. The continuing expansion and improvement of Soviet strategic defenses since that time has not led to any increase whatsoever in this number. Instead, the entire U.S. reaction to Soviet missile defenses has always focused on assuring successful penetration by existing forces.

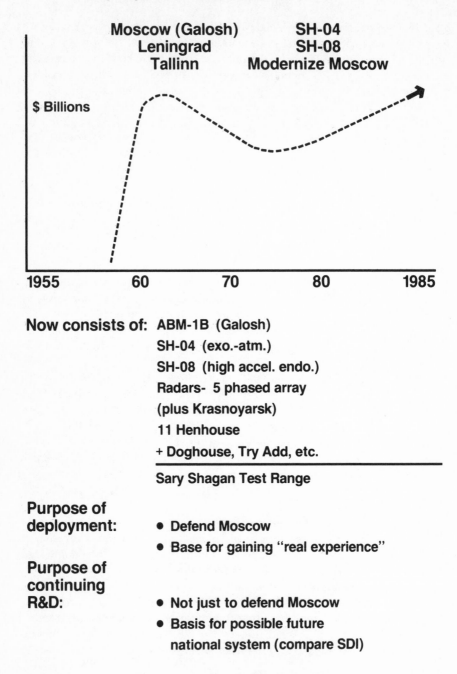

Now consists of: ABM-1B (Galosh)

SH-04 (exo.-atm.)

SH-08 (high accel. endo.)

Radars- 5 phased array

(plus Krasnoyarsk)

11 Henhouse

+ Doghouse, Try Add, etc.

Sary Shagan Test Range

Purpose of deployment:

● Defend Moscow

● Base for gaining "real experience"

Purpose of continuing R&D:

● Not just to defend Moscow

● Basis for possible future national system (compare SDI)

Figure 2-2. Soviet Missile Defense

Case 3: U.S. Air Defense, 1950–1965

The first U.S. effort to deploy strategic defenses came in response to a quick series of unwelcome technical surprises. In 1949 the Soviets exploded their first A-bomb; in 1955 they exploded their first H-bomb; and in 1956 they deployed their first long-range bombers, the so-called Bears and Bisons. The United States responded by attempting to construct an effective continental air defense system. By the late 1950s, the United States was putting in place extensive deployments of surface-to-air missiles (SAMs) and interceptor aircraft, all backed up by several lines of warning radars, mainly in the north. To provide the necessary command, control, communications, and intelligence (C³I) for these systems, the United States was planning to install a complex system call SAGE, which stands for Semi-Automatic Ground Environment. The essential core of SAGE itself was to consist of a small number of complex centers—perhaps six—housing large, powerful computers. These computers would analyze the data from the various sensors and then tell the interceptors— aircraft and SAMs—where to go and what to do.

By 1960 it had become evident that the task was hopeless. The Soviets had successfully developed their first-generation ICBM, and the United States was estimating that they would soon deploy many hundreds of them, and eventually, perhaps, thousands. The SAGE centers would be few in number and highly vulnerable, so it seemed likely that they would be among the first targets of a missile attack. And once they were removed, Soviet aircraft would essentially have a free ride. There seemed to be no way out of this and similar problems, so the United States, in effect, decided to abandon air defense at the very beginning of the missile era. At its peak in 1957, U.S. spending on air defenses (again in 1986 terms) reached nearly $10 billion (see figure 2-3). By 1962, spending on air defenses had already dropped to a small fraction of that amount, and it has fallen further since. The Alaska radar net and the Pinetree line (in Southern Canada) remain, but the mid-Canada line ceased operation in 1965. The United States now has no SAMs defending its territory or military bases, and only about three hundred interceptor aircraft, most of which are operated by the Air National Guard.

It is difficult to determine what the Soviet reaction, if any, to U.S. air defenses has been. Early on, even before the United States did, they placed their main emphasis on long-range ballistic missiles. That may have been done in anticipation of U.S. air defenses, but there is no concrete evidence to support this inference. More recently, the Soviets have started to equip their Bear bombers with long-range standoff systems (the ALCM-15). This action is probably a response to U.S. defenses, since their main value is that they make it unnecessary for the bombers themselves to penetrate close in to defended targets.

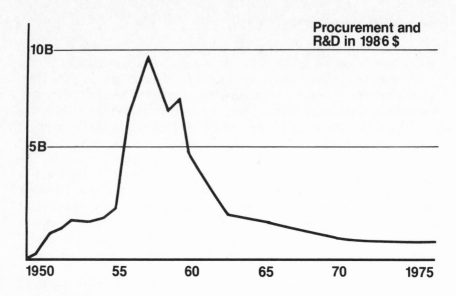

Consisted of (at peak)
SAMs (now none)
Interceptors (now 300)
Dew Line & other radars (now 118)
S.A.G.E

SOVIET RESPONSE

Early: emphasize missiles?	Bear & Bison	1956
Later: ignore?	Backfire	1974
	ALCM AS-4	1962 (Bear & Backfire)
	ALCM AS-15	1984 (Bear H)

in 1985: 325 A/C
(6% of Soviet Strategic Investment vs. 40% for U.S.)

Source: This figure is based on data presented in R.L. Maust, G.W. Goodman, Jr., and C.E. McLain, *History of Strategic Defense,* prepared by Systems Planning Corporation, Final Report SPC 742 (ARPA Order No. 4177), September 1981.

Figure 2-3. U.S. Air Defense

Case 4: U.S. Missile Defense, 1958–1972

By the mid 1950s, when it became clear that the Soviets were making a major commitment to the development of ICBMs, the U.S. began to explore the possibility of mounting a defense against them. By the end of the 1950s, the then-new Advanced Research Projects Agency (ARPA), since renamed the Defense Advanced Research Projects Agency (DARPA), was conducting a broadly based attack on the problem of ballistic missile defense. In the U.S. Army, the development of the first-generation ABM, the Nike Zeus, was well under way. Total annual expenditures, in 1986 dollars, exceeded $1.5 billion. Even at the early date, the army proposed to deploy a system based on hardware then in hand, but doubts about its efficacy led to a decision to defer deployment. R&D expenditure continued to expand; new ideas for missiles, radars, and other system components continued to turn up (see figure 2-4). By 1967, the system began to look more promising to some authorities in the Department of Defense, and it was tentatively decided to initiate deployment. Arguments among experts about the probable performance of the system,

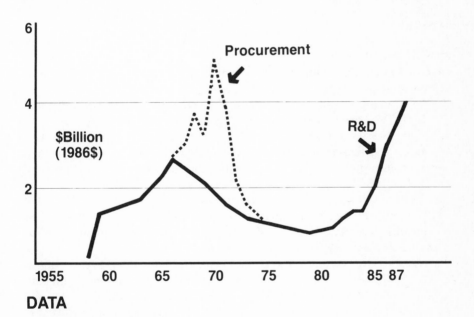

Source: This figure is derived from data presented in John Pike, *The SDI Budget and Program* (Washington, D.C.: Federation of American Scientists), February 1985.

Figure 2-4. U.S. Missile Defense

combined with public protests over proposals to deploy it at certain sensitive locations, caused the authorities to hesitate. In 1969, the U.S. Senate approved an initial deployment of ABMs at Grand Forks, North Dakota, by a 51-50 vote—not a very solid basis for proceeding much further.

In late 1969, the SALT I negotiations got under way, and in 1972 the resulting ABM Treaty was signed and ratified, placing severe limitations on further deployments. By the end of 1972, spending on the ABM had fallen to less than one-third of its 1970 peak of $5.0 billion. In March 1975, the Grand Forks site achieved initial operational capability. It was terminated by Congress that same year.

As in the air defense case, the Soviet response to these U.S. actions is unclear. Soviet MIRV deployment did lag behind U.S. ABM development by about a decade, but cause and effect are not provable. Testimony of U.S. government officials has made it very clear that the U.S. decision to provide MIRVs for its missiles was mainly a reaction to the Soviet ABM, but no such body of testimony or knowledge surrounds the corresponding Soviet decision.

Lessons

Many of the ideas, actions, and objectives that make up the new Strategic Defense Initiative are similar to those which characterize the historical cases just presented.

The pursuit of strategic defenses in the general sense is obviously not at all novel. The Soviets have been working on it steadily for forty years. The Swiss, the Swedes, and many other European nations have deployed substantial strategic defenses, including civil defense. From time to time, the United States has also promoted strategic defenses, but only in sporadic, short-term efforts.

The present size of the SDI R&D program—measured as a fraction of GNP, of total defense, or of total defense R&D—is also not at all unusual. Nor are the firm projections of spending on it for the period as far ahead as definitive fiscal planning reaches.

SDI objectives include intercepting reentry vehicles (RVs) in the terminal and late midcourse phases of their flight. The world has experience with both of these. Terminal missile defenses are currently deployed in the USSR, and they were deployed briefly in the United States. Exoatmospheric (that is, very late midcourse) interceptors have been developed and tested by both sides. Space-based observation platforms have been deployed by both sides for decades, and research designed to expand the capabilities of these observation platforms presumably has been under way throughout that period. Now called SEWS, or Satellite Early Warning Systems, these devices detect ICBMs during their boost phase and can provide some information about their pro-jected trajectories and targets. The SDI boost-phase intercept requires a very considerable expansion of the current capabilities but not something entirely new and different.

I draw three major lessons from a review of these parallels between past cases and the new initiative: first, the pursuit of strategic defense has been and very probably will continue to be futile; second, the pursuit of strategic defense could result in a new "arms race"; and third, the pursuit of strategic defense is not intrinsically incompatible with arms control.

1. The pursuit of strategic defenses has been largely futile. For nearly four decades, the Soviets have been investing vast sums on the deployment and improvement of air defenses. Never during all that time have they been capable of seriously blunting a U.S. air attack. To be sure, the United States has had to be continuously alert to what they were doing, and, on occasion, has had to develop new aircraft, new missiles, and new tactics in order to keep ahead of the Soviet defense capability; but the United States has always been able to do so and at much less cost than that of the defenses themselves. For almost as long, the Soviets have been trying to develop missile defenses. In this case, MIRV proved to be an easy and reliable means for coping with any missile defense the Soviets actually did build or even could have built. Despite their obvious ineffectiveness, the Soviets have continued to deploy and im-prove their strategic defense forces. Their reasons for doing so are not clear.

In each of the U.S. cases, after ten years of effort, the country finally came to recognize the futility of the enterprise, and in each case virtually abandoned further work.

Now the United States is about to embark on a third try. Some think that this time there is a better chance things will work out in a way that favors the defense. The past record of this contest between defense and offense does not give reason for much hope. For forty years, a never-ending contest between defensive measures, offensive countermeasures, counter-countermeasures, and so on, has always and easily resulted in an advantage for the offense. I find this general way of looking at the question more convincing than the usual argu-ments about the technical feasibility of particular devices or first-order discus-sion of measures versus countermeasures. We are not dealing here with a case of technological man against nature, but of man against man on a very familiar playing field. There are forty years of experience to review in that field, involving the expenditure, so far, of half a trillion dollars. The record clearly shows that the rules of the game and the nature of the field have always overwhelmingly favored the offense. There is nothing in sight to convincingly suggest that this relationship is at all likely to change in the foreseeable future.

The forgoing, however, is not quite the whole story. Even though the USSR has been unable to develop defenses that could stop U.S. aircraft and its weapons from striking Soviet targets, the deployment of defenses has not been totally without effect on the damage the Soviets must contemplate in the event of a U.S. attack. Since 1965, the total megatonnage programmed for delivery by U.S. strategic forces has fallen fivefold (see figure 2-5). To be sure, at the same time the number of warheads has increased somewhat, but not enough to make up for the decrease in total explosive power. Several factors have contributed to this net decrease, but the largest part of it is due to the way we have responded to Soviet air defenses. In effect, in order to assure continued penetration, we have replaced big bombs with smaller bombs and RVs, and by standoff missiles, ECM, and extra fuel. In addition, much of our strategic missile attack is targeted against the numerous and widespread air defenses, leaving less for other targets. As a result, while the total weight of a potential U.S. attack is still much more than enough to kill most of the Soviet urban population and destroy most Soviet cities, the decrease in megatonnage— and the concomitant decrease in radioactive fallout—could mean the difference between death and life for much of the small-town and rural population.

2. The pursuit of strategic defense could stimulate an arms race. Many analysts argue that the pursuit of any major new program, including strategic defense, automatically triggers an arms race. The history I have recounted confirms the existence of an action-reaction cycle in each of the two cases where the Soviets pursued strategic defense. The two U.S. cases are not so clear, however. The explanation, perhaps, is that each time the U.S. interest in strategic defense was expressed only in a short burst of activity that soon subsided. The stimulus simply did not last long enough to induce a clearly observable Soviet reaction.

Of all the cases cited, the most egregious in terms of its effects on the world at large is the first: the forty-year-long Soviet pursuit of an effective air defense. A reasonable estimate of total Soviet spending on this quest is $500 billion, in 1986 dollars. The U.S. reactions each cost less—only $50 billion or so—but they totaled well over a half trillion dollars. This is, by any standard, an enormous sum, yet it has produced very little net result.

Many opponents of Reagan's SDI have focused special attention on the potentially huge cost of a multilayer system of the type described in the Fletcher Report and subsequent architectural studies. Experienced commentators have made estimates of $1 trillion or more. The possible expenditure of such huge sums certainly must give pause. However, those who are seriously concerned about the diversion of such immense resources away from more important goals ought to focus at least as much attention on the actual current case as on

1a Strategic defense has not provided any substantial defense.

  2 Soviet cases

  2 U.S. cases

1b <u>But</u> it can affect the level of death and destruction.

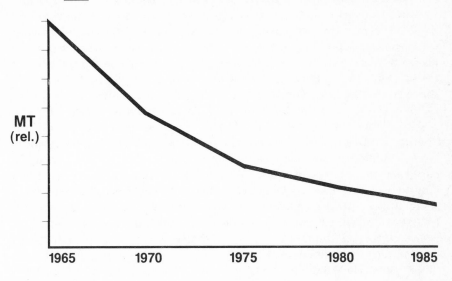

big bombs ➡ small bombs & RVs
stand off missiles
ECM
Fuel

Source: This figure is from the FY 1986 report of the Undersecretary of Defense for Research and Engineering (USDR&E).

Figure 2-5. Megatonnage Programmed for Delivery by U.S. Strategic Forces Since 1965

the hypothetical future one. This fiscal year, for instance, total U.S. and Soviet spending on strategic defenses, other than SDI, combined with spending on the reactions to those defenses, will be more than ten times the spending on SDI alone.

To summarize, the pursuit of strategic defense can indeed give rise to the kind of action-reaction cycle we call an arms race. One such cycle has been under way for forty years. The new initiative may give rise to another. So far, in terms of both actual program and firm projections, the new one is, and will remain for some years, much smaller than the earlier ones.

3. The pursuit of strategic defense is not intrinsically incompatible with arms control. Two past arms negotiations throw some light directly on this issue. The first instance involves the ABM Treaty of 1972 and the analyses and arguments supporting it. At the time, it was argued that there was a strong connection between the size of the strategic defenses one side possessed and the strategic offenses the other side would be obliged to build. A limit on ABM was seen as a necessary condition for limiting offensive forces.

The history of the development of the strategic offensive forces of the two sides does not confirm this claim. In fact, the number of strategic nuclear delivery vehicles (SNDVs) and the number of bombs and RVs existing today can be completely accounted for without any reference to the ABM Treaty. In particular, the number of U.S. SNDVs has been nearly constant since 1955, long before such treaties were even dreamed of. The number of Soviet SNDVs, some 20 percent larger than the U.S. number, is what a conservative Soviet analyst working in 1964, at the beginning of the Brezhnev regime, would have projected the U.S. number to be in 1984. And in each case, the number of bombs and RVs is determined largely, if not entirely, by the technological possibilities. The ABM Treaty may have affected these numbers, but, arguments based on plausibility aside, there is no concrete evidence that it did so.

The second instance involves SALT II, and it is simpler and more direct than the first. Briefly stated, the United States then accepted low limits on its bomber forces even though SALT II placed no numerical limits or any other constraints on Soviet air defenses. The U.S. delegation evidently did bring up a question about this, but no one felt strongly enough about the issue to pursue it very far. The current U.S. Strategic Arms Reduction Talks (START) position confirms this idea. Even if Soviet air defenses continue to be unrestrained, the United States will accept limits on the number of bombers, although not on their individual characteristics or on what they carry.

At the same time, it must be emphasized that the development of strategic defenses can easily be used to undermine the existing treaties. It is, as the Soviets would say, no accident that the strongest opponents of the existing treaty arrangements are among the leading proponents of the most exaggerated forms of strategic defense.

The START negotiations are not going well now, and I have little hope that they will go better in the future. Statements by the proponents of SDI, including President Reagan, have contributed to this impasse, but they are not an essential element of it. Even if SDI were to disappear through some sort of magic, there is no reason to believe that much would be accomplished in terms of arms reduction in the foreseeable future.

What's New and Different About Star Wars?

The really new and unique elements of SDI—the elements properly referred to as Star Wars—are the space-based systems intended to attack directly and destroy RVs or satellites. The world has no experience with such devices. The only arguable exception is the Soviet antisatellite (ASAT) system, but that system spends so little time in space and takes so long to destroy its target that it does not provide a basis for extrapolating to the new world of Star Wars devices.

The deployment of Star Wars systems—lasers of several kinds, neutral particle beams, "fighting mirrors," kinetic-energy kill devices—apparently would change the strategic situation in three radically novel ways: the "battle time line" would be very much shortened; the opposing defensive forces would be commingled; and the locale of the defensive shield would be unprecedented.

The Extremely Short Time Line

At present, terminal defenses have thirty minutes' warning time in which to react to an attack by ICBMs and fifteen minutes for an attack by SLBMs. We have had more than twenty-five years of experience with such conditions. During this time, there have been several occasions in which one or another of our detection systems has produced a false alarm. In each case, however, the officials in charge were able to turn to other systems and query them about the facts. In each case it became clear soon enough that the false alarm was indeed just that, and nothing further happened.

The Star Wars case would be radically different. To understand it, we must distinguish between two different modes of operation. One is counteroffensive, the other counterdefensive.

In the counteroffensive mode, the Star Wars battle stations seek to destroy enemy missiles while their rocket engines are still operating, that is, while they are in the so-called boost phase. For present designs, this phase lasts up to five minutes for certain large liquid-rocket systems. Projections of future designs, however, lead to estimates that this time may be reduced to as little as one minute. The kind of double-checking that is possible in the case of terminal defenses surely would be ruled out under such conditions.

The counterdefensive mode generates even more severe conditions. In it, the battle stations of Country A are set to attack those of Country B so that Country A's offensive missiles can get through to their targets. In the deployment architectures commonly discussed, most of the Star Wars units of the two sides spend most of their time within hundreds, or at most thousands, of kilometers of each other. For systems using lasers or particle beams, the battle time lines reduce to milliseconds. Clearly in either mode, but especially in the latter one, such systems have to be fully automatic, they have to make all their own decisions about when and at what to fire, and there is no room for human intervention. Everything we know about technology today tells us that this would be very dangerous. Perhaps things will change, but there is nothing in sight that gives us reason to believe they will.

Commingled Opposing Defenses

Today, the fighting components of the strategic defenses are separately located on opposite sides of the world. They cannot reach each other, they do not threaten each other; nor do they interact in any other way. Assuming a two-sided deployment, opposing components of Star Wars defenses would be located in the same general volume of space. They would be in constant touch with each other, observing each other with their sensors, "thinking" about each other with their on-board computers, and using their artificial intelligence to "ponder" what to do next. All this would be preprogrammed by human beings, but once the systems were in space they would necessarily be on their own, except, perhaps, for great "on/off" switches somewhere in each of the two headquarters. They would have to be equipped with what is often called a "hair trigger" in order to be sure they would work when they were supposed to. Under such conditions, how can we imagine that they would remain passive and stable indefinitely? Who can say what false alarm, beyond human veto, will set the whole thing off?

And even if the deployment were only one-sided, or nearly so, might it not suffer from a form of autoimmune disease and at some unpredictable moment suddenly start to shoot itself down?

Unprecedented Location of the Shield

In the case of terminal defenses, the shield is, so to speak, held out immediately in front of the defender's body. If the enemy hurls something in our general direction, we ward it off only just before it strikes us. Such postures have been common for centuries, and history has plenty to tell us about how to deal with them.

In the case of boost-phase defenses based on Star Wars systems, the shield is not immediately over the defender's homeland, but half a world away, directly over the other side's head. If the other side launches something into space for any purpose and in any direction, our shield stands ready to shoot it down. In a word, the United States is proposing to take its shield from in front of its "body" and shove it up against its opponent's nose even in peacetime. If the United States were on the receiving end first, would it consider such an act by the Soviets politically acceptable? It surely is novel, and the most positive thing that can be said in response to the question is that it is unknown how the other side would react.

Summing Up

Historical experience can give us much help in making projections about the future course of the world's various attempts to achieve effective strategic defenses. In many important ways, the new initiative is not so different from prior cases. The three special situations just cited, however, are so novel that we cannot look to the past for help in understanding them. We can only speculate about them, hoping that our political biases and our disaffections do not badly mislead us in the process.

3
Defensive Technologies for Europe

Gregory H. Canavan

T his discussion reviews the strategic defense technologies applicable to the European theater and assesses their expected performance there. It summarizes the more extensive discussions of defensive concepts and countermeasures found in "Theater Applications of Strategic Defense Concepts,"[1] as well as the more detailed treatment of cost-effectiveness, survivability, and stability in "Strategic Defense Concepts for Europe."[2] Where possible, the basis for numerical estimates is given in the text, but some estimates require more analysis, which is collected in "Quantitative Issues in Theater Missile Defense."[3]

Theater Objectives

Soviet objectives in the theater were recently reviewed by Albert Wohlstetter, who argued that the Soviets are prepared technically, organizationally, and doctrinally for the use of force, including nuclear weapons, against Western military forces and facilities that stand in their way—particularly in the event of reverses in a conventional invasion in the center of Europe. While the Soviets have shown little interest in the use of those weapons for bargaining, significant efforts have prepared them to use force selectively and under control, with the goal of avoiding both fratricide and unnecessary damage to the assets they want to take over and use. Primarily because of self-interest, they are least likely to use nuclear weapons in ways that could destroy the biosphere.[4]

In strategic exchanges, significant climatic damage might be caused by the detonation of about one hundred megaton-class weapons over a similar number of fuel-rich targets.[5] Since fuel densities are similar in the theater, thresholds should be similar to those for strategic engagements. Lacking

The author would like to acknowledge Dr. Albert Wohlstetter's role in stimulating his interest in theater applications, providing the formulation of Soviet objectives used, and constructively reviewing the resulting analysis. He would also like to acknowledge the comments of Drs. D. Yost, S. Cambone, C. Hartsell, and Ambassador Seymour Weiss on earlier drafts.

knowledge of their actual values, however, a conservative attacker might commit only a fraction of that number in the initial strike and increase or decrease the size of successive attacks on the basis of additional information. Escalatory pressure is also difficult to quantify, but it should be significant for attacks at any of these levels.

Such selective attacks would have to concentrate on military targets to have an acceptable probability of success, so partial defenses are measured by their ability to defend these targets. When defended, such targets become more difficult to destroy, and the attacker must commit more weapons to them. If the total number of warheads in the attack is limited, the number committed to nonmilitary targets must be reduced accordingly. Thus, at each stage of deployment, defenses reduce the expected damage to both classes of targets.

Framework for Analysis

The technical concepts for strategic defense[6] have been described in some detail in recent publications,[7] as have their demonstrated and projected performance[8] and the major considerations governing their integration into effective, multitiered strategic defensive systems.[9] This section reviews the main concepts and indicates how their performance changes in the theater. Multiple tiers remain useful in compounding attrition, complicating attacks, and preventing the saturation of lower altitude layers, so they are used to organize the discussion that follows.

The discussion of the concepts breaks naturally into separate discussions of the engagements in four tiers: boost phase, midcourse, high and low endoatmosphere. In the boost phase, neither reentry vehicles (RVs) nor decoys have yet been deployed, and there is significant leverage in destroying their missiles before they are. Including the time required for the deployment of RVs and decoys, the boost phase occupies roughly the first few hundred seconds of flight and first few hundred kilometers in altitude. In midcourse, which is above the sensible atmosphere, even light decoys are ballistic and hence credible targets. Since they can be numerous, their discrimination is pivotal. In the high endoatmosphere, reentering decoys are decelerated enough to permit at least partial discrimination by about 100 kilometers, which can support intercepts at 30 to 50 kilometers. In the low endoatmospheric regime, most large decoys have been discriminated by reentry. The remaining large, fast objects are likely to be RVs.

Range is an important variable whose impact is often misunderstood. Theater missile burnout velocities vary as the square root of the range—from 1 to 4.4 km/sec on optimal trajectories with ranges from 100 to 2000 kilometers.[10] Even the largest theater velocities are only about half the 7 to 8 km/sec typical of intercontinental ballistic missiles (ICBMs), and the rest are well below the 4 to 5 km/sec typical of submarine-launched ballistic missiles (SLBMs). The correspondingly lower reentry velocities make theater intercepts kinematically simpler.

They also lower the RV's apogee, the highest point of its trajectory, which is important because that determines the total atmospheric drag an object experiences. Apogee varies linearly, with range from 25 to 500 kilometers for 100- to 2000-kilometer ranges. RVs are decelerated noticeably by atmospheric drag at 80 to 100 kilometers; large, light decoys are slowed enough for discrimination at 120 to 130 kilometers.[11] Thus, short-range missiles such as the SS-21 and -23, whose apogees lie at 125 kilometers or lower, are limited to undecoyed operation, which makes them easier to identify and intercept.

Their trajectories could be lofted, but their flight times are uniquely determined by their apogees, so that lofting increases their apogees by increasing their response times to about those of long-range missiles, forgoing any advantage of surprise. In the antiballistic missile (ABM) debates[12] of the 1960s[13] and the present,[14] decoys have been the stressing threat. Without them, earlier ABM systems could have handled projected RV loads, but with them they could be saturated. Thus, short-range theater missiles, while kinematically demanding on account of their short flight times, produce a threat that could have been met by an even earlier generation of defensive technology.

Atmospheric deceleration and discrimination also impact long-range systems during their boost phase. Drag prevents buses from deploying decoys until they are above most of the atmosphere—about 120 to 130 kilometers. If the bus must drift up to this low-drag altitude before releasing its RVs and decoys, the resulting delay increases the effective boost-phase engagement times from the tens of seconds of the fast-burn boosters themselves to about 100 seconds, relatively insensitive to the acceleration or burn time of long-range missiles.[15]

Thus, the attacker can either try to coast buses up to the deployment altitude—taking a chance of being intercepted along the way—or deploy decoys at a lower altitude—evading the defense but unmasking the decoys to onlooking sensors. The former gives the boost-phase defenders an undiminished intercept opportunity; the latter eliminates decoys altogether, which gives midcourse and endoatmospheric defenders a bare threat that they should be able to intercept efficiently. Both options favor the defense.

Qualitative and quantitative aspects of the threat are summarized in recent publications.[16] Currently, there are a few hundred missiles in each range interval.[17] Complicating the assessment, however, are the diverse short-term projections[18] of the number of launchers expected in each range interval in the future. The assessment is further complicated by the fact that several of the missiles have a reload capability,[19] which could add three to four rounds per launcher. Such reloads would increase the number of short-range defensive interceptors that would have to be based in the theater, but reloading long-range theater missiles would have much less impact.

Midcourse and boost-phase concepts are less sensitive to the threat size than to the threat rate—the number of missiles launched simultaneously divided by the time during which they are vulnerable. As noted earlier, this engagement time can amount to several hundred seconds. Even reload times as short as a few minutes are long compared to them, which causes reloads to enter the analysis as sequential rather than parallel launches. They increase the number, but not the rate, of intercepts required. Thus, the ensuing discussion, which is primarily concerned with the long-range missiles, concentrates on launchers rather than reloads.

Similar considerations apply to multiple independently targetable reentry vehicles (MIRVs). Currently, only longer-range missiles and SS-20s are MIRVed, since drag makes MIRV buses difficult for shorter-range missiles. The principal defenses against long-range missiles are limited by the engagement time, which is unaffected by the number of RVs per missile. To maximize the number of RVs penetrating such a defense, the attacker should actually distribute the RVs over as many missiles as possible, that is, de-MIRV. Thus, the number of missiles is the main parameter of the MIRV threat as well.

Currently, there are several hundred missiles in each range interval. But the important question is what their number and distribution will be when defenses could be deployed. The references previously cited suggest how those levels might increase over the next few years. But the time scale for the development and deployment of strategic defenses is measured in decades. Over that interval, almost any change is possible. In that situation the threat is best estimated not by extrapolating current trends but by examining the relative effectiveness of the offense and defense. If the defenses are cost-effective, they will produce incentives for both sides to shift to defensive deployments, which would inhibit the further growth of offenses. In such stable situations—which are the ones of primary interest in assessing defensive deployments—it is appropriate to use roughly current offensive levels to estimate defensive performance.

Boost-Phase Technologies

In the boost phase, it is possible to attack the missiles and buses, which are significantly softer than the RVs they deploy, providing many-for-one kills on MIRVed launchers and eliminating their decoys altogether. Strategic boost-phase concepts have been discussed widely;[20] this section primarily treats their application to the theater. There are five main technologies: space-based lasers, ground-based lasers, particle beams, kinetic energy weapons, and nuclear concept.

Space lasers focus their energy into small spots to burn holes in targets. Ground-based lasers use space-based mirrors to focus energetic pulses and punch holes in targets, and particle beams deposit their energy within targets, disrupting or destroying the electronic, explosive, and structural elements of missiles, buses, or warheads. Kinetic-energy projectiles kill boosters and buses by homing to and colliding with them. Nuclear-driven directed-energy concepts are also being studied. The paragraphs that follow sketch the principles of operation, scaling, and countermeasures to the main technologies.

Space lasers burn rocket fuels to produce their power, which is delivered to distant targets by large focusing mirrors. Research and studies have indicated that laser powers in the order of tens of megawatts and mirror diameters of tens of meters should be attainable.[21] Satellites with 20-MW lasers and 10-meter mirrors—the "20-10" concept often discussed for strategic defense—could kill targets hardened to the practical limit at a range of 1000 kilometers at a rate of several targets per second.[22]

There is now reasonable agreement that the simultaneous, distributed launch of a few thousand missiles would require about ten satellites of nominal performances in the battle, although the total constellation would need to be larger by about a factor of 10 to account for the "absentee" satellites that are out of sight when the missiles are launched. Thus, a total constellation of about one hundred satellites would be required to achieve strategic defensive goals.[23]

There has been little serious question of whether or not the lasers and mirrors could be built. Most criticism has focused instead on whether they would be cheaper to deploy or to countermeasure. The principal countermeasures are hardening or spinning the missiles, decreasing their burn time, decreasing the size of the launch area, and attacking the defenses themselves. Hardening requires additional ablative materials to provide structural elements with more protection against laser radiation. If the ablator were needed only right under the laser beam, it could have significant impact. But the beam can move over the missile, so practical schemes must add ablator over the whole missile. The missile's area is one hundred to one thousand times larger than that of the laser beam, so the laser's focused spot more than offsets the ablator's 100-fold advantage in specific energy. For similar reasons, spinning the booster only reduces by about a factor of 2 the tenfold net advantage of lasers, whose beams can track the hot spot on the target.

The preceding estimates used a 100-second engagement time, even though today's boosters have burn times about twice that. Since their buses also have equally long deployment times, the total engagement time is about 400 to 600 seconds. Ideally, fast-burn boosters could reduce theater-burn times to under a minute. But if multiple warheads or decoys are required, their deployment would still produce effective engagement times of about 100 seconds—even if the buses could be made both sufficiently hard during the drift phase and sufficiently fast during deployment to survive. Neither requirement is obvious, since the bus faces the same hardening penalties as the missile and has to expose its soft interior in order to deploy its payload as well.

It is mathematically advantageous to the attacker to concentrate his launchers in a compact launch area—ideally a point—and attempt to punch a hole in the defensive constellation. With mobile theater launchers, such concentration is theoretically possible. But there are drawbacks. Simultaneous-point launch onto anything but single, crowded trajectory to a given target produces nonsimultaneous arrival, relaxing the time lines for midcourse and endoatmospheric defenses. Conversely, simultaneous arrival for structured attacks requires nonsimultaneous launch, which lengthens the boost phase engagement time, increasing the effectiveness of defenses.

To get away from the "point trajectory" associated with point launch, it is necessary to depress or loft the RVs and spread their apogees vertically. But the fractional change in a theater RV's flight time is half that in its apogee. The flight time and apogee of an RV on an optimal 1000-kilometer trajectory are 450 seconds and 250 kilometers. Spreading the trajectories by just 100 kilometers vertically would spread their flight times by about 90 seconds, which could either increase the time available for atmospheric engagements by a factor of 5 or increase the engagement time available to boost-phase defenses by 100 percent. The former would reduce saturation of the simpler and less expensive endoatmospheric defenses; the latter would offset the advantage to the attacker for using point launch in the first place. It should also be noted that point launches extract no penalties from—and provide some advantages to—the efficient, area-insensitive pop-up basing modes available to theater defenses.

Point launch also increases the vulnerability of the launchers to nuclear effects, since all the missiles in a compact launch area could be prevented from launching by the detonation of nuclear weapons above. Thus, pindown becomes both more efficient and plausible in the theater. Point launch's concentration of targets in space and time increases the leverage of nuclear weapons for both kill and discrimination—particularly for structured launches that require simultaneity in space and time in both launch and arrival, which could be put at risk by a single weapon. For such point launches, the whole theater threat would be discriminated by roughly a dozen weapons.

If the attacker could not penetrate the defenses without prohibitive losses, he could attempt to suppress them by attacking the defensive platforms before launch. For lasers, the treatment of suppression largely repeats the earlier discussion of countermeasures, since the suppressing missiles would have to be protected by the same techniques to have any chance of reaching the satellites. But those techniques fail in suppression for the same reasons that make them ineffective as countermeasures. Against isolated satellites they extract some penalty, but against deployed constellations, particularly those that can kill boosters and discriminate decoys, suppression is extremely costly to the attacker.

Ground-based lasers obey roughly the same scaling as space lasers, although their shorter wavelengths produce a given brightness with mirrors a factor of 10 smaller and 100 lighter. Thus, hybrid deployment—in which ground-based lasers provide power to space mirrors—minimizes the mass in orbit as well as the total cost. Operation in a pulsed mode minimizes their sensitivity to many of the countermeasures to continuously operating lasers. Ground facilities must be made survivable and be provided with an unobstructed propagation path to space, which adds cost because of the need for redundancy. But in other respects, the discussion of the survivability of hybrids with predeployed mirrors largely follows that of space-based chemical lasers. Hybrids whose mirrors are popped up on warning avoid both survivability and absenteeism concerns.

Particle beams obey roughly the same scaling—with favorable modifications because of their greater lethality. They can damage electronic components and destroy warhead and structural components at fluences that are factors of 100 to 1000 below those required for lasers. Thus, particle beams could kill targets at the same rate as lasers one hundred to one thousand times brighter. Countermeasures to particle beams are difficult. Stopping a weapon energy beam requires about 4 centimeters of lead, a hardening penalty sixty times that for lasers. For a 1-meter bus, the hardening penalty would be over a ton of lead—roughly its whole payload. Spinning the bus only exposes more area; it does not reduce the interior deposition.

Fast-burn boosters are more of a problem, since they can burn out as low as 70 to 80 kilometers, while particle beams only penetrate down to 120 to 130 km. But that still leaves a window for particle beams to engage the buses, which delay deployment to about the altitudes particle beams can reach in order to avoid drag. The particle beam's engagement time would then decrease to the buses' deployment time, which might only be a few tens of seconds. But even that is useful, since the buses cannot afford any disruption during deployment.

Kinetic-energy concepts are based on cheap missiles and infrared (IR) sensors. Their constellations scale somewhat differently than those for directed energy. For distributed launches, they scale as the number of missiles divided by the launch area, producing constellation sizes about the same as those for directed energy. For point launch, the engagement time determines the scaling, which produces constellations an order of magnitude larger, which could, however, still be acceptable if defensive missiles were to meet cost goals.

Countermeasures to kinetic-energy platforms are limited. Hardening has little effect, owing to the high closing velocities involved; spinning has none. Fast-burn boosters are compromised by their buses' need to deploy at altitudes the defensive missiles can reach. The fact that this 20- to 30-kilometer window permits only a few tens of seconds for engagement is not overly constraining, since nonnuclear kill (NNK) engagements are simultaneous rather than sequential.

In summary, boost-phase defense offers significant leverage, since the RVs and the decoys are killed with the boosters. And in the theater, smaller threat rates make defensive constellations cheaper, smaller, and less sensitive to countermeasures, new technology, and changed deployments. Each directed-energy concept shares these advantages to some extent. Ground-based lasers should minimize both the cost and mass in orbit; particle beams have unique advantages in lethality. Kinetic-energy weapons offer inexpensive lethality in the near term while retaining an acceptable engagement window for the long. Boost-phase concepts should be able to reduce the numbers of RVs and decoys to levels at which midcourse technologies could discriminate the threat, designate a fraction for intercept by NNK missiles, and identify for endoatmospheric interception a residue against which they should be effective. Thus, defensive concepts, particularly when integrated into multiple layers with balanced attrition, should be effective in the theater.

Midcourse Technologies

Strategic midcourse technologies have also been discussed in some detail.[24] Lasers and standard nuclear weapons are not attractive for killing RVs in the midcourse because the RVs are harder by factors of 10 to 100 than boosters and buses to the lasers' thermal and impulsive loads. But kinetic-energy concepts bypass that hardening. Since they kill by impact, they have about the same lethality against RVs as boosters.

The main kinetic-energy concepts currently under development are ground- and space-based NNK missiles. The former are being developed for an Exoatmospheric Reentry Intercept System (ERIS), which is intended to launch the missiles with sufficient accuracy for their small field-of-view IR homing sensors to reacquire targets that have already been discriminated. ERIS is an attempt to concert the technologies demonstrated in the Homing Overlay Experiment (HOE) into a practical system by substituting smaller missiles and production sensors for the experimental versions used in the HOE. Limited range, small field of view, and limited on-board discrimination should permit the sensors and processors to be small; long flyout times should make the missiles efficient. If those goals are met, ERIS should make ground-launched midcourse intercepts attractive.

Space-based buses called Porcupines, carrying many small, solid rockets that could be launched quickly in any direction, could also be attractive, depending on the cost of the missiles and the number of platforms needed. The buses could either be deployed by pop-up missiles or predeployed in space. The goal for each is to reduce the interceptors to little more than IR-guided air-to-air rockets by offloading most of the acquisition, track, and discrimination functions from the individual missiles and shifting them either to the bus or to another satellite altogether. In the former case, their cost could be shared by the ten to one hundred missiles on the bus; in the latter case, it could be shared by all of the missiles in the engagement. If ERIS and Porcupine achieve their cost targets of less than $1 million per intercept, they would be cost-effective by a factor of 10-100:1 relative to theater offensive missiles, as discussed in more detail shortly.

In midcourse, the ability to discriminate decoys has significant leverage, since it determines the number of interceptors that must be expended to hit a target. Discrimination concepts can be classified as either passive or active. The former includes imaging and radiometric systems; the latter includes techniques ranging from low-power inspection to high-power interrogation. Passive and low-power techniques should be adequate for initial theater threats. But with time, theater decoys can be made to look like RVs—and RVs to look like decoys—to passive and low-power techniques, so that active measures will eventually be required.

Current candidates for active discrimination include pulsed lasers and particle beams. Each uses a familiar mechanism to probe distant objects. Lasers probe with impulse. When a laser delivers a short pulse of energy to an object, it blows off material, whose recoil imparts a velocity to the object. The ratio of the impulse delivered to the velocity measured gives an estimate of the object's mass. If the recoil velocity is significant, the object is almost certainly a decoy.

The appropriate lasers for impulsive interrogation are visible wavelength excimers.[25] A megajoule pulse of visible light would impart a velocity of about 1 m/sec to a 100-kilogram weapon or 0.1 km/sec to a 1-kilogram decoy. Both velocities are readily detectable, so their difference should be a robust discriminant. Impulsive interrogation also deflects the objects irradiated. If the impulse were applied early in a 1000-kilometer trajectory, it could deflect an RV about 1 m/sec × 450 sec = 500 m, which is comparable to its kill radius. The deflection increases with the laser's energy and the missile's range, so it might be possible to use midcourse lasers not just to discriminate but also to negate long-range RVs.

Basing the lasers presents some problems. Although the lasers approach an overall efficiency of 10 percent at scale,[26] it would be difficult to produce the roughly 10-MJ electrical input pulses required on satellites or aircraft. Ground-based lasers are less sensitive to engineering problems, since they could either tap into the electric grid or generate the required power with peaking units. Such lasers could interrogate many targets directly, since they could see the deployment phase of launches up to 1000 kilometers away and the apogees of even more distant launches. Direct illumination, however, involves long slant ranges through the atmosphere, which produce beam distortions that require sensitive corrections.

To avoid those long paths—and exploit all of midcourse, rather than just part of it—ground-based lasers could instead deliver their energy to mirrors on aircraft or satellites above the bulk of the atmosphere, which would redirect the energy to the target—the so-called hybrid mode of operation. Aircraft basing of the mirrors would be practical in the theater, where range reduces the size of the redirecting mirrors down to the order of a meter, which should be acceptable for airborne applications.

Aircraft basing avoids many problems, but it is still susceptible to surprise in short conflicts and attrition in extended engagements. Space basing avoids aircraft survivability and operational constraints, but it does so at the price of new concerns about satellite survivability. In the theater, both problems can be avoided by using pop-up deployments, in which the defender would, on detection and confirmation of attack, launch the hybrid on an approximately vertical trajectory. The mirrors could be monolithic, so they would require little preparation; on reaching altitude they could begin operation immediately. Almost all of the midcourse would then be available for discrimination; the thirty seconds to pop the mirror up would decrease the observation time only by about 10 percent. Pop-up basing extends the mirror's range far beyond the ranges that are possible with either ground or air-based systems, without incurring the absentee and survivability penalties of predeployment in space.

The ground-based lasers would need to be survivable. Scaling from current prototypes suggests that they would have dimensions on the order of 5 to 10 meters—large but not incompatible with modularization for dispersal. Even with the prototype scaling costs of $100 per joule for the largest such laser built to date,[27] a one-MJ discrimination laser would cost about $100 million. Prorated over several hundred RVs, that would give an increment to the cost per kill comparable to that from the interceptors. The mirrors would add to the cost, but experience with larger space optics indicates that their contribution should be no larger than that from the laser.

Threat rate determines the discrimination rate required. But even if the attack involved one hundred RVs with ten decoys per RV, interrogating each during the 240 to 460 seconds available in midcourse would require rates only of a few objects per second, which is within the capability of a single repetitively pulsed laser and mirror. Since these performance levels are orders of magnitude below those for strategic concepts, theater midcourse discrimination could be its earliest application.

Particle-beam discriminators irradiate objects with high-energy hydrogen beams, which produce neutrons, gammas, and x-rays that are detectable by remote sensors. The strengths of those signals are approximately proportional to the object's mass. That permits the discrimination of the heavy RVs from the light decoys, which give essentially no return. Nominal beam parameters can support the required interrogation rates and ranges. The beam's energy is determined by the RV's mass, but its current and dwell time can be varied. Thus, traffic permitting, particle beams could not only discriminate decoys but also destroy any RVs found—quite effectively with respect to both lasers and kinetic-energy concepts. Neutral particle-beam platforms would probably have to be predeployed in space on account of their size, but they should still be survivable because of their ability to detect and destroy even heavily decoyed attackers.

In the past, the principal problem in the midcourse has been discriminating the numerous credible decoys possible. Passive techniques appear adequate for the near term, active probes for the long term. For the latter, pulsed lasers and particle beams look promising, since they produce strong interaction signals that should be robust discriminants. Pop-up basing looks attractive for hybrid lasers; predeployment for particle beams. The interceptors that support them could be modest NNK missiles launched from the ground or survivable predeployed space platforms.

High Endoatmospheric Technologies

In the high endoatmosphere, that is, below 100 to 120 kilometers, decoys decelerate because of atmospheric drag, making at least partial discrimination possible. Since nuclear detonations in that regime need not produce catastrophic degradation of targets on the ground, both nuclear and nonnuclear intercepts are permissible. The key developments for the former are improved radar and IR sensors that avoid the background and survivability problems of previous systems. Improvements in homing IR seekers could make autonomous intercepts affordable. Both approaches depend on improvements in discrimination to provide the commit altitudes needed to exploit fully the potentially inexpensive interceptors available in this regime.

Radars for high-altitude intercepts are susceptible to widespread nuclear effects, jamming, and saturation. And their size reduces their mobility, which adversely impacts their survivability. Earlier radar-based systems were susceptible to nuclear effects, which set an upper limit on the altitude at which RVs could be detected of about 100 kilometers.[28] With that, even high-performance missiles could not intercept at altitudes over 20 to 30 kilometers, producing a crowded battlespace. Lower-commit or higher-intercept altitudes drove the interceptor's velocity and mass higher than those of the offensive launcher. To minimize the cost per intercept, it is desirable to discriminate at the greatest range possible and intercept with a low-performance missile. To do so, it is necessary to capitalize on the longer flyout times made possible by improved discrimination by either IR sensors or midcourse sensors.

The leading interceptor candidates in this tier are NNK missiles with homing IR sensors, which could eliminate external guidance and still achieve the miss distances required for NNK. For NNK concepts guidance is pivotal. The ability of IR homing missiles to intercept individual ballistic objects in this regime was demonstrated in the HOE. Prototype interceptors using that technology are being developed as components of the High Endoatmospheric Defense System (HEDS) for strategic engagements. Theater versions could use smaller and cheaper sensors and missiles. The targets' IR signatures would be smaller in the theater because of their reduced velocities, but that is largely offset by the target's simpler kinematics. Thus, HEDS technology should transfer directly to the theater.

Lasers have also been studied for this regime. But it is impractical for them to deliver enough energy to overcome an RV's massive intrinsic thermal and impulse protection. Railguns are also at a disadvantage in the intercept of undecoyed threats, since chemical rockets have both adequate performance and lower expendables in this regime. If, however, discrimination altitudes were depressed to 60 to 80 kilometers by nuclear effects or countermeasures, the interceptor's flyout times would be significantly reduced, which would place velocity at a premium, favoring railguns.

Adequate sensors and interceptors are in development and appear to support a reasonable progression. It would probably start with mobile radars and lead to IR acquisition and discrimination sensors on aircraft. The main leverage in the high endoatmosphere would appear to be the development of exoatmospheric discrimination techniques that could sufficiently increase intercept altitudes to exploit all of the high-altitude battlespace with interceptors of modest performance.

Low Endoatmospheric Technologies

In the past, the major problems with defensive concepts for the low-atmospheric regime were sensor blackout, saturation, and vulnerability—all of which could arguably now be overcome. For radars, new developments include hardened antennas imbedded in concrete slabs, disposable radars, and mobile platforms that survive because of the attacker's uncertainty about their location.[29] If the radars only have to control low-altitude intercepts, their power-aperture requirements are reduced sufficiently for them to be truck-mounted, in which case survivability could be attained through mobile sensors and interceptors carried on off-road vehicles that could be as dispersible and survivable as the targets themselves.

The choice of a warhead depends on tradeoffs between sensor performance, warhead lethality, and launcher survivability. Current radars could command-guide existing missiles with kiloton-range warheads to high-confidence endoatmospheric intercepts. The Sprint missile was developed to do just that for the Safeguard system of the 1960s.[30] But the price was a disturbed environment, immobility, and reduced survivability. IR-homing NNK interceptors could relax each of those constraints. NNK produces no fratricide, faces no obstacles to mobility, and hence should have significantly greater survivability. NNK should also be quite effective. Low altitude greatly increases the target's signature in the short IR wavelength intervals for which the homing sensors are simpler. NNK concepts have received some development, and ones that have already passed significant testing are said to have the "propulsion functions [and] maneuvering systems aimed at low cost"[31] needed to make NNK intercepts economically attractive. Both missile and sensor technologies scale, so strategic developments should transfer readily to the theater.

Sophisticated threats complicate the evaluation, however. Maneuvering reentry vehicles (MARVs) change course by generating lift during terminal approach. Currently, such maneuvers are used for accuracy, but at low altitudes they could also be used to evade the interceptors. Velocities are high enough to make pursuit difficult in strategic engagements. But they scale roughly as the square of the RV's velocity, so that in the theater, accelerations are reduced by factors of 10 and 100 relative to those in strategic engagements, which should permit even modest interceptors to engage successfully.[32]

The second issue is salvage fusing. An attack RV can fuse, or trigger, its warhead when it detects the impact of relatively low-velocity NNK projectiles.[33] At low altitudes, such salvage detonations could produce much of the desired damage on the target as well as significantly degrade its defenses. Since producing an NNK warhead that can prevent fusing is difficult, somewhat paradoxically, the nuclear degradation from an NNK intercept could be greater than that from a low-yield nuclear intercept. That suggests a mix of the two, in which NNK intercepts are used at high altitudes, where salvage fusing is least damaging, and nuclear intercepts are used at low altitudes, as a last resort, since a low-yield detonation need not be devastating to targets 10 kilometers below. MARVs and salvage fusing are serious problems, but in the theater they appear to have solutions.

It has been noted that an interim theater antiballistic missile (TABM) capability for this regime could be provided by upgrading the Patriot air defense missile, much as the Soviets have upgraded the SA-X-12.[34] There are, however, practical problems. Air-defense systems are designed to react to large subsonic targets with modest transverse acceleration by launching their missiles as soon as the targets unmask from the terrain. Thus, their sensors stress low angles, clutter, and mobility at the expense of the sensitivity required to intercept multiple, high-angle, ballistic targets of small cross section at nuclear keepout ranges. While air-defense components could be modified, an NNK system designed specifically for TABM could be cheaper.

An exception is the potential impact of NNK on nonnuclear theater ballistic missiles (TBMs). In the absence of defenses, they are attractive vehicles for early, selective strikes, since they could disrupt or destroy key installations and linkages with minimal collateral damage or preemptive pressure. But their conventional warheads would have to be larger and heavier than nuclear warheads to accommodate the required sensors, guidance, and explosives. Thus, it would be more difficult for them to evade, and the penalty for doing so could be significant. NNK interceptors could be well suited to intercepting them—or simply pursuing them and degrading their accuracy.

The NNK interceptors needed would also be available during the early stages of the battle, when selective nonnuclear attacks would otherwise have the greatest impact. Such a capability might be particularly useful in the Middle East, where a steady rain of nonnuclear TBM could deny access to key facilities and delay mobilization unacceptably. These arguments apply with little modification to chemical and biological weapons, which are also an integral part of Warsaw Pact planning, as well as to cluster munitions released high in the atmosphere. NNK could provide timely and appropriate responses to several otherwise awkward threats.

Other advanced technologies such as lasers and railguns have been discussed for low-altitude intercepts.[35] But lasers face fundamental propagation constraints that limit the fluence they can deliver in the low endoatmosphere to less than that required to kill an RV. Even if railguns could efficiently accelerate projectiles to over 10 kilometers per second, simple rockets would still have a lower mass and cost per shot. "Simple-novel" schemes such as cluster rockets and dust clouds from nuclear detonations have been suggested as interim measures for hard-point defense in the strategic arena. But the former, because of their short ranges, can defend targets only with hardnesses approaching those of silos, which are rare in the theater. And the latter would be less effective against lower-velocity theater RVs. They would also be less palatable—particularly in extended attacks, in which the dust clouds would have to be replenished frequently.

In addition to the potential weaknesses of the defense's warheads, interceptors, and launchers, the attackers could also attempt to exploit the weaknesses of the sensors. If radars were used as near-term sensors, the attacker could respond by developing radar-seeking MARVs. An appropriate defensive response would then be the development of passive acquisition and track sensors, probably ones operating in the IR. Because they have no emissions, such sensors are hard to detect and are intrinsically more survivable. IR sensors do, however, have to be deployed above the weather. For that, an airborne platform analogous to the one being developed for strategic defense could be appropriate—particularly since its mobility should also make it more survivable. Thus, there is an adequate array of sensors for the low-endoatmospheric regime, whose development appears relatively straightforward. There is also a logical progression in their deployment, in which mobile radars should be adequate in the near term, and passive retrofits should be available from strategic programs when needed.

Evaluations and Extensions

The performance of space-based lasers in strategic exchanges has been extensively analyzed.[36] For nominal performance, predictions agree to within a few tens of percent[37] that constellations of fifty to one hundred strategic satellites would be required to negate the simultaneous launch of fourteen hundred fully hardened ICBMs from their current distributed configuration.

In the theater, differences between predictions are smaller. If the defensive satellites were dedicated to the theater only, larger constellations of smaller, less bright satellites could actually be more efficient. Their constellation size can be obtained by scaling previous results to the somewhat smaller launch areas and much smaller threat rates of the theater. If the satellites' brightness is reduced by about a factor of 10, for example, by deploying "10-5" satellites rather than the 20-10 strategic satellites discussed above, the theater constellation would need about thirty satellites, which is only a factor of 3 larger than the number of 20-10 satellites that would be required. Large satellites would be so widely separated that the launch area would look compact to them; only a few satellites would be close enough to contribute effectively. The smaller, more numerous satellites would be over the missiles at the time of launch, reducing their average range and restoring the favorable scaling associated with distributed launches.

Smaller satellites should also be much less sensitive to retargeting and engineering issues, which primarily scale on brightness.[38] And if a satellite's cost was roughly proportional to its brightness, the cost of a 10-5 theater satellite would be about an order of magnitude less than that of a 20-10 strategic platform. Since the number of satellites is reduced from strategic constellations by about a factor of 3 and the cost of a satellite by a factor of 10, the overall reduction would be about a factor of 30. If strategic satellites were to cost a few hundred million dollars apiece, those for theater defense would cost a few tens of millions, and theater constellations would cost about 30 satellites × $30 million/satellite = $1 billion—although development and support costs would increase that figure by a factor of 2 to 4. Smaller satellites should also be faster to develop; some have argued that they could be deployed immediately. That is open to debate, but it is plausible that more modest levels of technology would support earlier deployments.

The preceding estimates also permit a rough estimate of lasers' cost effectiveness. If the offensive systems have typical costs of $20 million per launcher,[39] and the whole constellation is written off against a nominal one-hundred-launcher attack, the cost exchange would be roughly $2B:$1B = 2:1 in favor of the defense. If, however, the engagement consisted of a number of such launches spread out over many minutes or days, the defense's cost-effectiveness would increase in direct proportion to the overall size of the attack. All the defense requires to counter serial attacks is additional fuel, whose launch cost is only about $1K/kg. Since only a few tens of kilograms of fuel are required, the cost to kill a hardened booster in an extended engagement drops significantly. For a one-thousand-missile attack, a laser's cost per kill would drop to about $1 million—a 20:1 marginal advantage. These low-variable costs even make it possible to consider the use of lasers against other targets, which is discussed later.

Similar scaling obtains for the hybrid laser, which benefits as well from reduced absenteeism in pop-up modes, and whose fuel costs are negligible, since it—like the laser—remains on the ground. Particle beams benefit from greater lethality, but they are penalized by their shorter engagement times. The two effects roughly offset one another. For the current distributed launch configurations, kinetic-energy interceptors would require about one hundred missiles over the launch area and hence a few thousand over the whole globe. If the defensive missiles each cost $1 million, a one-hundred-launcher attack would again have a cost-effectiveness of about 2:1. Subsequent attacks could, however, be met by missiles that were already in space but out of range of earlier engagements. If a total launch of one thousand missiles exhausted all the defensive missiles, the overall exchange ratio would again be 20:1.

The effectiveness of midcourse systems depends critically on their ability to discriminate. If that ability were perfect, NNK missiles costing about $1 million each would have an effectiveness of 20:1. But if discrimination were only 5 percent effective, the engagement would be cost-neutral. That illustrates the benefits of discrimination, but its cost must also be included in the evaluation. Amortizing a $500-million hybrid laser or particle beam over one hundred RVs would add $5 million to the cost per kill, which is awkward at low rates, though not at high rates or in extended engagements. For extended engagements, the increment drops to about $1 million per kill. Since the concepts discussed earlier could support high levels of discrimination, it would appear that both boost-phase and midcourse concepts can be cost-effective in both preemptive and extended engagements.

Endoatmospheric engagements benefit from interceptors that could cost under $1 million and discrimination platforms that are air- or ground- rather than space-based. By largely eliminating absentee platforms, these concepts could reach advantages of 10-100:1. But that level of performance is contingent on effective intercepts throughout the regime. If many RVs entered the atmosphere simultaneously, the defenses could be saturated, strongly reducing their effectiveness. Given significant attrition or discrimination by other layers, however, the endoatmospheric layers could be quite effective.

The low incremental costs per kill just estimated could make lasers effective against other targets, such as bombers and cruise missiles. Given the ability to detect them, either could be attacked from space for the incremental cost of the fuel required.[40] Space lasers could engage tactical aircraft at cost advantages of about 100:1 and could also negate certain soft battlefield targets.

The preceding discussion concentrated on theater missiles. If the suppression of that threat caused the Pact to consider the use of SLBMs or ICBMs in support of the theater, the same defensive assets could be applied to them as well. Theater defenses are oversized for nuclear-powered ballistic missile submarines (SSBNs). Constellations sized to negate one hundred missiles in 100 seconds—one missile per second—are oversized by an order of magnitude for the simultaneous launch of all the missiles on an SSBN. That would generate only 20 missiles/100 seconds = 0.2/second—a fifth of the defense's capability. Since that coverage is global, it would also apply to launches of up to one hundred ICBMs from the Soviet fields.

These conclusions are contingent on the survivability of the defensive constellations, but even predeployed platforms do appear to be survivable. Near-term suppression attacks can be met by a combination of hardening and maneuver. At the next level, attackers—even those with terminal guidance— could be countered by self-defense missiles launched from the defensive platforms at an advantage of about 20:1.[41] The stressing threat to isolated defensive platforms is a warhead hidden in a cloud of decoys. But if the midcourse technologies would be used to discriminate the threats to the defensive platforms as well, they should be able to unmask the decoys and reduce the engagement to that with a bare attacker, which favors the defense.[42]

Given survivability, the performance levels estimated earlier cannot be compromised by suppression. That means that defensive deployments should also be crisis stable, that is, they should not give either side an incentive to preempt in a crisis, given reasonable sequential deployments.[43] That, together with their cost-effectiveness, means that such defenses should also be arms-control stabilizing, since their introduction would remove any incentive for further increases in offensive forces—generating pressure for their reduction, instead. Under those conditions, theater defenses and arms control should be mutually supportive in providing pressure for offensive-force reductions.

Summary and Conclusions

Previous sections discussed a framework for the analysis of the performance of strategic defense technologies in the theater, concluding that boost-phase concepts benefit significantly from the shorter ranges, lower velocities, and more efficient, survivable pop-up basing modes available in the theater. They appear to be effective in the near term and seem as well to retain a useful engagement window for the far term. Midcourse defenses benefit from the use of laser and particle beams for discrimination and nonnuclear IR homing missiles for intercept. Similar interceptors could produce cheaper kills in the high endoatmosphere. Against short-range missiles, endoatmospheric concepts benefit from the absence of decoys and the enhanced survivability of the hardened, mobile sensors and interceptors.

Theater constellations should also have a strong capability against nonnuclear theater ballistic missiles, nuclear and NNK air-breathing vehicles, and ICBM or SLBM threats from outside the theater. Thus, their introduction into the theater should be stabilizing as well as effective, serving to discourage preemption, inhibit additional offenses, and suppress conflicts at other levels.

Notes

1. G.H. Canavan, "Theater Applications of Strategic Defense Concepts," *Los Alamos National Laboratory Report* LA-UR-86-818, May 1986.

2. G.H. Canavan, "Strategic Defense Concepts for Europe," *Los Alamos National Laboratory Report* LAUR-85-963, March 1986, to be published in A. Wohlstetter, F. Hoffman, and D. Yost, eds., *Swords and Shields: New Choices for Offense and Defense*," (Lexington, Mass.: Lexington Books, D.C. Heath & Co.).

3. G.H. Canavan, "Quantitative Issues in Theater Missile Defense," *Los Alamos National Laboratory Report* LAUR-86-1616, May 1986.

4. A. Wohlstetter, "Between an Unfree World and None: Increasing Our Choices," *Foreign Affairs, 63*(5) (Summer 1985), pp. 962-94.

5. G. Carrier, chairman, "The Effects on the Atmosphere of a Major Nuclear Exchange," (Washington: National Academy of Science, Academy Press, 1985). See also S.L. Thompson and S.L. Schneider, "Nuclear Winter Reappraised," *Foreign Affairs, 64*(5) (Summer 1986), pp. 981-1005, for a summary of more recent work, which reduces the severity of earlier predictions.

6. "The Strategic Defense Initiative: Defensive Technologies Study," U.S. Department of Defense (Washington: Government Printing Office, April 1984).

7. J.C. Fletcher, "The Technologies for Ballistic Missile Defense," *Issues in Science and Technology, 1* (1), pp. 15-29, Fall 1984, and G.A. Keyworth, "The Case for Strategic Defense: An Option for a World Disarmed," *Issues in Science and Technology, 1,* 1 (Fall 1984), pp. 30-44.

8. J. Abrahamson, interview, "Space-Based Defense: The View from the Top," *Geopolitique, 9,* 1985, pp. 6-28, discusses the current status, and G. Yonas, "Strategic Defense Initiative: The Politics and Science of Weapons in Space," *Physics Today* (June 1985), pp. 24-32, discusses the prospects for new concepts.

9. G. Canavan, H. Flicker, L. Hantel, O. Judd, D. Roeder, K. Taggart, and J. Taylor, "Alternative Concepts Evaluation for Strategic Defense," *Los Alamos National Laboratory Report* LA-UR-85-2210, July 1985.

10. G.H. Canavan, "Quantitative Issues," pp. 2-4.

11. Ibid., pp. 6-13.

12. A. Carter and D. Schwartz, eds., *Ballistic Missile Defense* (Washington: the Brookings Institution, 1984).

13. R.L. Garwin and H.A. Bethe, "Anti-Ballistic-Missile Systems," *Scientific American* (March 1968).

14. S. Drell and W. Panofsky, "The Case Against Strategic Defense: Technical and Strategic Realities," *Issues in Science and Technology, 1* (1) (Fall 1984), pp. 45-65, and H.A. Bethe and R.L. Garwin, "Space-Based Ballistic-Missile Defense," *Scientific American, 251,* 4 (Oct. 1984), pp. 39-49.

15. G.H. Canavan, "Quantitative Issues," pp. 6-9.

16. *The Military Balance* (London: International Institute of Strategic Studies, 1985), and *Soviet Military Power* (Washington: U.S. Department of Defense, 1985).

17. G.H. Canavan, "Theater Applications," pp. 12-14 and Table I.

18. R.M. Gates and L.K. Gershwin, "Soviet Strategic Force Developments," testimony before a Joint Session of the Subcommittee on Strategic and Theater Nuclear Forces of the Senate Armed Services Committee and the Defense Subcommittee of the Senate Appropriations Committee, 26 June 1985.

19. D.S. Yost, "Soviet Ballistic Missile Defense and European Security," in H.J. Neuman, ed., *The American Strategic Defense Initiative: Implications for West European Security* (Netherlands Institute of International Relations, 1986).

20. G. Yonas, "Strategic Defense Initiative," pp. 28-32, gives an introduction to the concepts and references.

21. "The Strategic Defense Initiative," U.S. Department of Defense. For an expanded, unauthorized discussion, see *Aviation Week and Space Technology* for 17, 24, and 31 October 1984.

22. H.A. Bethe and R.L. Garwin, "Space Based Ballistic-Missile Defense," and the Union of Concerned Scientists reports on which it is based, estimated much lower rates, but they were the product of an incorrect evaluation of the average engagement ranges, which impacts the kill rate quadratically.

23. H. Bethe and A. Petschek, "Scaling of Defensive Laser Satellite Constellations in 'Star Wars,'" *Los Alamos National Laboratory Report* LA-UR-85-2675, August 1985, and G. Canavan, "Further Comments on Defensive Constellation Scaling," *Los Alamos National Laboratory Report* LA-UR-85-3014, August 1986.

24. G.H. Canavan et al., "Alternative Concepts," pp. 27-36.

25. G.H. Canavan, R.O. Hunter, and A.M. Hunter II, "Development and Application of Advanced High Energy Lasers," *Los Alamos National Laboratory Report* LA-UR-83-0202, January 1983, to be published in H. Mark and L. Wood, "Energy in Physics, War, and Peace: a *Festschrift* Celebrating Edward Teller's 75th Birthday," *International Science,* Israel.

26. G.H. Canavan et al., ibid., p. 2.

27. Ibid., pp. 13-15 and Table I.

28. R.L. Garwin, "Anti-Ballistic-Missile Systems."

29. G.H. Canavan et al., "Alternative Concepts," pp. 7-8.

30. R.L. Garwin, "Anti-Ballistic-Missile Systems."

31. J. Abrahamson, "Space-Based Defense."

32. G.H. Canavan et al., "Alternative Concepts," pp. 25-27.

33. Ibid., pp. 15-16.

34. R.M. Gates and L.K. Gershwin, "Soviet Strategic Force Developments," p. 5.

35. J. Abrahamson, "Space-Based Defense."

36. See G. Canavan, H. Flicker, O. Judd, and K. Taggart, "Comparison of Analyses of Strategic Defense," *Los Alamos National Laboratory Report* LA-UR-85-754, February 1985; "Comments on the OTA Paper on Directed Energy Missile Defense in Space," *Los Alamos National Laboratory Report* 85-3572; and R.L. Garwin, "How Many Orbiting Lasers for Boost-Phase Intercept?" *Nature, 315,* 23 May 1985, pp. 286-90.

37. H. Bethe and A. Petschek, "Scaling of Defensive Laser Satellite Constellations"; G. Canavan, "Further Comments"; and G. Canavan and A. Petschek, "Satellite Allocation for Boost Phase Missile Intercept," *Los Alamos National Laboratory Report* LA-UR-85-4114, August 1986.

38. G. Canavan, ibid., pp. 23-24.

39. G.H. Canavan, "Theater Applications," pp. 79-80.

40. Ibid., pp. 95-102.

41. G.H. Canavan, "Survivability of Strategic Defensive Concepts," *Los Alamos National Laboratory Report* LA-UR-85-1583, April 1985, and G.H. Canavan, "Survivability of Neutral Particle Beam Platforms," *Los Alamos National Laboratory Report* LANL-85-2476, July 1985.

42. G.H. Canavan, "Survivability of Strategic Defensive Concepts," p. 39.

43. G.H. Canavan, "Simple Discussion of the Stability of Strategic Defense," *Los Alamos National Laboratory Report* LA-UR-85-1377, April 1985.

4

SDI and Cooperation within Western Europe: Developing Extended Air Defense

François Heisbourg

T he question of Western European cooperation in relation with, or in the framework of, the U.S. Strategic Defense Initiative, is a complex one. This complexity is due to at least two sets of considerations. The first set relates to the content of SDI itself, which corresponds to several possible definitions, for example, President Reagan's long-term vision of a world where nuclear weapons would be "impotent and obsolete"; a new high-technology research program; or a pulling together under a common organization of pre-1983 U.S. endeavors in ballistic missile defense (BMD). The second set of considerations concerns the varied nature of Western Europe's interests in the face of SDI. In this regard, evaluations will very much depend on the issues addressed: doctrinal, technological, military, and so on.

To reduce the analytical problem to manageable proportions, this chapter will not address all of these issues. It will deal neither with doctrinal implications nor with the "long-term vision": these two areas have been covered extensively in the literature since 1983, pro and con; they also happen to be areas where the room for cooperation between the United States and Western Europe is, to put it mildly, the least promising.

Therefore, the focus will be on the technological and military aspects of SDI as a research program, whether it be "new" or a continuation of the pre-1983 BMD programs. Although there is naturally a considerable degree of overlap between the purely technical side and the potential military applications, these categories will be analyzed separately, given the distance between upstream research efforts and the actual deployment of weapons systems.

Europe and SDI as a High-Technology Program

Whatever may be the future of SDI in terms of objectives or practical developments, it has already served as a catalyst to concentrate European minds on the extraordinary growth of U.S. military R&D expenditure. Between 1979 and 1986, U.S. spending for military R&D has grown by 64 percent, or close to two-thirds in real terms.[1] For 1986, military R&D budgetary outlays will have been four times greater in the United States than in the allied countries of Europe considered as a whole: $34.3 billion versus less than $9 billion (at spring 1986 exchange rates).[2] There may be some doubt in the United States about the wisdom of this concentration of American efforts on the military side of R&D; indeed, from a macroeconomic viewpoint, it may not be an optimal course. Such considerations, however, do not alleviate concerns about the impact of this overwhelming American advantage in military R&D on the future competitiveness of Western Europe's defense and aerospace industries.

This situation was not brought about by SDI, which, even today, represents less than 10 percent of U.S. military R&D. However, President Reagan's initiative has jolted Europeans not only because of the spectacular, media-oriented manner in which it has been presented and managed; the shock has been amplified by the intrinsic character of the program. SDI as a research program should be compared not to the total sum of military R&D expenditure but only to that fraction which is devoted to research. SDI is, in effect, the free world's largest research program.

Even more important, SDI money is spent not only on the prospective active defense systems (directed-energy and kinetic-energy weapons) but, to a similar extent, on the sensing, data processing, and battle management aspects: SATKA (Surveillance, Acquisition, Tracking, and Kill Assessment) and BM/C³ (battle management/command, control, and communication) are supposed to absorb more than two-fifths of the funding. These are fields where progress will be largely of a generic nature: super-sensitive/high-speed sensing; ultra-miniaturized/large-capacity data processing; artificial intelligence/ advanced software; and so on. All of this will be relevant outside of the framework of SDI. Certain of the benefits of this research could be of primary importance to the conventional defense of the European continent; hence, the real interest which the SDI research program has evoked in Western European industrial military circles.

However, events have tended to demonstrate that the existence of this interest does not in itself pave the way for Euro-American cooperation on SDI, even in those cases where intergovernmental agreements do exist.[3] The reasons for this are relatively straightforward and also rather difficult to surmount. A description of the problems suggests, in itself, some of the do's and don'ts of possible cooperation:

1. SDI is a U.S. program. The fact that the Reagan administration has committed itself to extending to its allies the protection derived from SDI does not in itself transform the American nature of the endeavor. The U.S. taxpayer is funding it, and, therefore, practically all of the related procurements—

including those in the research phase—will come from U.S. laboratories and industries. Even if no degree of explicit or implicit protectionism whatsoever existed, this would be the natural result of a U.S.-run and U.S.-funded enterprise.

Market analyses by specialized U.S. establishments have usually come up with estimates for foreign shares of 1 percent or less of the research program's funding, that is, less than $300 million over the 1985-1989 period. This does not in itself eliminate U.S. motivation to secure technological cooperation with SDI on the part of the Western European defense industry, but it certainly reduces the financial incentive.

2. European firms can cover only limited segments of the SDI spectrum. This is due only in part to a lack of expertise or competence. After all, the Western European defense industry and its supporting laboratories have proved, on many occasions, that they meet the American level of expertise, and sometimes they have even exceeded it (for example, French superiority in ramjet propulsion or carbon materials). However, Europe's quasi-complete inactivity in the military uses of outer space puts it at a marked disadvantage vis-à-vis U.S. firms in the space-based segments of SDI.[4]

Another comparative disadvantage stems from the tendency of European R&D institutions to focus on the defense of the European theater. Other than for theater defense, therefore, the interest, and possible cooperation, of Western European research and industrial entities will (and should) therefore tend to polarize on relatively narrow and precise technological niches: certain types of microelectronic components, different varieties of software, optics and optoelectronics, and so forth. Progress here will, however, remain within tight limits if existing trends in the field of technology transfer continue to prevail.

3. Technology transfer within the alliance is increasingly constrained. The tightening of technology transfer controls toward Warsaw Pact countries and their "fellow travelers" since the beginning of the 1980s has been a much needed change, given past abuses and excesses. The positions of the United States and France in this area have been quite similar in their refusal to squander the West's advantage in innovation and creativity to the benefit of its potential adversaries. Conversely, creativity should not be stifled by impeding the timely flow of scientific and technical data between allied countries. Unfortunately, this is a real problem today, for SDI as for other cutting-edge programs. The mundane procedures relating to technology transfer (for example, export licences, authorizations to visit classified establishments, personnel clearances, and so on) make cooperation on SDI a grueling process, independently of the existence of intergovernmental memoranda of understanding on SDI. The British have been especially critical of this situation.[5]

This set of difficulties is a consequence not only of the regulations them-selves but probably more so of the psychological climate in which the regula-tions are applied: openness is not a quality that is currently encouraged at the working level in a U.S. defense establishment understandably shocked not only by the familiar media leaks but also by a variety of espionage cases, several of which involve non-Warsaw Pact countries.

For SDI, the constraints may be worse than for other projects, because of the added limitations set by the ABM Treaty regarding the transfer of technol-ogy and information to third countries (see Article IX of the treaty and the corresponding U.S.-Soviet understanding). One can sympathize with U.S. pre-cautions; but one is also forced to observe that they do turn cooperative ventures into punishing and time-consuming obstacle courses: they may be worth running, but few will cross every hurdle.

In these conditions, one can summarize a few conclusions: Western European interest in many of the SDI-related technologies is high; the Ameri-can nature of SDI program management and funding reduces the scope of opportunities for European firms; the number of technological niches in which the Europeans have a chance to participate is relatively limited; and technology transfer problems may well be the single most important obstacle to Euro-American cooperation in SDI-related technologies.

SDI and the Defense of the European Theater

If one leaves the purely technological side of the SDI program and considers its military relevance in terms of theater defense, a potentially more promising landscape unfolds. After all, SDI is also a regrouping of the "traditional" ballis-tic missile defense programs run by the U.S. armed services before 1983, which basically involve ground-based terminal defense of military assets. This is increasingly relevant to the European situation.

The issue will be discussed here from three angles: the evolving threat assessment in Europe; the evaluation of extended air defense needs in West-ern Europe and the corresponding capabilities; the policies needed to build up extended air defenses in connection with, or independently of, the U.S. SDI research program.

A New Conventional Threat Situation?

In the past thirty years, NATO has built up a robust and diversified air defense in Western Europe: interceptor aircraft; hardened aircraft shelters; counter-strike aircraft; the NATO Air Defense Ground Environment (NADGE) surveil-lance network; Airborne Warning and Control System (AWACS) early warning aircraft; the Hawk barrier and other surface-to-air missiles (SAMs) of short (Roland, Crotale, and so on) or longer ranges (Patriot).

This continental scale "macro-system" offers Europe and the U.S. forces stationed there a degree of protection against the Soviet-manned air threat. Although it does not, at the present time, shield the theater against unmanned delivery vehicles, that is, Frog, Scud, and Scaleboard missiles, this lacuna has not been of major significance, since these rockets have lacked the precision to threaten Western assets without the use of weapons of mass destruction. The USSR would have to cross the nuclear threshold to use these systems effectively; and the answer to that would be, in either NATO or French doctrine, a nuclear riposte. Deterrence by threat of nuclear response was, and still is, the only known answer to such a threat.

The deployment of a new generation of Soviet missiles—SS-21s, 22s, 23s, and air- or sea-launched cruise missiles—has begun to transform the situation. Progress in guidance and precision will probably give the USSR a large-scale deep-strike conventional attack capability by the mid-nineties, using both manned and unmanned delivery vehicles. The latter will include a wide array of tactical ballistic missiles (TBMs); depressed trajectory ballistic missiles; cruise missiles—that is, air-launched cruise missiles (ALCMs), sea-launched cruise missiles (SLCMs), probably also ground-launched cruise missiles (GLCMs); and, not least, air-launched standoff missiles. In other words, the tactical ballistic missile threat, although technically one of the most challenging to defend against, will be only one facet of a much wider array.

The adversary's primary objective would be to eliminate in a very short span of time Allied air bases and other air-defense assets (radars and command centers) so as to allow him to prosecute the land battle under conditions of air supremacy.

This menace has given rise to the concept of extended air defense (EAD) forged almost simultaneously in France *(défense aérienne élargie)*[6] and in West Germany *(Erweiterte Luftverteidigung)*. Formulas such as European Defense Initiative (EDI)[7] or European SDI have usually been dropped from official statements, because of their potential for controversy and/or confusion with the long-term vision expressed by President Reagan.

European Theater Defense: Requirements and Capabilities

The basic requirement for an extended air defense macro-system would be to arrive at levels of overall performance approximating those of existing air defense against the existing manned air threat. Therefore, one is looking at:

1. Partial efficiencies (there will be, as with the air threat, a significant proportion of "leakers") for active systems as a whole.

2. A maximization of command, control, communication, and intelligence (C^3I) capabilities, to enhance force multiplication on the one hand (AWACS is a good example here), to allow graceful degradation on the other—as is the case, in a comparable area, for battlefield tactical command and control (C^2) of the Réseau Intégré de Transmissions Automatiques (RITA) or the Ptarmigan variety.

3. A stress on modular architectures, to enable partial system improvement over an extended period of time. Cost constraints combined with rapid technical change both push in this direction. The prime example here is that of Hawk, which, through multiple improvements, will probably have in the end a useful lifetime of around half a century.

4. Last, and maybe foremost, the studies concerning the architecture of extended air defense will need to consider the whole range of counter-measures in a coherent manner if an optimal balance is to be struck between cost and effectiveness. Hardening, dispersion, camouflage, and spoofing will often be of greater relevance, although maybe technically less exciting, than building up a multilayer active defense.

If the threat situation is the principal justification for change, consideration will nevertheless have to be given to replacement needs as an element for determining a deployment calendar. Since the Hawk barrier will probably be due for gradual phasing out during the last years of the century, this should be a major horizon for the introduction of a new medium-range SAM with antimissile capabilities. Similarly, the NADGE long-range surveillance system will need updating and replacement: such is one of the aims, over the next fifteen years, of the Air Command and Control System (ACCS) under NATO.

In the face of these requirements, what are the corresponding capabilities?

First of all, Western Europe and the United States have a long-standing record of successful cooperation, within the NATO framework, on air defense systems, be it SAMs (for example, Hawk) or the radars for NADGE.

Second, France's particular position within NATO has not prevented it from being completely involved in the alliance's air defense activities (Air Defense Committee, NADGE, Hawk improvement program), excluding AWACS.[8] The systematic, theaterwide nature of air defense has been long appreciated in France, and this has kept it "in" after 1966 while it moved out of most other military areas of NATO. Extended air defense may impose increased integration in terms of command and control; such questions should be addressed as they occur in the elaboration of a system (rather than posed in general a priori terms). The French are more pragmatic when faced with practical issues than they are sometimes thought to be—as long as they are not put under overt and/or political pressure.

Third, Western Europe's defense industry has a lead in the Western world in short-range air defense systems. The United States has yet to develop the equivalent of Crotale and Roland (used for the defense of U.S. bases in West Germany). Through the Hawk improvement programs, French, German and Italian defense firms have kept up in terms of medium-range systems and have learned to work with U.S. companies.

Lastly, in a different order of issues, developments at sea provide an anticipated, practical demonstration of the evolution of the overall threat. Since the sinking of the Israeli destroyer Eilat in 1967 by a Soviet-made Styx antishipping missile, the conventional tactical missile has been a practical rather than a theoretical threat at sea. The deployment of anti-sea-skimmer missile systems by the United States (Aegis), France (Crotale-Naval), the U.K. (Sea Wolf), and so on, is in the present rather than the future tense.

The development of naval vertical-launch antimissile systems to counter high-velocity/high-angle-of-reentry missiles is already in progress within several navies. Although there are obvious limits to transferability from sea to land, both in terms of threat and countermeasures, much duplication can be avoided by tying the existing naval state of the art to planning extended air defenses for the land theater.

Paths for Cooperation

The items previously described overlap to no small extent with the concepts, technologies, and potential combat systems evolving within SDI. This is particularly true in two fields: terminal-phase point defense and theaterwide integrated C³I. The congruence between SDI and extended air defense is therefore potentially quite large, even allowing for major differences in the threat situations and in the aims assigned to defense.

In practice, several paths need to be followed simultaneously by the Western Europeans, between themselves and/or with the Americans, to achieve progress. The multiplicity of approaches is not only imposed by the political facts of life; at this stage, it is also desirable, since the shape and structure of extended air defense is, as yet, undetermined—as is, therefore, the nature of the institutions that should build it up.

In this context, the following observations can be made, moving from the national level to the alliance as a whole, via European-based institutions:

National Endeavors. At present, only France has actually initiated the exploratory development of a possible Hawk replacement, with an antitactical missile (ATM) and an (at first residual) antitactical ballistic missile (ATBM) capability. The Surface/Sol Air Futur (SSAF)[9] could have its Initial Operational Capability (IOC) around 1994 for the naval version, preceding a planned ground-based variant. Other Western countries are still at the "paper program" stage: Mittleres Fla-Rak-System (MFS), or medium-range SAM, in the Federal Republic of Germany (F.R.G.), Medium-SAM in the United Kingdom.

The United States is also giving thought to a medium-range SAM project; but one should not forget that there is real work being done on major SDI-related projects with theater defense potential, such as the Low Endoatmospheric Defense Interceptor (LEDI) and High Endoatmospheric Defense Interceptor (HEDI).

European Cooperation. In practical terms, the position of the F.R.G. is crucial to any theaterwide extended air defense venture, given its geographical position and the fact that a significant portion of the possible target array is located there: 40 percent of Hawk batteries are based in the F.R.G. French/German cooperation as a core would make good technical and industrial sense, with possible inclusion of Italy (already involved in Hawk improvement) and the U.K. (which will need to replace its Bloodhound SAMs), around an SSAF/MFS-type system.

Beyond possible cooperation on prospective weapons systems fitting into extended air defense, the Western Europeans would do well to do some of their own concept elaboration and architecture planning. For the time being, this seems to be done only within national establishments and within NATO or U.S.-led ventures (for example, Strategic Defense Initiative Organization-(SDIO) initiated theater architecture studies). The Independent European Program Group (IEPG, which comprises all of the alliance's European members except for Iceland) would be the right sort of forum for this. In the absence of such European-initiated thought, the governments—and firms—of Western Europe should not be surprised if the operational, technical, and industrial solution for extended air defense will be determined by the United States. Such a situation would be all the more paradoxical since the threat is to a major extent specific to the European theater, and the U.S. taxpayer will legitimately consider that he should not have to shoulder more than a fraction of that burden.

U.S.-European Cooperation. A number of operations which have already been initiated directly between the United States and European countries have at least potential bearing on theater defense. The European architecture studies ordered by SDIO, either on a government-to-government basis (the U.S./U.K. study) or as competitive bids, come under this category, as do the U.S.-German discussions on the upgrading of Patriot (the plan here is to give Patriot some ATBM self-defense capability).

Such ventures are useful if they do in effect speed up progress, even if critics could be tempted to consider them as constituency-builders on the U.S. domestic front and/or as instruments that preclude Western European progress. The relative absence of European initiatives makes it particularly tempting for European firms or governments to enter into such competitions or arrangements. The limits here may actually be set by the United States itself, which, especially in the case of SDIO-led studies, may feel constrained by ABM-treaty or security considerations (for example, what kind of threat assessment does one share with others?) as the joint studies move through their various phases.

If and when decisions are made with respect to elements of extended air defense, such as the replacement for Hawk, industrial considerations will come to the forefront. If one is to have a theaterwide capability, and if one takes into account U.S. forces in Europe, the venture has to be of transatlantic dimensions. The question concerns the nature of U.S. industrial participation: as a leader (as had been the case in Hawk), or as co/subcontractor? The notion of a European leadership—implying European-originated concepts and architectures—is desirable both on political grounds (the financial burden being essentially European) and on legal grounds (no possible conflict with the U.S.-Soviet ABM Treaty). The defense industry of Western Europe has the competence to perform such a task. The natural locale for the implementation of cooperation, whatever its terms, should be NATO, for the same strategic and operational reasons that have put previous macro-systems such as NADGE and Hawk under its aegis.

Notes

1. This figure combines U.S. Department of Defense with U.S. Department of Energy military R&D expenditures.

2. The figures are $3.7 billion for the U.K., $3 billion for France, and $1 billion in the Federal Republic of Germany (F.R.G.), counting only public expenditures.

3. At the time of this writing, such agreements do exist with the U.K., the F.R.G., and Israel.

4. Exceptions are British and French involvement in military telecommunications satellites and France's incipient orbital observation program.

5. See excerpts of the speech by Mr. Orman (head of the official British SDI participation office) at Huntsville, Alabama, on May 12, 1986 (quoted in *Star Wars Intelligence Report*, May 13, 1986.)

6. See Heisbourg, "De la SDI à la Défense Aérienne Elargie," in *L'Armement* (March 1986).

7. *Europaische Verteidigungsinitiative* (European Defense Initiative) was briefly used by the German Ministry of Defense in the second half of 1985.

8. In the field of air defense, France is at least as tightly involved as the U.K. (which has attempted to develop its own AWACS-Nimrod and has not acquired Hawk).

9. The Surface/Sol Air Futur program is managed by Thomson-CSF (as industrial leader) and Aerospatiale (which is responsible for the "Aster" missile).

5

Alliance Strategy and Ballistic Missile Defense

David S. Yost

Research programs in ballistic missile defense (BMD) have been reorganized in the United States as elements of the Strategic Defense Initiative (SDI) and have been allocated increased funding as a consequence of President Ronald Reagan's March 1983 speech. The question of whether the SDI research programs will eventually lead to U.S. BMD development and deployment decisions is hypothetical. The USSR, in contrast, has operational BMD capabilities today (within ABM Treaty constraints) and is continuing to improve an infrastructure capable of supporting large-scale deployments of BMD systems of traditional ground-based types. Soviet research and development activities in more advanced BMD and space-warfare technologies and Soviet investments in active and passive forms of strategic defense have long been complemented by vigorous offensive-force modernization and expansion. The continued improvement of Soviet BMD and Soviet ballistic missile strike capabilities seems likely to help sustain the SDI research programs, and could eventually contribute to justifying BMD deployment decisions in the United States and Western Europe.

The potential implications of BMD for alliance strategy and Western security are not self-evident. They will depend on a large number of factors that may well evolve in unpredictable ways. Five factors stand out as especially significant: (a) which BMD technologies may prove feasible at militarily effective levels and at costs deemed affordable by Western governments, given the opportunity costs posed by other demands on national and defense budgets; (b) the effects of other advanced technologies that may be introduced more or less simultaneously with BMD capabilities (for example, low-observable "stealth" delivery systems and highly accurate long-range conventional munitions); (c) the future of existing arms-control limitations on BMD (above all, the ABM Treaty) and the results of current and subsequent negotiations; (d) the political resolve with which the United States and allied governments

The views expressed are those of the author alone and should not be construed to represent those of the Department of the Navy or any U.S. government agency.

pursue treaty-permitted BMD research and respond to Soviet BMD activities and Soviet ballistic missile strike capabilities; and (e) the specific challenges to Western security posed by Soviet BMD programs, in combination with other Soviet capabilities.

The latter factor comprehends the most explicitly strategic questions. While it is obviously artificial to isolate strategic questions from considerations of technological feasibility, cost and cost-effectiveness, arms control, national and allied decision-making, and so forth, the potential strategic risks and opportunities deserve special attention. When SDI was first announced, the president's visionary goals—to explore the technical feasibility of "rendering these nuclear weapons impotent and obsolete" and "eliminating the threat posed by strategic nuclear missiles"[1]—tended to lead commentators on strategic issues to focus on the potential implications of a transition to a defense-dominant U.S.-Soviet relationship. It was sometimes feared, for example, that Western Europe could take on the appearance of a potential battlefield between protected superpowers.[2]

It is now more widely recognized, however, that a situation of defense dominance is not likely to be a matter of practical concern for at least two decades. The United States does not envisage strategic BMD development decisions until the early 1990s, with production decisions—and deployment— foreseen for later periods, if then;[3] for the results of the research may not meet official criteria of survivability and cost-effectiveness,[4] and arms control and economic constraints (to say nothing of altered strategic assessments) could also affect deployment choices. For at least two decades to come, therefore, the Atlantic Alliance is far more likely to be concerned with imperfect defenses than with systems of such high effectiveness that a defense-dominant situation could be established.

Moreover, the most likely BMD deployments in the next decade would consist of ground-based interceptors of essentially traditional types. While the operational reliability and effectiveness of such systems would be relatively uncertain, the systems would be based on known technologies. At present, the USSR appears to be better placed than the West to engage in large-scale deployments of such systems.[5] Since this is a much more plausible medium-term challenge for Western strategy than a situation of U.S.-Soviet defense dominance, it deserves more sustained attention than hypothetical and distant conditions. This preliminary exploration will therefore briefly consider three questions:

1. What is the military strategy of the Atlantic Alliance?
2. Given Soviet strategic priorities, what would be the implications for Western strategy if the USSR obtained a substantial lead in deployed BMD capabilities?

3. What functions could BMD research programs and, ultimately, BMD deployments in North America and Western Europe perform to meet Western security requirements?

The emphasis on BMD could be misleading, despite the importance of ballistic missiles as a means of delivering nuclear and—increasingly—conventional and chemical munitions. BMD should ideally not be isolated from the overall context of other forms of defense (active and passive) or from offensive-force developments or from the means of command, control, and communications (C^3) that would direct the employment of active defenses and offensive forces in operational contingencies. Moreover, comprehensive analyses would go beyond speculation about the implications of differing force inventories and levels of defensive capabilities to consider additional factors that are quite relevant to deterrence and war outcomes: strategic planning, operational tactics, deception and surprise, training, endurance, intelligence, maintenance and logistics, force reconstitution assets, and so on.[6]

The Military Strategy of the Western Alliance

The predominant objective of Western strategy is deterrence of Soviet aggression. This extends beyond discouraging direct attack to neutralizing Soviet power pressures in peacetime so that attempts at coercion and intimidation cannot succeed. If the Western Alliance failed in its deterrent objective, it would try to prevent the expansion of any armed conflict and to manage the crisis—regaining any lost territory as rapidly as possible and with as little violence as possible. The overriding aim has been to provide the Soviet leadership with incentives to settle the conflict on terms consistent with Western security interests.

The strategy of "flexible response," which was adopted in 1967, is not intended to guide NATO in winning a hypothetical NATO-Warsaw Pact war but rather to deter aggression and, if necessary, to obtain a cessation of hostilities and restore prewar boundaries by convincing the USSR that unacceptable risks of uncontrollable nuclear escalation could result from failure to desist in aggression and withdraw. In the words of the Defense Planning Committee's 1975 Ministerial Guidance,

> The primary aim is to deter an attack before it is launched, by making it clear to any aggressor that any attack on NATO would be met by a strong defense and might initiate a sequence of events which cannot be calculated in advance, involving risks to the aggressor out of all proportion to any advantages he might hope to gain. . . . Should aggression occur, the military aim is to preserve or restore the integrity and security of the NATO area by employing such

forces as may be necessary within the concept of forward defence and flexibility in response . . . the conventional forces should be strong enough to resist and repel a conventional attack on a limited scale, and to deter larger scale conventional attacks through the prospect of an expansion of the area, scale and intensity of hostilities, which could lead to the use of nuclear weapons. . . . The purpose of the tactical nuclear capability is . . . to convince the aggressor that any form of attack on NATO could result in very serious damage to his own forces, and to emphasize the dangers implicit in the continuance of a conflict by presenting him with the risk that such a situation could escalate beyond his control to all-out nuclear war.[7]

While not an official statement on behalf of the alliance, a West German defense white paper included a particularly concise description of the scenario envisaged by NATO:

The initial tactical use of nuclear weapons must be timed as late as possible but as early as necessary, which is to say that the doctrine of Forward Defense must retain its validity, the conventional forces of the defender must not be exhausted, and incalculability must be sustained so far as the attacker is concerned. The initial use of nuclear weapons is not intended so much to bring about a military decision as to achieve a political effect. The intent is to persuade the attacker to reconsider his intention, to desist in his aggression, and to withdraw. At the same time, it will be impressed upon him that he risks still further escalation if he continues to attack. Such further escalation would mean that [U.S.] strategic nuclear weapons would be used against the attacker's own territory. Such weapons would initially be used selectively against military targets.[8]

The guidelines worked out by NATO's Nuclear Planning Group since its establishment in 1967 have concurred with these principles for any initial as well as follow-on use of U.S. nuclear weapons that Soviet aggression might force on NATO.[9] Dependence on U.S. nuclear retaliatory threats has remained high, partly because the Western allies have consistently chosen for over three decades not to build up conventional forces comparable to those of the USSR and its allies. As a result, the alliance's situation continues to be that described by the Supreme Allied Commander Europe (SACEUR), General Bernard W. Rogers, in 1982:

Instead of possessing the variety of capabilities which would truly translate into flexibility in response, NATO is left in a posture that in reality can only support a strategy more accurately labeled a 'delayed tripwire.' The amount of delay following a conventional Warsaw Pact attack before the tripwire would be activated and NATO would face resorting to the nuclear option would depend on such variables as length of warning time and the timeliness and appropriateness of decisions taken by political authorities.[10]

Ballistic missile defense has historically been of little operational importance in Western strategy. Indeed, since the conclusion of the ABM Treaty in 1972, a widespread presumption in the West has been that East-West strategic stability and Western security depend on prolonging a situation of mutual vulnerability to nuclear attack. Because of this presumption (and on grounds of technical feasibility, cost, and cost-effectiveness), the West has invested relatively little in passive defenses (civil defense, hardening, mobility, and so forth), in BMD research, or in deployments of air defenses against Soviet aircraft and cruise missiles—in comparison to Soviet defenses against such delivery systems, and in relation to the evolution of the Soviet threat.

The air defenses of North America are especially thin; and air defenses are not much thicker in the northern and southern flank areas of Western Europe. Even in Central Europe, where Western air-defense efforts have been most earnest, there are serious deficiencies. Major General Jörg Bahnemann of the West German Air Force, who is also vice chairman of the NATO Air Defense Committee, recently noted that NATO's Central Region air defenses are currently incapable of intercepting Soviet ballistic missiles or cruise missiles (the radar cross sections of the latter are too small for deployed Western radars). NATO defenses are also inadequate for dealing with the Warsaw Pact force of "about 1,000 armoured helicopters and their anticipated surprise jump operations" and the "about 4,000 [Warsaw Pact] combat aircraft in offensive roles."

> NATO could win in most of the individual duels but massive air raids, coming in well timed waves, could saturate and break through our air defenses and attack vital assets, command centers, and logistic installations of our forces. . . . Unfortunately we have not made the necessary investments for the respective command, control, communications [C³] and information systems. We have not even been able to agree on concepts and technical approaches for an identification system, not to speak of the stringent need to have survivable sensors and operations centers, secure and ECM [electronic countermeasure] resistant communications and sufficient redundancy of the system.[11]

Soviet Strategic Priorities

The Soviet concept of deterrence differs from the one that is dominant in Western thinking in that the Soviets are not guided by a concept of strategic stability based on rough parity in offensive-force capabilities and mutual societal vulnerability; instead, for the Soviets, deterrence is an ability to "restrain" or coerce their adversaries by marshalling a superior array of war-fighting and damage-limiting capabilities as part of an overall "correlation of forces" increasingly favorable to the USSR. The priority attached to avoiding war has been accentuated by nuclear conditions. But, if war were to become unavoidable, the

Soviets would aim to limit the scope of operations and pursue political aims with regard to postwar configurations of power.

It is doubtful whether the Soviets ever single out strategic nuclear forces for the isolated attention typical of Western analyses. Soviet strategic-force planning appears to be embedded in—and practically inseparable from—comprehensive planning for the management of threats and the advancement of Soviet political aims without war, to the maximum extent possible.

While U.S. strategic nuclear planning tends to neglect or even "to forget about what might be the local outcome of the regional conflict that probably precipitated the strategic exchange,"[12] Soviet planning remains resolutely political and focused on war outcomes—that is, how the USSR could gain political control in the specific contiguous regions of greatest interest for the Soviet power position in the postwar period. Of all the potential theaters of military operations contiguous to the Soviet Union, none is more important than Western Europe. As Fritz Ermarth has remarked, "The U.S.S.R. tends to see intercontinental forces, and strategic forces more generally, as a means to help it win an all-out conflict in its most crucial theater, Europe."[13]

It is plausible that as Soviet strategic nuclear forces have become more numerous and survivable, Soviet military theorists have reasoned that a situation could be created in which nuclear conflict at any level of intensity could lead to a worse outcome for the Atlantic Alliance than for the USSR. By matching and even exceeding U.S. nuclear capabilities in specific areas, the USSR could hypothetically discourage the United States from initiating the use of nuclear weapons under any circumstances—or perhaps, at least, convince the United States not to strike targets in the USSR, for fear of Soviet retaliation against the U.S. homeland. According to Lieutenant General M.M. Kir'yan, the constant launch readiness of the Strategic Rocket Forces is intended to function as "the main restraining factor against the aggressive aspirations of hostile forces."[14] While the intercontinental ballistic missile (ICBM) force has specific advantages in terms of readiness and accuracy, Soviet authorities have described their submarine-launched ballistic missile (SLBM) and long-range bomber fleets as forces that also contribute significantly to "restraining" the "imperialists."[15]

The Soviet doctrinal interest in achieving operational effectiveness in all relevant categories of combat potential does not imply any inclination to initiate a nuclear war, or indeed any war. Military prowess is intended to provide backing for Soviet peacetime diplomacy in various ways. Highly effective war-waging capabilities (including active and passive forms of strategic defense) are seen as likely to deter the initiation of war by any adversary of the Soviet state, and such capabilities might enable the USSR to make political gains through intimidation. If war should nonetheless arise, the Soviets would intend to try to limit it to the operations necessary to achieve their essential political objectives, and to deter the United States and other nuclear-armed governments from using nuclear weapons or (if one or more opposing governments had initiated such use) from expanding the geographical extent of nuclear operations.

Soviet leaders certainly recognize the reality of Soviet vulnerability in nuclear war; however, "Even within the confines of mutual vulnerability, Soviet military strategy still focuses on how to wage a nuclear war and defeat the enemy, if such a war should occur."[16] One means for improving Soviet prospects of victory in nuclear war is to reduce Soviet vulnerabilities. In the Soviet view, mutual vulnerability need not mean equal vulnerability. The Soviet Union has accordingly invested far more than the West in countermilitary strike capabilities and in active and passive defenses. This has included BMD, within the constraints of the ABM Treaty.

Soviet Ballistic Missile Defense

As Sayre Stevens, a former deputy director of the Central Intelligence Agency, has noted, there remain "many uncertainties about the Soviet BMD program, its achievements, technical objectives, and overall intent."[17] Many of these uncertainties derive, of course, from Soviet secrecy and efforts to deny Western intelligence services any knowledge of Soviet BMD. Other uncertainties derive from the difficulty of establishing whether the Soviets intend to use specific systems for BMD purposes or for other purposes (for example, attacking aircraft or satellites, or simply for surveillance). "We will probably never have absolute proof short of their performance in actual battle."[18] Even if the intended function were clear, the reliability and effectiveness of the system in combat would still be unclear—even, to a lesser degree, to the Soviets themselves.

It is nonetheless clear that Soviet BMD investments steadily increased after the ABM Treaty and its 1974 Protocol limited the United States and the Soviet Union to a single BMD site each. In contrast, U.S. investments in BMD activities fell after the conclusion of these agreements and after the 1975 congressional directive to close down the Safeguard system in North Dakota. Some experts estimate that the allocation of resources shifted from an approximate 2 to 1 advantage favoring the United States in BMD technology and development spending in the late 1960s to a possible Soviet advantage of 5 to 1 in 1980.[19] Soviet investments have been concentrated on upgrading the Moscow system, developing potentially BMD-capable surface-to-air missiles, deploying new large phased-array radars, and pioneering exotic technologies, such as directed-energy weapons.

Modernization of the treaty-permitted Moscow system became apparent in 1978. The original 64 Galosh interceptors are being replaced by improved exoatmospheric Galosh interceptors and by new SH-08 Gazelle high-acceleration endoatmospheric interceptors.[20] The Gazelle is especially significant because it can rely on atmospheric sorting to discriminate real warheads from decoys. According to an official statement prepared by the British Ministry of Defense, this endoatmospheric interceptor "will enable discrimination against all but the most elaborate penetration aids."[21] The Gazelle is based in silos that may be equipped with an underground automatic reload system.[22] The Soviets could reach the treaty-permitted total of one hundred launchers in the Moscow site by 1987.[23] While the modernized Moscow system (also known as ABM-X-3) includes fixed radars such as the enormous new Pushkino installation, in some ways the Pawn Shop missile guidance radars and Flat Twin tracking radars are more impressive, because of their modular construction. The Flat Twin is readily transportable, and could be mass-produced, concealed, and deployed fairly rapidly at sites requiring relatively little preparation.[24]

Three Soviet surface-to-air missiles (SAMs) may have some BMD capability: the SA-5, SA-10, and SA-X-12. Although the SA-5 has been repeatedly improved since the 1960s and was tested some fifty times in conjunction with ballistic missile flights in the early 1970s,[25] the approximately two thousand SA-5 launchers probably still represent only a marginal BMD capability. The SA-10 is deployed in about eight hundred launchers, more than half of them near Moscow, and mobile SA-10s are currently being deployed. According to the U.S. Department of Defense, both the SA-10 and the extensively tested experimental SA-X-12 "may have the potential to intercept some types of U.S. strategic ballistic missiles."[26] All three SAMs are more likely to be able to intercept older-generation SLBM warheads than ICBM warheads, because the former are generally slower and offer larger radar cross sections. This is significant because U.S. ICBMs are subject to attack on the ground, while U.S. SLBMs at sea are presumed to be less vulnerable.[27]

The SA-X-12 may also be an antitactical ballistic missile (ATBM), in that the U.S. Department of Defense judges that the SA-X-12 "may have the capability to engage the Lance and both the Pershing I and Pershing II ballistic missiles."[28] The SA-X-12 has reportedly been successfully tested against Soviet intermediate-range missiles, such as the Scaleboard.[29] The SA-X-12 is also notable because its mobility could enable the Soviets to build thousands of them and conceal them in storage until they were ready to deploy them relatively rapidly.[30]

The new large phased-array radars (LPARs) under construction in the USSR are significant because they could supplement older radars with hand-over early warning and pointing data for the new ABM-X-3 Moscow system and the potentially BMD-capable SAMs. In February 1985 the U.S. government announced its judgment that one of the new Soviet LPARs, near Krasnoyarsk, is a violation of the ABM Treaty, given its location hundreds of miles inland and its inward orientation.[31] When the Krasnoyarsk LPAR and the five others like it become operational in the late 1980s, the final gaps will be closed in the

Soviet BMD radar coverage network.[32] According to the U.S. Central Intelligence Agency, the LPARs will provide the USSR with "a much improved capability for ballistic missile early warning, attack assessment, and targeting" and will be "technically capable of providing battle management support to a widespread ABM system."[33] In December 1986, the discovery of three additional modern LPARs in the western USSR was revealed; these are expected to become operational in the early 1990s, and will supplement the coverage provided by existing radars.[34]

Soviet BMD research based on exotic technologies—from hypervelocity kinetic-energy railguns to directed-energy systems (lasers, particle beams, and radiofrequency signals)—began in the mid-1960s. In 1979, the U.S. Department of Defense estimated that Soviet spending on high-energy lasers was five times that of the United States.[35] The laser programs are especially significant because they represent the earliest weaponization prospects.[36] The ground-based lasers at Sary Shagan today seem capable of interfering only with low-altitude U.S. satellites. Ground-based laser BMD prototypes should not be expected until the late 1980s. Space-based laser BMD systems are not likely until after the year 2000, and will probably be preceded by space-based anti-satellite lasers.[37]

The United States retains superiority in various BMD-relevant technologies, including microelectronics and high-speed data processing; but the USSR has taken precedence in applying such technologies to BMD and in getting BMD capabilities fielded. As long ago as 1978, U.S. Secretary of Defense Harold Brown remarked that the U.S. lead in BMD technology had been "greatly diminished" since the ABM Treaty had been approved in 1972.[38] The modernization of the Moscow complex, the potentially BMD-capable SAMs, and the new LPARs make it plausible that the Soviets could achieve significant partial BMD coverage in the next decade, well before the United States could achieve comparable capabilities. Because of the transportable and concealable nature of many of the components, the actual deployments could be made in months if the new LPARs were in place—as they are expected to be.[39]

The ABM Treaty has therefore not prevented the USSR from making progress toward substantial BMD capabilities. Whether one wishes to characterize the activities as a gradual "creep-out" from the ABM Treaty or as the groundwork for a potential decision for a relatively rapid "breakout,"

> The Soviets have the major components for an ABM system that could be used for widespread ABM deployments well in excess of the ABM Treaty limits. . . . They could undertake rapidly paced ABM deployments to strengthen the defenses at Moscow and cover key targets in the western USSR, and to extend protection to key targets east of the Urals, by the early 1990s.[40]

In other words, the strategically relevant BMD asymmetry between the United States and the USSR in the near term (that is, the next decade) does not reside in either side's advantage in specific technologies but in the Soviet option for widespread BMD deployments. These deployments would not consist of space-based "exotic" systems but of ground-based radars and interceptor missiles of essentially traditional types. The continually enhanced BMD infrastructure gives the USSR, as Sayre Stevens has noted, an option "to deploy limited ABM defenses widely and rapidly at a time of its choosing. The United States has no comparable option and is at least five years away from having one."[41] James A. Schear has added that

> there is little dispute that components of the ABM-X-3 system, which is essentially ready to deploy, could be proliferated nationwide fairly rapidly—perhaps over a period of one to three years—if the Soviets (for whatever reason) decided to take the step. From the strategic standpoint, a grater capacity for rapid deployment of ABM components—even within the confines of the treaty—does confer some break-out advantage. . . . Such a capacity would become especially significant in the context of other developments, such as the mass production and stockpiling of components, the further construction of LPARs, or the preparation of possible deployment sites at priority target areas.[42]

The technological quality of the BMD systems deployed by the USSR in such circumstances would probably be inferior to the more exacting standards of the United States; but this technical inferiority would not necessarily rule out the acquisition of strategically useful capabilities. The Soviet lag in microelectronics, for example, need not be a major hindrance: "Much of the necessary hardware needed can get along quite well using older circuitry and components. This use of older technologies can even demonstrate some benefits such as greater 'hardness' with respect to the effects of Electromagnetic Pulses generated by nuclear detonations (EMP)."[43]

Potential Consequences for the Alliance

A significant Soviet advantage in deployed BMD capabilities would supplement a Soviet military posture already keenly attuned to the risks of nuclear war. Paradoxical as it may seem, the extensive Soviet investments in active and passive defenses and in offensive forces probably testify to the seriousness with which the Soviets approach nuclear war, and to their desire to avert and avoid it. In the event of war involving the Soviet armed forces, the Soviet leadership would presumably wish to prevent nuclear strikes on Soviet soil and, to the maximum extent possible, to keep any operational use of nuclear weapons under control. It makes sense for the Soviets to try to maximize their chances of achieving victory through conventional means alone. The use of nuclear weapons would increase uncertainties about the outcome of an East-West war in Europe. The development of Soviet nuclear war-waging capabilities appears therefore to be intended to degrade the credibility of NATO's nuclear threats and to give the USSR more discriminate and controllable nuclear options, in case they are required to achieve victory.[44]

The apparent Soviet preference for conducting only conventional and, if need be, limited nuclear operations does not imply any Soviet willingness to conform to the scenario postulated in NATO's strategy of flexible response. (As noted earlier, the declared intent of NATO strategy in planning for initial and follow-on use of nuclear weapons is "to persuade the attacker to reconsider his intention, to desist in his aggression, and to withdraw."[45]) It is rather the reverse: Soviet strategy aims to convince Western governments to desist in their resistance by being better prepared than NATO to prevail at any and all higher levels of violence. The "objective conditions" of existing-force balances and capabilities—including Soviet superiority in strategic defenses and survivable nuclear weapons and operational military assets—might persuade NATO governments not to initiate nuclear use or not to engage in more extensive use after the failure of initial selective strikes. It would be in the interests of the Soviets to maximize the probability of escalation control, or stalemate, at the intercontinental level, and thus to confine war to more manageable levels of intensity, with more attainable and more politically meaningful results.

In order to highlight some of the key implications for the Atlantic Alliance of an expansion in Soviet BMD capabilities, this brief discussion will concentrate on a hypothetical and, it is hoped, improbable situation of a large Soviet unilateral BMD advantage. The four principal implications represent extreme and "pure" cases to the extent that they are not qualified by Western countermeasures.

1. The credibility of NATO's strategy of "flexible response" could be reduced. NATO's flexible response strategy includes the threat of selective employment of nuclear weapons against targets in the USSR and elsewhere in the Warsaw Pact, but elements of this threat could be directly countered by Soviet BMD. To the extent that NATO's selective nuclear-strike options depend on U.S. ICBMs, SLBMs, and shorter-range ballistic missiles such as the Pershing I, Pershing II, and Lance, Soviet BMD could erode the credibility of NATO strategy.

The degree to which U.S. "extended deterrence" guarantees would be undone would depend in part on the level of effectiveness of Soviet BMD, in combination with other active defenses, in denying U.S. ballistic missiles and other nuclear and nonnuclear delivery means access to the Soviet Union and the Warsaw Pact as a whole. Traditional ground-based BMD deployments might, however, be effective against the types of nuclear attacks NATO would be most likely to mount—selective and restrained attacks, as Kevin Lewis has suggested:

> Since ICBMs probably will remain the instrument of choice for limited strategic attacks over the near term, it could very well be the case that *even a fairly modest new Soviet ABM deployment could jeopardize our limited employment capability*. Unfortunately, constraints on the azimuth of the ICBM threat to the USSR, the extended flight times of U.S. land-based missiles (compared with some INF [intermediate-range nuclear forces] and SLBMs), and other factors would combine to render U.S. land-based missiles incapable of some, perhaps many, limited employment missions should new Soviet ABM deployments take place.[46]

The value of U.S. ballistic missiles as a deterrent to Soviet aggression and as a lever to enforce intrawar restraint on the USSR could thus be reduced. Air-breathing systems (aircraft and cruise missiles), perhaps equipped with "stealth" technology to reduce signatures visible to Soviet radars, could still be used to attack targets in the USSR; but they would have to penetrate the extremely dense and sophisticated Soviet air defenses (SAMs and fighter-interceptors). The "thicker" and more effective the combination of Soviet BMD and air defenses, the higher the level of weapons attrition per target for NATO would be—and the harder it would be for the United States to honor the "flexible response" guarantees. If Soviet BMD and air-defense programs resulted in at least partial neutralization of U.S. extended-deterrence guarantees to NATO Europe, Western Europe would be more vulnerable to Soviet attack or intimidation, since it would be harder for the United States to threaten retaliation for Soviet aggression.

Three alternatives to trying to penetrate Soviet BMD and air defenses with limited strikes can be imagined. One would be to attack relatively peripheral targets in areas not covered by defenses of the Warsaw Pact and the Soviet zone of interior—for example, Soviet naval forces at sea, such as nuclear-powered ballistic missile submarines (SSBNs), or Soviet forces in Vietnam or Cuba. This threat would, however, probably not offer as much value in deterring the Soviets as threatening targets in the USSR proper.

A second alternative would be to use much larger commitments of ballistic missiles, aircraft, and/or cruise missiles to try to overwhelm Soviet BMD and air defenses and thus deliver the selective strikes envisaged in NATO strategy. Soviet BMD and air defenses might well prove inadequate in the face of a large-scale U.S. attack. This alternative would, however, be less than entirely satisfactory or plausible, because it would then be much harder for NATO to communicate restraint in intent, which is one key to controlling escalation.[47]

A third alternative would be attacking poorly defended targets in the USSR. These targets would be, by definition, of lesser value to the Soviets, and such a choice of targets by the United States might fail to impress the Soviets with the imperative of early war termination on terms acceptable to the Atlantic Alliance.

In short, Soviet ground-based BMD deployments could raise serious problems for the selective nuclear strikes envisaged in NATO's flexible response strategy. Targeting flexibility could be constrained; damage expectancies could be even more unpredictable; weapons requirements could be increased; and escalation control prospects could be made even more uncertain. Given the difficulties and dilemmas Soviet BMD would clearly pose for NATO strategy, and the corresponding strategic advantages for the USSR, it seems plausible that the Soviets long ago recognized these potential advantages and have purposefully sought to realize them. Soviet BMD programs are probably partly motivated by a desire to erode the credibility and effectiveness of NATO's flexible response strategy.

The effective neutralization of key elements of NATO's ability to threaten selective nuclear strikes must have a certain attraction for the Soviets, because NATO needs such limited options more than the USSR does. The USSR has built up the Warsaw Pact's conventional capabilities to such a degree that for deterrence and, if necessary, for conflict management, NATO is heavily dependent on threats of escalation to such limited nuclear strikes—on the assumption that the Soviets would eventually desist rather than face further escalation. The Soviets have already narrowed the flexibility of U.S. nuclear choices by building "counter-deterrent" retaliatory capabilities. Moderately effective ground-based BMD in the USSR could further constrain this flexibility.

2. Potential Soviet control over the escalation process could be enhanced. Various Western observers have argued for several years that the Soviets may already enjoy a degree of "escalation dominance," owing to the virtually complete vulnerability of the U.S. homeland and land-based U.S. strategic forces to Soviet ballistic missile attack. Manfred Wörner, for example, prior to becoming West Germany's minister of defense, argued that "the ability by the United States to control the process of escalation in the event of a conflict in Europe" was critically dependent on the U.S. ICBM force: "For the foreseeable future, land-based ICBMs represent the most reliable, quickly reactive and accurate strategic weapons, especially in terms of systems applicable to a conflict in Europe. Only survivable ICBMs fill the NATO requirement of keeping open the options of first and selective use of nuclear weapons."[48]

Uwe Nerlich drew this conclusion in more explicit terms: "Without invulnerable American ICBMs, extended deterrence ceases to be a rational objective. . . . The possibility of a [Soviet] strike against American ICBMs in response to a limited strategic strike in a European contingency is likely to constrain strategic flexibility from the outset."[49] Since U.S. ICBM vulnerability has now been widely acknowledged to be far more serious than Soviet ICBM vulnerability[50] (though the significance of this situation is still debated), it can be argued that the Soviets could already be at an advantage in exerting escalation control in a crisis or war.

This does not necessarily mean that the Soviets would conduct an actual attack against all or part of the U.S. ICBM force. Indeed, the Soviets would probably prefer not to conduct such an attack, because of the high risks involved. Although a Soviet first strike against U.S. ICBMs and other vulnerable U.S. nuclear forces would dramatically shift the "correlation of forces" and make Soviet "escalation dominance" more concrete, the issue here is Soviet escalation dominance in crises and more limited conflicts, owing in part to Western assessments of Soviet operational prowess and relative Soviet and Western vulnerabilities. Some observers have rejected the concept of escalation dominance with the argument that relative degrees of operational superiority are meaningless in the nuclear age; but Soviet and Western assessments of comparative strengths and vulnerabilities could have undeniable political significance for influencing decisions in concrete circumstances.

By this logic, the credibility of U.S. guarantees has been in decline since the late 1950s, when the United States first became vulnerable to prompt Soviet nuclear retaliation against the U.S. homeland in response to any U.S. use of nuclear weapons in defense of Western Europe; and the disappearance of U.S. nuclear superiority during the SALT I period (1969-1972) has led to further deterioration, owing to the continuing advance of Soviet capabilities to retaliate in kind for any U.S. nuclear employment against Soviet interests. Uncertainties about the credibility of the U.S. extended-deterrence guarantees articulated in NATO's flexible response strategy and about the U.S. ability to exert control over the escalation process have in fact been widespread and increasing in expert circles in the West for many years. According to Hans Rühle, the head of the Planning Staff in the West German Ministry of Defense,

> The previous clear-cut superiority of the U.S. in the realm of strategic nuclear weapons has been replaced by an approximate parity. . . . In the sphere of intermediate-range nuclear systems the Soviet Union has come to enjoy a clear superiority—even when all the NATO states will have implemented the dual-track decision of 1979. The nuclear escalation dominance of the U.S. has thus been lost, while escalation control has become extremely difficult [for the U.S.]. The effectiveness of extended deterrence has thereby necessarily been diminished. . . . This implies on the other hand that the Soviet Union's ability to threaten Western Europe militarily and intimidate it politically has increased considerably.[51]

If the Soviet Union were to gain a unilateral BMD advantage significantly larger than the one it currently possesses, the increased asymmetry in the already important differences in relative U.S. and Soviet vulnerabilities could endow the USSR with a more clear-cut ability to try to influence U.S. nuclear employment decisions—that is, to control escalation by "deterring the U.S. deterrent." This might occur because a BMD "cap" composed of ground-based interceptors could significantly complement the USSR's other active defenses (air defenses, antisatellite systems, and so forth) and passive defenses (in addition to civil defenses, command and control and force protection measures based on hardening, redundancy, concealment, dispersion, and mobility) to further reduce the relative vulnerability of the USSR's most valued assets in war. John Gardner, then director of defense systems for the U.S. Department of Defense, testified in 1983 that given the USSR's air defenses and passive defenses, ". . . if we fail to be able to contain the Soviet Union from providing active ballistic missile defenses, then of course we put ourselves in some serious jeopardy with respect to our ability to retain a significant damage capability against them."[52]

The practical effects of this reduction in vulnerability could be manifested in various ways. It is probable that the Soviets would still prefer to achieve their political objectives without war and would still be highly conscious of the risks and uncertainties of war in the nuclear age. On the other hand, the situation would be changed to the extent that the Soviet leadership and NATO governments believed the USSR capable of countering a U.S. ballistic missile attack. The reduction in Soviet vulnerability could therefore lead to: (a) fewer Soviet inhibitions in contemplating aggression; (b) increased Soviet advantages in intrawar bargaining and war-termination negotiations; and, most important, (c) an improved Soviet ability to control directly the scope of nuclear escalation, owing to an enhanced ability to counter and absorb selective U.S. nuclear attacks against the Soviet Union, with the U.S. less well defended against possible Soviet attacks.

The latter effect would be most important for Western Europe in war, because it would imply an improved Soviet ability to carry theater offensives forward. The Soviets might be able to project military power into Western Europe with less fear of (or hindrance from) U.S. long-range strike forces based on ballistic missiles. This could in turn increase the operational and political importance of Soviet conventional and shorter-range nuclear force advantages. Strategic defense, including BMD, is vital to the USSR, partly because "it is imperative as a backdrop for managing theatre warfare of the kind she is preparing for."[53]

While there are significant asymmetries in U.S. and Soviet capabilities for intercontinental nuclear war, the more likely cases of crisis and limited conflict would probably involve threats of limited and selective nuclear employment. In such cases, the relative vulnerabilities of the Atlantic Alliance and the USSR could affect decision making as to escalatory options. The USSR would have a logical incentive to maintain strategic nuclear war-waging capabilities that could act as a counter-deterrent to dissuade the United States from escalating any eventual war to the intercontinental level, and that could thus work to confine wars to levels of violence short of nuclear strikes against Soviet territory. At the same time, the USSR could aim to be as well prepared as possible for the extension of war to greater regional depth and higher levels of destructiveness and, as a worst case, to intercontinental exchanges. These capabilities could help to hold down the level of violence and enable the USSR to terminate conflicts on Soviet terms.

The Soviets may also foresee that increasing the significance of their conventional and shorter-range nuclear force advantages could logically lead NATO governments to recognize increased requirements for similar forces in the West. The Soviets could anticipate that this would exacerbate already divisive intra-NATO debates on burden sharing with respect to conventional-force efforts and on requirements for modernizing shorter-range nuclear forces—at a time when some political trends in NATO favor withdrawing such nuclear forces, and when the Soviets are increasing their nuclear artillery and short-range missile capabilities. Further theater-force expansion could be attractive to the Soviets, in order to capitalize on this situation, even in the context of new Soviet arms-control proposals in Geneva and at the Vienna negotiations on Mutual and Balanced Force Reductions.

Moreover, the Soviets could well speculate that another effect of heavy unilateral BMD and air defenses in the USSR could be the virtual reduction of NATO military options to short-range nuclear and nonnuclear battlefield weapons. This would imply a war limited to Europe—a concept that would be more welcome to the Soviets than a war involving the Soviet homeland; but this concept is unlikely to be approved by Western European governments. For most Western Europeans, a threat to use a large number of battlefield nuclear weapons (and thus create a "radiation zone" 50 km or so wide) would be no solution; for even if that threat would deter the Soviets (and defeat a Warsaw Pact offensive), the cost to West Germany and Western Europe as a whole would be too high to be sustained before public opinion. Enhanced radiation warheads could limit collateral damage and residual radio-activity, but these distinctions would probably not make the concept more attractive to Western European governments.

It would be all too clear that NATO had only this single military option if possible long-range U.S. strikes were virtually neutralized by Soviet BMD and air defenses and if NATO as a whole proved politically incapable of generating sufficient conventional forces to deter and defeat Warsaw Pact aggression. The cohesion of the Atlantic Alliance could therefore be severely undermined. If any eventual war seemed virtually certain to be confined to Europe and likely to be intense and protracted, some Western Europeans might find surrender preferable to armed resistance.

3. Soviet prospects for victory in conventional operations could be improved. Prospective improvements in Soviet escalation-control capabilities are clearly closely related to the declining credibility of the selective nuclear-strike threats intrinsic to NATO's flexible response strategy. The improvements in Soviet offensive nuclear capabilities over the past two decades may have already had the effect of creating a certain counter-deterrent to U.S. threats to use nuclear weapons in defense of Western Europe. If Soviet BMD led to the direct neutralization of U.S. ballistic missile-delivered nuclear threats and enhanced Soviet prospects for escalation control, this would increase the probability that any future war in Europe might remain at the conventional level of operations. The USSR has actively sought this development, because it would reinstate the importance of Soviet conventional force superiority. NATO strategy has since the outset countered Soviet conventional superiority with nuclear threats, and the USSR has tried to neutralize these threats.

The Soviet interest in keeping any eventual war in Europe at the conventional level of operations has been more clearly recognized in recent years. The expansion and modernization of all types of Soviet nuclear forces may be partly explained by an aspiration to undermine the credibility of potential U.S. nuclear responses to Warsaw Pact conventional aggression. At the same time, Warsaw Pact conventional forces, particularly those of the USSR, have become increasingly capable of conducting rapid air and ground offensives with short and ambiguous warning that might well be intended to neutralize promptly most NATO nuclear capabilities in Europe by nonnuclear means. This is obviously not the only Soviet option, nor even necessarily the most likely one in certain specific contingencies; but it is a particularly troubling one, because it implies reduced risks for the USSR.

While Soviet nuclear capabilities would be protected to the maximum extent possible and kept ready for operational employment, if necessary, the USSR could hope to win a war in Europe by conventional means. As John G. Hines and Philip A. Petersen have described this possibility, Warsaw Pact conventional "forces would strive to quickly fragment NATO's forward defense and occupy key political and economic centers in an effort to induce the perception among NATO allies that continued resistance or nuclear escalation would be futile."[54] The roles that Soviet BMD could play in such a Soviet strategy for conventional victory in Europe would include, as suggested above, helping to protect the Soviet nuclear means of attack and helping to convince NATO governments that resistance and/or nuclear escalation would be point-less.

Less obvious and more operational implications would stem from the functions ATBM (antitactical ballistic missile) forms of BMD could perform in support of Soviet tactical air defenses. Soviet tactical air defenses are already the most comprehensive in the world, with over 4,600 SAM launchers and 12,000 antiaircraft artillery pieces deployed at regimental through front level.[55] In 1979, the U.S.-Soviet gap in battlefield air-defense systems was already assessed at "approximately three-to-one in favor of the U.S.S.R. . . . and likely to widen further," with a Soviet "technological edge."[56]

The importance the Soviets attach to tactical air defense in Europe is evident in the fact that the "largest concentration of SAM launchers and AAA [antiaircraft artillery] pieces—over 8,100—is found opposite European NATO."[57] The relationship to BMD is apparent in light of the fact that "the standard weapon at army and front level is the SA-4, which should shortly begin being replaced by the SA-X-12. The SA-X-12 will probably also have a capability against tactical ballistic missiles."[58] According to the CIA, the SA-X-12 will be deployed with Soviet ground forces beginning in 1985-1986.[59] The apparent decision to equip operational ground force units with the SA-X-12, a mobile system potentially capable of intercepting strategic and shorter-range missiles, implies that the Soviets attach a high priority to the success of any offensive they may eventually conduct in Europe.

The Soviets have undoubtedly noticed that various NATO "emerging technologies" programs and concepts—for example, Counter-Air 90, Follow-on-Forces Attack (FOFA) and the Army Tactical Missile System (Army TACMS)—call for using precision-guided ballistic missiles such as Lance or Pershing II (or entirely new missiles) to deliver advanced conventional sub-munitions against Warsaw Pact airfields and other military targets.[60] But ATBM-equipped Soviet ground forces could directly counter such ballistic missile systems and reduce their credibility and effectiveness. BMD at this level of operations could therefore be most valuable to the USSR in trying to gain and hold air superiority—an indispensable key to victory.

A central element of the Soviet campaign for conventional victory would be an offensive air operation conducted with various types of fighter and bomber aircraft, artillery, and missiles, and by airborne and special-purpose troops. Shorter-range Soviet ballistic missiles (SS-21s, SS-22s, and SS-23s) of high accuracy and responsiveness, equipped with conventional warheads, would play a large role in such an air offensive. The more accurate ballistic missiles "have allowed the Soviets to obtain a greater potential for suppressing NATO's air and nuclear assets without nuclear means, while still having the ability to complete the task with nuclear means if that should be necessary."[61] While the Atlantic Alliance has only 300 launchers for missiles in these ranges categories, the Warsaw Pact has over 1,600 such launchers and has probably "accumulated substantial stocks of reload missiles."[62] Advanced conventional warhead designs and improved accuracies are expected to permit nonnuclear attacks against NATO's nuclear storage sites and nuclear delivery systems, and key air defense command centers, communications sites, and reinformcement assets.[63]

These new ballistic missile options—with conventional, nuclear, and/or chemical warheads—are to be coupled with ATBM in the form of the SA-X-12 to defend Soviet strike capabilities against any NATO attempt to use ballistic missiles to interfere with the Soviet offensive air operation and the Soviet conquest-of-air superiority. The Soviets appear to have developed an ATBM concurrently with their development of improved shorter-range ballistic missiles strike options, just as they initiated strategic BMD development work in the late 1940s and early 1950s at the same time that they began their work on the world's first ICBMs and SLBMs.

4. The credibility of the British and French nuclear deterrents could be diminished. A final notable advantage for the USSR in improved unilateral BMD would be lowering the credibility of the British and French independent nuclear deterrents. If the U.S. Department of Defense is correct in its view that the SA-X-12 may have "the potential to intercept some types of U.S. strategic ballistic missiles" as well as shorter-range missiles such as the Pershing II,[64] the Soviets can already expect to have some capability against the British SLBMs and the French SLBMs and intermediate-range ballistic missiles (IRBMs).

If this capability against the British and French forces became impressive, it would be an important bonus for the Soviets on top of the other strategic advantages in BMD sketched previously. Once again, Soviet risks of sustaining damage in war could be reduced. The Soviets could also gain greater control over the possibility that British or French (or, for that matter, Chinese) use of nuclear weapons could function as a "trigger" or catalyst for nuclear escalation by the United States or another government. Effective BMD could make the "trigger" threat inherent in a situation of multiple centers of independent nuclear decision making more manageable for the USSR, and related Soviet risk calculations would be simplified. Moreover, Western Europe would be effectively deprived of forces that could furnish one of the practical bases for greater defense unity in the long-term future.[65]

Further advantages for the Soviets could stem from British and French efforts to preserve the penetration credibility of their forces. The British and French would probably develop their own advanced penetration aids, posing discrimination requirements for Soviet BMD distinct from those likely to be posed by U.S. systems. The British have so far maintained that they plan no increase in warheads on their prospective Trident II D-5 SLBMs beyond what had been planned for Trident I C-4 SLBMs.[66] In November 1985, the French defense minister announced an intention to develop miniaturized warheads "almost invisible to radars" to overcome "the most immediate and serious threat" of an expansion of improved Soviet terminal defenses.[67] An official report to the minister of defense in January 1986 indicated that even if the Soviets deployed space-based chemical laser BMD systems around the year 2010, "the French deterrent capacity would remain sufficient, at the price of a limited increase in the number of ballistic missiles as well as hardening measures whose cost would be difficult to estimate, but probably within our reach."[68]

In addition, the French have shown a renewed interest in developing cruise missiles. General Jeannou Lacaze, then chief of staff of the Armed

Forces, said in May 1985 that in order to penetrate Soviet BMD and air defenses, France must consider ways to diversify her delivery means:

> This does not exclude the use of cruise missiles, especially if one can make them supersonic and use them in sufficient numbers to saturate air defenses. . . . It is advisable to improve constantly the effectiveness of ballistic systems, extending as necessary possible hypotheses for their employment, while maintaining a technological watch over the cruise missile. It seems prudent, in fact, whatever its mode of penetration might be, to develop a new strategic delivery means capable of remedying, if necessary, a placing into question of the sea-based delivery means.[69]

The "sea-based delivery means"—France's SLBMs—could be threatened not only by Soviet antisubmarine warfare capabilities but also by Soviet BMD.

If Britain and France cut back on conventional spending to increase their numbers of ballistic missiles, warheads, and penetration aids (and nonballistic nuclear delivery means), the reduced level of conventional capability in Western Europe could facilitate the realization of Soviet plans for conventional victory in the event of war.[70] If London withdrew the British Army of the Rhine (BAOR) and RAF (Royal Air Force) Germany from the Federal Republic as a cost-saving measure, it could stimulate similar withdrawals by other allies maintaining forces in West Germany. In the French case, increased nuclear investments at the expense of conventional forces could tend to undermine recent positive trends toward enhanced Franco-West German defense cooperation and reconfirm French allegiance to nationalistic nuclear "sanctuary" concepts.[71]

The four principal strategic implications discussed previously could also affect Western security in peacetime, since peacetime perceptions are affected by opinions about likely events in war. Improved unilateral BMD capabilities could be of great value to the Soviets in advancing their strategy for victory without war, precisely because of the effects that would be anticipated from Soviet BMD in war. If the USSR were to achieve a large unilateral advantage in BMD, Western vulnerability to Soviet military power would be increased, because Soviet vulnerability to retaliation would be reduced. By reducing the credibility of British and French as well as U.S. ballistic missile means of attack, the Soviets could hope to persuade Western Europeans that they have no reliable nuclear deterrent options, either in alliance with the United States or through Western European capabilities.

Western students of Soviet political-military affairs have long recognized that the Soviets would prefer to achieve political hegemony in Europe without war, by demoralizing public opinion with the display of superior military power and by making it increasingly difficult for Western governments to maintain adequate deterrent postures. As Hannes Adomeit has pointed out, one of the principal purposes of the Soviet military buildup is "to influence

Western perceptions . . . to convey the impression that Western Europe *cannot* and therefore, *will not* be defended."[72] The possibility that the Soviets might try to use BMD deployments of doubtful technical effectiveness for peacetime political effects should be recognized. As the January 1986 report to the French minister of defense noted,

> Aside from these purely technical considerations, it is essential not to forget the psychological aspects that govern public opinion: the mere mention of space-based weapons has already produced a profound effect, as has been apparent for some time. It is even more serious that the demonstration by the USSR of a powerful laser in space seems perfectly conceivable to us in the next few years, given the working methods of the Soviets: it would of course only be a simple experimental device, of perhaps debatable utility, and not a practical basis for a possible deployment; but this could be a skillful political *coup,* for such an experiment could seem to undermine very seriously our concept of deterrence in the eyes of the public. It would be very difficult to make understood the considerable differences between scientific feasibility, technical capacity, and effective deployment.[73]

A Soviet "Breakout"?

The basic premise of the foregoing discussion—that the USSR could achieve a large unilateral advantage in deployed BMD of essentially traditional types— has a certain technical plausibility; for the United States and other Western countries are not prepared to respond rapidly with equivalent deployments. As Sayre Stevens noted:

> One possibility is that the Soviet Union might conclude that the situation is ripe—because of the vulnerability of U.S. ICBMs, the hiatus before new U.S. forces come on line, and a significant Soviet advantage in lead time to BMD deployment—to effect a dramatic shift in the strategic balance that would produce great political leverage. That initiative might consist of a nationwide deployment of several thousand interceptors. Although such a move might trigger a U.S. response, it could not be a rapid one.[74]

A fundamental disparity between East and West is that unlike the USSR, neither the United States nor any other Western country has any deployed or readily deployable BMD capability. On the intercontinental level, the United States lacks an operational complex comparable to the Moscow system and does not deploy any SAMs for air defense of the continental United States,[75] much less SAMs capable of being upgraded for BMD. The United States is constructing new ballistic missile early warning radars (Pave Paws) but these are "much less capable than [the new] Soviet large-phased-array radars."[76]

On the European level, the only U.S. candidate system for upgrading to an ATBM role is the Patriot. It has been reported that Patriot upgrading will entail "major propulsion modifications" in the missile,[77] software changes in the radar, and a new conventional warhead designed "to produce larger fragments with greater energy."[78] It appears that the upgraded Patriot will have only a limited self-defense capability against the slowest of the modern Soviet shorter-range ballistic missiles (that is, the SS-21 and SS-23).[79] According to the International Institute for Strategic Studies, "The upgraded Patriot will only be successful against conventionally-armed short-range missiles, since it will lack the acceleration to intercept a nuclear or chemical warhead high enough to ensure destruction without collateral damage."[80] The French Sol Air Futur (also known as Aster 30) and other possible Western European systems might be able to perform in an ATBM role as well;[81] but none of these systems (including the ugraded Patriot) would be available until the 1990s.

Once again, a certain asymmetry is evident, in that successful tests of the SA-X-12 in an ATBM role have been reported in the past few years. The disparity in deployed and promptly deployable BMD capabilities favoring the USSR argues against any suggestion that Soviet BMD programs are simply a "hedge" against possible future U.S. BMD deployments. On the other hand, this disparity does not necessarily imply a Soviet intention to "break out" of the ABM Treaty's constraints.

If one of the Soviet motives in approving the ABM Treaty was to constrain U.S. competition in a critical area of high-technology strategic defense,[82] the USSR would probably still prefer to avoid such competition. The USSR could not obtain the theoretically maximum advantages of a large unilateral BMD deployment without raising high risks of eventual responses by the United States and its allies. The Western response could not, however, be as rapid as any Soviet breakout, given current capabilities. This could endow the USSR with potentially great advantages in a future crisis or conflict.

But unless the outcome of that crisis or conflict somehow dramatically altered international political configurations and/or basic technological and industrial strengths, the West would be likely to respond to a Soviet breakout in order to prevent harmful consequences such as those just discussed. If the hypothetical breakout advantages did not lead to decisive events favoring the USSR, a breakout could raise risks of unpredictable Western responses, including a high degree of U.S. and allied unity on crash programs—offensive and defensive—to counter the effects of the Soviet breakout. CIA officials have testified that while the Soviets "could undertake rapidly paced ABM deployments to strengthen the defenses at Moscow and cover key targets in the western USSR, and to extend protection to key targets east of the Urals, by the early 1990s," they will "have to weigh the military advantages they would see in such defenses, against the disadvantages of such a move, particularly the responses by the United States and its Allies."[83]

As in 1972, when the ABM Treaty was concluded, one of the principal disadvantages for the USSR could be the alleviation of U.S. ICBM vulnerability, since this application is often at the top of U.S. BMD priorities. Reduced U.S. ICBM vulnerability would probably be viewed by the USSR "as an undesirable threat to its preemptive counterforce capabilities."[84] Keeping U.S. BMD under control through the ABM Treaty simplifies the attainment of Soviet targeting objectives, while U.S. BMD deployments could dramatically increase Soviet offensive-force requirements and create uncertainties with potentially severe practical consequences for Soviet attack planners.[85] The consequences would, of course, be even more stringent if, in the more distant future, the United States were to deploy effective multilayer BMD systems, including space-based elements for midcourse and boost-phase intercepts.

On the other hand, the large Soviet ICBM force, with its substantial throwweight and warhead advantages over the United States, could possibly enable the Soviets to overwhelm a U.S. BMD system consisting solely of ground-based terminal defenses, depending on the scope and effectiveness of the U.S. system. If a revision of the ABM Treaty limited the United States to such defenses and allowed the Soviets to expand their network of ground-based terminal defenses, the outcome might well be to the net advantage of the USSR—given the more defensible character of Soviet strategic forces and other valued assets, the superior Soviet potential for a relatively rapid and extensive deployment of such traditional BMD systems, and the Soviet advantage in prompt counterforce capabilities (to overwhelm U.S. defenses). But the Soviets would probably prefer to retain the ABM Treaty regime for the time being, even if an arms-control regime licensing large-scale deployments of traditional ground-based BMD might be to their overall advantage, partly because of the risk that the United States could not be kept limited to ground-based systems of traditional types in the long term. A shift to a position favoring a revision of the ABM Treaty to permit ground-based BMD of traditional types, perhaps for ICBM defense or other limited purposes, could nonetheless be plausible if Soviet assessments of likely U.S. behavior accorded greater probability to actual U.S. BMD deployments.

Another major Soviet incentive for maintaining the ABM Treaty—and hence an inhibition with respect to the breakout option—is the fact that the USSR has been able to do a great deal to improve its BMD potential under the ABM Treaty. Soviet policy has perhaps been calculated to develop as much breakout potential as possible and even to "creep out" (via SAM upgrades and new LPAR deployments) without provoking the United States and its allies into a vigorous BMD competition. The Soviets may see it as a sensible objective to enhance their lead over the United States in promptly exploitable BMD capabilities without endangering U.S. compliance with the ABM Treaty by engaging in violations or ambiguous activities that the United States would find intolerable. Soviet BMD activities may therefore be calibrated to "a scale designed to minimize U.S. objections and claims of SALT violations."[86] Indeed, the Soviets appear to be interested in negotiating additional constraints on U.S. research and development activities in BMD and in military space systems. A creepout from the ABM Treaty via ambiguous activities would therefore appear more likely than an explicit breakout.

Implications for Western Strategy

Continued development of the Soviet BMD potential appears certain, whatever the fate of U.S. BMD research projects, because the Soviets would like to undermine the credibility of NATO's flexible response strategy and gain other critical strategic advantages. On the other hand, the circumstances in which the Soviets might exercise the option of exploiting their currently superior ability to proliferate traditional ground-based BMD interceptors in an unambiguous large-scale breakout from the ABM Treaty are not entirely predictable. The balance of evidence suggests that the Soviets would at present probably prefer not to engage in a breakout that might energize Western BMD efforts and ultimately place the USSR at a disadvantage. The Soviets may be especially concerned that the United States could in the long term develop space-based systems that could essentially nullify Soviet ICBM throwweight advantages and partially compensate for U.S. and allied deficiencies in other forms of strategic defense (air defenses and passive defenses such as hardening, mobility, deception, and so on).

But Soviet decision making is not entirely predictable.[87] There is a tendency to assume that even if the USSR is better positioned for post-ABM Treaty breakout than the United States, the Soviets will not exercise this option and will expand their BMD capabilities only if provoked by the U.S. SDI. A recent British analysis, for example, stated that "should this [ABM] Treaty collapse as a result of the Strategic Defense Initiative, given that the Soviet Union is best placed to take advantage of such a collapse, the credibility of the UK deterrent may be called into question."[88]

There are two difficulties with this assumption. The first is the fact that a great deal of BMD progress has been made by the Soviets since the ABM Treaty came into force. Above all, the USSR has modernized the Moscow system with missiles and radars suitable for relatively rapid proliferation, has developed potentially BMD-capable mobile SAMs (for example, the SA-X-12), and has constructed most of a network of large phased-array radars capable of early warning, attack assessment, and battle management for a large-scale BMD deployment. Further improvements in this BMD potential can be expected, and relative Soviet superiority in rapidly exploitable BMD options could therefore increase.

This leads to the second difficulty with the assumption of Soviet inaction. It is unwise and imprudent to allow the Soviet BMD breakout potential to continue to improve without taking compensatory steps. For the Soviets could at some point calculate that they could gain a meaningful strategic advantage by exercising a breakout option that had grown tempting, owing in part to their counterforce superiority and investments in active and passive defenses. The West should therefore prepare its own BMD deployment options, including ATBM in Europe, and improve its capabilities for penetrating Soviet BMD.

Western BMD Deployment Options

However remote the contingency may seem, the strategic advantages the Soviets could gain vis-à-vis the Atlantic Alliance through a large unilateral expansion of their BMD capabilities make it clear that the United States and its allies should prepare for this contingency by conducting their own R&D programs on BMD. The West should be prepared to respond to the contingency of a fairly rapid expansion of existing Soviet BMD capabilities in a sufficiently timely fashion. Such research efforts could also help to deter the Soviets from further violations of the ABM Treaty and/or from undertaking a clear-cut breakout from its constraints. As the President's Commission on Strategic Forces (the Scowcroft Commission) noted,

> Vigorous research and development on ABM technologies—including, in particular, ways to sharpen the effectiveness of treaty-limited ABM systems with new types of nuclear systems and also ways to use non-nuclear systems— are imperative to avoid technological surprise from the Soviets. Such a vigorous program on our part also decreases any Soviet incentive—based on an attempt to achieve unilateral advantage—to abrogate the ABM treaty.[89]

It would be unwise to assume that a vigorous BMD research and development program in the West would provoke a dangerous arms race or "provoke" the USSR into rash actions. SDI has probably already had a certain deterrent effect with respect to any Soviet inclinations to capitalize on their currently superior capability to rapidly deploy a widespread network of traditional ground-based BMD interceptors. In the BMD area, as in many other areas of the East-West competition, properly directed Western countermeasures would be stabilizing, would promote Soviet restraint, and would be less dangerous than inaction in the face of Soviet offensive-force expansion and related Soviet efforts in BMD and other forms of strategic defense. The West could enhance the credibility of its deterrent posture by affecting Soviet assessments of its will to reduce its vulnerabilities and resist the expansion of Soviet power.

The requirements of a Western BMD research program with these purposes—dissuading the Soviets from creepout and preparing the West for that contingency—should be clear. The United States and its allies should identify both near-term and longer-term deployment options. This is, in fact, one of the objectives of the Strategic Defense Initiative (SDI) established by the Department of Defense and the Department of Energy. The March 1984 report by the Secretary of Defense, based on intensive studies of BMD technologies and their policy implications, concludes that SDI "does *not* represent a deployment attempt. . . . Rather, it will create the technological base for sound deployment decisions."[90]

It would be a mistake for the United States and its alliance partners to pursue only the longer-term, high-leverage concepts of midcourse and boost-phase intercepts with space-based BMD systems and system components. While these concepts must be thoroughly investigated, it is equally necessary to be prepared for the contingency of a Soviet breakout from the ABM Treaty and to hedge against the continuing activities that may constitute an ambiguous creepout from the treaty's constraints. The Western Alliance should therefore reduce the current asymmetry in capabilities to proliferate promptly, and benefit from, ground-based terminal defenses of traditional types. (Research in both the traditional and advanced technology areas of BMD is, of course, permitted by the ABM Treaty.) The Soviet advantage in rapidly deployable BMD will continue to grow if the United States abstains from competing in this area. Because of U.S.-Soviet asymmetries in offensive forces as well as in active and passive defenses, the United States should also prepare for the possible need to deploy fairly promptly systems more complex than traditional terminal defenses, with space-based supporting assets.

If the United States and other Western countries did eventually deploy BMD capabilities in response to Soviet BMD and ballistic missile expansion, the consequences would be scenario-dependent, in that the specific systems, the targets defended, and other factors could be quite variable. On the other hand, some general principles are evident. The first and most fundamental is that BMD in the West would probably affect Soviet attack planning in ways helpful to deterrence and strategic stability.

Western BMD capabilities would cast doubt on the prospects for success of Soviet offensive attack plans. The Soviets have to date been able to size their offensive forces against a Western Alliance without active defenses, except for limited air defenses, and with very little passive defense. This has enabled them to plan to seize Western Europe in a matter of weeks through ground and air offensives supported by selective long-range targeting of assets critical to the defense of NATO Europe, possibly including U.S. reinforcement means such as key airlift and sealift assets and general-purpose forces in addition to nuclear-weapons sites and other vital targets in Europe. BMD and air defenses in the

West would significantly affect Soviet calculations of prospects for victory, because the price of successful attacks would be raised in a potentially dis-proportionate manner. The higher likelihood of survival of critical Western military assets should enhance deterrence and make attempts at coercion (and war) more improbable. As Stephen M. Meyer has pointed out, "Even a modest ability to blunt an initial Soviet attack might produce enough *additional uncertainty* in the minds of Soviet political and military leaders so as to make pre-emption a more remote strategic option."[91] Moreover, it should be recalled that

> the damage-limiting effectiveness of Soviet strategic offence and strategic defense are interdependent. This synergy, which works to Soviet advantage in a world without American strategic defences, also implies that SDI could actually reduce the effectiveness of Soviet active and passive strategic de-fenses, as well as that of Soviet strategic offensive forces. Reducing the effec-tiveness of the initial Soviet offensive strike . . . places a greater burden on the Soviet Union's strategic defences with respect to both the level of threat they must counter and their own survivability. From the Soviet military per-spective, then, the deployment of SDI systems threatens a far broader range of Soviet defence investment than just ballistic re-entry vehicles.[92]

Although Soviet declaratory policy has often implied that any use of nuclear weapons would lead inevitably to escalation to all-out nuclear war (partly in order to demoralize Western publics), Soviet military doctrine for actual combat operations has shown significant interest in selectivity in nu-clear employment. Some of the most likely targets of Soviet missiles—that is, U.S. ICBMs and hardened command centers—are also the most defendable in the near term. Even if U.S. BMD capabilities were initially limited to defending offensive retaliatory forces and associated command and control capabilities in Europe and the United States, Soviet attack-planning uncertainties (which are already significant) would be increased by the challenge of overcoming U.S. BMD. The Soviet calculus for victory through counterforce strikes would therefore be complicated. Deterrence of war and strategic stability could thus be reinforced, because confidence in the predictability of attack results would be denied. It should be recalled, however, that the nature and number of Soviet strategic and intermediate-range missile forces could enable the Soviets to overwhelm limited terminal defenses more readily than the United States could overwhelm Soviet defenses of the same type.

It would nonetheless be more expensive for the Soviets to multiply numbers of missiles and warheads than some observers have claimed. Soviet military doctrine calls for large reserve forces for various purposes, including the exertion of influence over possible NATO decisions to respond to Soviet employment of nuclear weapons. Partly because Soviet doctrine requires high numbers of reserve weapons, BMD in the West could aggravate resource allocation strains that are already acute, owing to the high burden of defense spending on the Soviet economy. Investments in additional missile forces to try to counter BMD in the West could come at the expense of Soviet conventional-force improvements or even Soviet BMD. Soviet resources are no doubt finite in various ways, including the materials that would be required to proliferate warheads. In other words, BMD in the West could impose costs that would make it more difficult for the Soviets to build up destabilizing positions of military superiority.

Indeed, strategic instability would probably be the least likely consequence of Western BMD programs in response to those of the USSR. What would be destabilizing would be a Western failure to pursue BMD research and development in order to be prepared to respond to the contingency of fairly rapid Soviet BMD deployments in a sufficiently timely fashion. One of the soundest arguments in favor of improved Western BMD research and development programs is the necessity for a prudent hedge against the possibility of a relatively rapid unilateral Soviet deployment of BMD systems.

Because of the currently unknown effectiveness and possible vulnerability to countermeasures of BMD systems, anxiety about a destabilization of the existing situation of mutual vulnerability seems premature. It is doubtful whether either U.S. or Soviet leaders would be so highly confident of the operational effectiveness of their BMD systems that a first strike would appear tempting, especially given the high national fatalities that would result even if the systems worked rather well and only a relatively low number of nuclear weapons penetrated the defenses. A significant degree of nuclear vulnerability will obviously persist indefinitely. Moreover, even if relatively comprehensive multilayer defenses were deployed, practical obstacles to testing the entire system in realistic conditions would limit confidence in its reliability to some degree. Crisis stability could nonetheless be reinforced in that retaliatory systems could be more survivable, with fewer vulnerabilities to attract strikes.

The fact that Soviet BMD would probably have reduced the variety and credibility of some U.S. limited strike options should be set against the fact that the virtually complete vulnerability of the U.S. homeland and land-based U.S. strategic forces to Soviet ballistic missile attack has already eroded the credibility of those options. The greater the effectiveness of active defenses (BMD plus defenses against aircraft and cruise missiles) in the United States, the smaller the degree of U.S. vulnerability and the higher the level of U.S. deterrent credibility would be in threatening implementation of NATO's flexible response selected-strike options—even though actual implementation would be complicated by the requirement to overcome or evade Soviet BMD. Flexible response would be revised to the extent that the alliance could improve its direct, active defenses and decrease its continuing dependence on threats of retaliation via limited-strike options.

Antitactical Ballistic Missiles

One form of BMD that is particularly urgent for the West is defense against Soviet shorter-range ballistic missiles. As noted earlier, the Soviets have developed an antitactical ballistic missile (ATBM) capability in the form of the SA-X-12 concurrently with more accurate shorter-range ballistic missiles. With foreseeable accuracy improvements, the USSR could use conventional-warhead shorter-range ballistic missiles (in conjunction with air-launched missiles and other systems) to destroy an extensive array of critical military installations in Western Europe without having recourse to nuclear weapons and without causing high numbers of civilian fatalities.

Countermeasures against this threat are required. Counterforce strikes against Soviet missiles and aircraft cannot be fully relied upon, since dependence on such means could promote incentives for preemption in a crisis. Moreover, planning for such strikes could be politically difficult to sustain in the alliance. Modern Soviet short-range missile launchers represent difficult targets to acquire, in any case, because of their "improved mobility, faster reaction time and reduced support requirements."[93] Nor are hardening, dispersal and deception measures likely to be sufficient means of protection. Relatively few alliance assets in Europe have been hardened (a few C^3 and weapons sites). Dispersal plans depend on warning and the political will to act on warning; the latter may not be available, given likely fears of "provocation" and aggravation of the crisis.[94]

ATBM defenses would be more consistent with NATO's defensive posture than reliance on counterforce strikes, and more stabilizing than dependence on dispersal. If NATO deployed ATBM capabilities, it could reduce Soviet confidence in the Warsaw Pact's ability to gain victory on conventional terms in two ways: first, by protecting NATO's command posts, ports, airfields, air defenses, and logistic and C^3 sites; second, by helping to assure the survival of NATO's nuclear assets, in that time would be gained to allow for dispersal. ATBM could also protect against limited nuclear attacks. ATBM could decisively reinforce the improved air defenses and passive defenses (hardening, mobility, and so on) that are needed in Western Europe. If effective and deployed in sufficient numbers, ATBM could help to make a rapid victory on Soviet terms infeasible and could increase the sustainability of NATO's defense capabilities; ATBM would thus bolster deterrence.

Without better air defenses and BMD, the survivability and sustainability in combat of NATO's military posture is questionable. Even limited defenses of selected critical targets could increase Soviet uncertainties about the effectiveness and controllability of nuclear or nonnuclear attacks, and thus enhance deterrence. ATBM defenses could make the West more capable of focused retaliation and sustained military operations. Western Europe would remain much more vulnerable in war than North America, owing to the threat of land invasion and less warning time regarding air and missile attack; but ATBM could help to attenuate differences in vulnerability between Western Europe and North America, and thus prevent an accentuation of long-standing discrepancies in risk exposure.

The development of ATBM capabilities would probably have to go beyond possible upgrading of the Patriot air defense system, since it may not be capable of reaching more than a limited self-defense capability. While the upgraded Patriot could be helpful, a more robust system would be necessary to counter foreseeable shorter-range ballistic missile threats.

The obstacles to developing ATBM are more likely to be financial and political than technical.[95] The most significant political obstacle may be differing interpretations of the ABM Treaty. As noted earlier, the USSR has been able to expand its BMD infrastructure by enlarging and upgrading its air-defense network and developing potentially BMD-capable SAMs. While upgrading SAMs to BMD capability by testing them in "an ABM mode" is forbidden by the ABM Treaty, the SA-X-12 has reportedly demonstrated its ability to perform in an ATBM role—a capability that is not explicitly limited by the ABM Treaty. The Soviets have thus been able to profit from the blurring of distinctions between air defense and tactical and strategic BMD. Sayre Stevens suggests that the Soviets could use mobile ATBM systems like the SA-X-12 to gain strategic BMD capabilities:

> Their rapid deployment in large numbers (possibly from covert storage) would constitute another means whereby the Soviet Union could extend its defensive forces, very possibly within the provisions of the ABM Treaty. Although the treaty does prohibit giving non-ABM systems the capability to intercept strategic ballistic missiles, it would be extremely difficult to make an airtight case that it had occurred if the Soviet Union denied the allegation.[96]

Soviet spokesmen have not only denied that the SA-X-12 could be capable of intercepting strategic ballistic missiles; they also deny that it is capable of serving as an ATBM, and maintain that it is simply an air defense missile.[97] These denials are consistent with their position that developing U.S. ATBM systems for deployment in defense of Western Europe would be a violation of the ABM Treaty.[98] Soviet statements that acknowledge that the USSR has developed and ugraded antitactical ballistic missile (ATBM) capabilities are quite rare.[99]

The U.S. government's position appears to be that the SA-X-12 would be legally allowable under the ABM Treaty if the SA-X-12 were only capable of intercepting shorter-range ballistic missiles, because the treaty only limits capabilities against "strategic ballistic missiles." Treaty compliance issues arise to the extent that the SA-X-12 may be useful in defense against U.S. ICBMs and SLBMs. In 1983, the deputy under secretary of defense for strategic and theater nuclear forces, T.K. Jones, testified that "it appears the Soviets are developing that [the SA-X-12] to counter the shorter-range ballistic missiles and the ABM Treaty was drafted so that that is a legal development and they could deploy it fully. However, at the margin, a system that has good capability against something like the Pershing II would also have reasonable capability to defend reasonable areas against our ICBMs and submarine-launched ballistic missiles."[100] On similar grounds, the Office of Technology Assessment reported in 1985 that ATBM systems are "not prohibited" by the ABM Treaty, though ATBM systems capable of intercepting SLBMs and ICBMs would "undercut" its provisions.[101]

In these circumstances, the Atlantic Alliance should reject Soviet attempts to argue (a) that ATBM is prohibited by the ABM Treaty, or (b) that the ABM Treaty should be amended to outlaw ATBM explicitly. The ABM Treaty, as previously noted, defines an ABM system as "a system to counter strategic ballistic missiles or their elements in flight trajectory" (Article II). Since the USSR has long held in arms control negotiations that its intermediate-range missiles are incapable of threatening the continental United States and are therefore not "strategic,"[102] defenses against such missiles should be seen as legal, even by Soviet definitions.

The main instrument available to the Soviets to contend that ATBM capabilities are forbidden is Article IX of the ABM Treaty, which states that "each Party undertakes not to transfer to other States, and not to deploy outside its national territory, ABM systems or their components limited by this Treaty." Agreed Interpretation G indicates that Article IX "includes the obligation of the US and the USSR not to provide to other States technical descriptions or blueprints specially worked out for the construction of ABM systems and their components limited by the Treaty." The Soviets and some Western opponents of ATBM have used Article IX and this agreed interpretation to argue that ATBM in Western Europe would represent an attempt to circumvent the ABM Treaty.[103] Even though the treaty's language does not explicitly exclude ATBM (which suggests that it is not covered by the treaty), the Soviets and some Western critics of the ATBM concept are attempting to promote the view that ATBM in Western Europe would contradict the treaty.

ATBM in Western Europe would not contradict the ABM Treaty, however, unless the systems and components deployed were originally designed by the United States for defense against Soviet "strategic ballistic missiles." Western Europeans are legally at liberty to develop their own ATBM systems; and the United States would be free to assist the Western Europeans in doing so, so long as the systems at issue were not originally developed for defense of the United States. The United States is likewise legally free to deploy ATBM to protect U.S. and allied forces and other assets in Western Europe.

Because of the ABM Treaty's silence on ATBM, the Soviets may at some point propose that the treaty be revised to close this "loophole." Although a well-devised and verifiable ATBM accord might have some theoretical attractions, Soviet behavior with respect to intermediate-range missile systems, BMD, and other forms of strategic and theater defense has made an equitable agreement on ATBM appear most unlikely.

As on the intercontinental level, the Soviets have deployed far more intermediate-range missiles and warheads directed against Western Europe than the United States has deployed for the defense of Western Europe. Similarly, the military assets of the United States and its allies in Western Europe, the targets the USSR would threaten, are more vulnerable than the corresponding target set in the USSR, owing to superior Soviet investments in various forms of active and passive defense. Above all—to complete the parallel with the intercontinental situation—the Atlantic Alliance currently lacks any ATBM capability and has not yet decided to develop and deploy ATBM systems, while the USSR has developed and is about to deploy the SA-X-12, a system with ATBM and strategic BMD potential.

An ATBM agreement providing for equal numerical levels of ATBM systems would therefore not favor the Atlantic Alliance. The West's military assets are so vulnerable that they would require much more ATBM protection for "parity" in defense. Soviet superiority in intermediate-range missile and warhead numbers would at the same time place asymmetrical burdens on Western ATBM. The Atlantic Alliance would find it politically difficult to increase its intermediate-range missile capabilities beyond those foreseen in the December 1979 modernization plan.[104]

Qualitative restrictions on ATBM development and deployment might also be proposed by the Soviets and could pose equally problematic implications for Western security. The net result of such qualitative constraints, given prevailing verification uncertainties and compliance practices, might well be to exacerbate East-West asymmetries in active and passive defenses. To guard against this possibility, the Atlantic Alliance must retain its freedom to deploy ATBM in Western Europe, and avoid subjecting ATBM to quantitative or qualitative restrictions that would asymmetrically favor the USSR.

Capabilities for Penetrating Soviet BMD

If in years to come the USSR were to gain a large unilateral advantage in BMD, the adverse implications could be partially addressed through improved U.S. abilities to penetrate Soviet BMD. As was pointed out by the Scowcroft Commission in April 1983, it is particularly important to be able

> to counter any improvement in Soviet ABM capability by being able to maintain the effectiveness of our offensive systems. The possibility of either a sudden breakthrough in ABM technology, a rapid Soviet breakout from the ABM treaty by a quick further deployment of their current ABM systems, or

the deployment of air defense systems also having some capability against strategic ballistic missiles all point to the need for us to be able to penetrate some level of ABM defense. This dictates continued attention to having sufficient throwweight for adequate numbers of warheads and of decoys and other penetration aids.[105]

Improved U.S. abilities to penetrate Soviet air and ballistic missile defenses against intercontinental, intermediate- and shorter-range systems (bombers, cruise missiles, and ballistic missiles) would help to prevent the Soviets from gaining a great advantage in escalation control capabilities. Improved penetration means could also hinder Soviet efforts to undermine the credibility of NATO's flexible response strategy and to defeat NATO's "emerging technologies" programs. The same principle would apply to maintaining the penetration credibility of British and French forces, so as to continue to complicate Soviet risk calculations. It is important to persuade the Soviets that the risks in miscalculating the consequences of aggression could be intolerable, and that they cannot gain any usable superiority in means of escalation control.

Developing and maintaining adequate penetration capabilities will not be easy or inexpensive. To begin with, the United States is already at a disadvantage with respect to numbers of intercontinental missiles (ICBMs and SLBMs) and shorter-range missiles and with respect to the throwweight of both types of missiles. This asymmetry means that U.S. prospects for multiplying numbers of warheads and penetration aids are more limited than Soviet options.

Public skepticism about offensive-force improvements will restrict spending on such forces, as will financial constraints—limits on national budgets as well as defense budgets. Modernizing offensive forces in order to be able to overcome projected improvements in Soviet BMD and other active and passive Soviet defenses may not win great support during a time of budgetary stringency. Public attitudes and financial constraints, together with arms control, will condition the extent to which the United States and its allies can develop a balanced mix of offensive and defensive capabilities.

Conclusion

The object in developing improved capabilities to penetrate Soviet BMD and to deploy BMD in the Atlantic Alliance would, of course, remain deterrence and war prevention. As Paul Nitze has argued,

> What we must do is give the Soviets grounds for concluding that we in the West are prepared to maintain sufficient political will and military capability to ensure deterrence of any possible aggression, conventional or nuclear. We must bring them to realize that their buildup cannot and will not be translated into an exploitable military or political advantage.[106]

In other words, the West must prevent dangerous Soviet assessments as to simplified risks and thus avert Western susceptibility to coercion. This can be done only through a balanced program of improved options for offensive and defensive deployments, to be implemented as necessary for the maintenance of stable deterrence. It would be imprudent and destabilizing to leave Soviet offensive and defensive investments unanswered. To leave the BMD field to the USSR alone would be a prescription for strategic instability and Western vulnerability to Soviet military power.

The implications for alliance strategy and Western security in an interaction of more or less simultaneous large-scale Soviet and Western deployments of BMD and offensive countermeasures have yet to be fully explored. The balance sheet of potential benefits and disadvantages for the West in such an interaction would depend in part on the scope and effectiveness of the specific BMD systems deployed in the Atlantic Alliance and the Warsaw Pact, but it would also depend heavily on the effectiveness of other forms of active and passive defense and on the available offensive systems—and on the strategy for their use.

In investigating the possible interactions between Western and Soviet efforts to develop defenses against ballistic missiles as well as enhanced ballistic missile strike capabilities, analysts should exercise caution with respect to popular assumptions about trade-offs and the arms race. The term "trade-offs" might be construed to imply that Western choices could be based on confidence in the West's ability to influence the development of the Soviet force posture—for example, that a Western decision to pursue certain types of BMD capabilities (and gain certain benefits from such defenses) would provoke certain specific Soviet responses (and thus entail certain predictable disadvantages for the West); and that, in making a decision to refrain from investing in BMD (or in other military capabilities), the West could count on corresponding Soviet inaction. By this logic, forgoing the potential benefits of a BMD research program (or eventual BMD deployments) might be worthwhile, since the trade-off or compensation would be an avoidance of the anticipated disadvantages for the West in an expansion of Soviet BMD and ballistic missile strike capabilities. Similarly, the term arms race is sometimes understood to imply that the West may choose not to compete in specific areas of military technology and may be assured of parallel Soviet restraint.

The implicit theories about arms competitions and Soviet behavior behind such assumptions appear to be flawed on at least two basic grounds. First, the theories oversimplify the origins of arms-competition behavior by suggesting that external example is the principal determinant of force posture development. As Andrew W. Marshall has noted, "It is probably both less biased and more perceptive to see military force postures of nations as evolving under the influence of many factors and to see the simultaneous evolution of the forces of potential adversaries as interactive in some ways and as autonomous in others."[107] The most detailed historical analyses of the post-1945 development of the U.S. and Soviet force postures have found, Marshall adds, that

> the interactive process is slower paced and more complex than usually assumed . . . no one consistent pattern of interaction exists. . . . The hypothesis that the United States or Soviet Union develop their forces only or mainly in direct and immediate reaction to what the other does is at best difficult to maintain.[108]

Second, simplistic theories of bilateral arms competitions would tend to equate the strategic objectives and force development patterns of the Western Alliance and the Warsaw Pact. However, as has been noted, Soviet strategic objectives differ profoundly from those of the Atlantic Alliance, and this has been reflected in contrasting military posture investments. In virtually all areas of strategic defense—BMD, air defense, hardening, mobility, deception, civil defense, and so on—the West's restraint has not been matched by imitative Soviet forbearance. On the contrary, Soviet efforts in these domains have been marked by steady expansion and modernization, reinforced by complementary offensive-force programs.

Notes

1. President Ronald Reagan, cited in *New York Times,* March 24, 1983.
2. Fears of "psychological decoupling" and the creation of "zones of differing security" within the alliance remain prominent in some circles. For an overview of initial reactions to SDI, see David S. Yost, "European Anxieties about Ballistic Missile Defense," *Washington Quarterly,* vol. 7 (Fall 1984).
3. The research program is to "run into the early 1990s, when decisions could be made by a future President and Congress on whether or not to enter into systems development." *Report to the Congress on the Strategic Defense Initiative* (Washington, D.C.: Strategic Defense Initiative Organization, 1985), p. 10.
4. The best-known articulation of these criteria is Paul Nitze's speech, *On the Road to a More Stable Peace,* Current Policy no. 657 (Washington, D.C.: Bureau of Public Affairs, Department of State, February 20, 1985), pp. 1-3.
5. According to the Office of Technology Assessment, "although the state of Soviet 'traditional' BMD technology probably does not exceed our own, the Soviets are almost certainly better positioned in the near-term to deploy a limited-capability ballistic missile defense system than we are." U.S. Congress, Office of Technology Assessment, *Ballistic Missile Defense Technologies,* OTA-ISC-254 (Washington, D.C.: Government Printing Office, September 1985), p. 243.
6. Andrew W. Marshall, "A Program to Improve Analytic Methods related to Strategic Forces," *Policy Sciences,* vol. 15 (1982), pp. 47-50.

7. Annex to the Final Communiqué, Defense Planning Committee Ministerial Meeting, May 1975, in *NATO Facts and Figures,* 9th ed. (Brussels: NATO Information Service, 1978), pp. 348-49.

8. *White Paper 1975/1976: The Security of the Federal Republic of Germany and the Development of the Federal Armed Forces* (Bonn: Federal Minister of Defence, 1976), pp. 20-21.

9. J. Michael Legge, *Theater Nuclear Weapons and the NATO Strategy of Flexible Response,* R-2964-FF (Santa Monica, Calif.: Rand Corporation, April 1983), p. 27.

10. General Bernard W. Rogers, "The Atlantic Alliance: Prescriptions for a Difficult Decade," *Foreign Affairs,* vol. 60 (Summer 1982), p. 1152.

11. Major General Jörg Bahnemann, "Air Defense in Central Europe," *NATO's Sixteen Nations,* vol. 30 (December 1985), p. 42.

12. Fritz Ermarth, "Contrasts in American and Soviet Strategic Thought," *International Security,* vol. 3 (Fall 1978), p. 147.

13. Ibid.

14. Lieutenant General M.M. Kir'yan, *Voyenno-tekhnicheskiy Progress i Voorzhennyye Sily SSSR* (Progress in Military Technology and the Armed Forces of the USSR) (Moscow: Voyenizdat, 1982), p. 296.

15. For a systematic survey of Soviet discussions of the roles of the Strategic Rocket Forces, the SLBM fleet, and long-range aviation in nuclear deterrence and in war, see James John Tritten, *Soviet Naval Forces and Nuclear Warfare: Weapons, Employment, and Policy* (Boulder, Colo.: Westview Press, 1986).

16. Sidney D. Drell, Philip J. Farley, and David Holloway, *The Reagan Strategic Defense Initiative: A Technical, Political, and Arms Control Assessment* (Cambridge, Mass.: Ballinger Publishing Company, 1985), p. 18.

17. Sayre Stevens, "The Soviet BMD Program," in Ashton B. Carter and David N. Schwartz, eds., *Ballistic Missile Defense* (Washington, D.C.: Brookings Institution, 1984), p. 183.

18. Malcolm Wallop, "Soviet Violations of Arms Control Agreements: So What?" *Strategic Review,* vol. 11 (Summer 1983), p. 18.

19. E.C. Aldridge, Jr., and Robert L. Maust, Jr., "SALT Implications of BMD Options," in *U.S. Arms Control Objectives and the Implications for Ballistic Missile Defense,* Proceedings of a Symposium held at the Center for Science and International Affairs, Harvard University, November 1-2, 1979 (Cambridge, Mass.: Puritan Press, 1980), pp. 55-66.

20. U.S. Department of Defense, *Soviet Military Power 1986* (Washington, D.C.: Government Printing Office, 1986), pp. 42-43.

21. Ministry of Defense paper, "The Soviet Ballistic Missile Defence Programme," presented to the House of Commons by John Stanley, Minister of State for the Armed Forces, in Great Britain, Parliament, *Parliamentary Debates* (House of Commons), vol. 87 (November 26, 1985), col. 562.

22. *Aviation Week and Space Technology,* August 29, 1983, p. 19; and *International Defense Review,* September 1983, p. 1193.

23. U.S. Department of Defense, *Soviet Military Power 1986,* in n. 20, p. 43.

24. *Aviation Week and Space Technology,* November 14, 1983, p. 23; and *A Quarter Century of Soviet Compliance Practices under Arms Control Commitments:*

1958-1983 (Washington, D.C.: General Advisory Committee on Arms Control and Disarmament, October 1984), pp. 9-10.

25. Testimony regarding "some 50" violations of the ABM Treaty in such tests was given by Admiral Elmo Zumwalt (chief of naval operations at the time of the tests), who added that "the Soviets should have gotten all the information they need from those tests." Zumwalt testimony in U.S. Senate, Committee on Appropriations, *SALT II Violations, Hearing* before a Subcommittee, 98th Congress, 2nd sess., March 28, 1984 (Washington, D.C.: Government Printing Office, 1984), pp. 68-69.

26. U.S. Department of Defense, *Soviet Military Power 1984* (Washington, D.C.: Government Printing Office, 1984), p. 34.

27. Stevens, "The Soviet BMD Program," in n. 17, pp. 215-16.

28. U.S. Department of Defense, *Soviet Military Power 1985* (Washington, D.C.: Government Printing Office, 1985), p. 48.

29. Hubertus G. Hoffmann, "A Missile Defense for Europe?" *Strategic Review,* vol. 12 (Summer 1984), p. 53; and Michael R. Gordon, "CIA is Skeptical that New Soviet Radar Is Part of an ABM Defense System," *National Journal,* March 9, 1985, p. 524.

30. Robert Cooper, director of the Defense Advanced Research Projects Agency, cited in *Washington Times,* March 9, 1984, p. 3A.

31. *The President's Unclassified Report to the Congress on Soviet Noncompliance with Arms Control Agreements* (The White House, Office of the Press Secretary, February 1, 1985), p. 8.

32. U.S. Department of Defense, *Soviet Military Power 1985* in n. 28, p. 46.

33. *Soviet Strategic Force Developments,* testimony before a joint session of the Subcommittee on Strategic and Theater Nuclear Forces of the Senate Armed Services Committee and the Defense Subcommittee of the Senate Committee on Appropriations, June 26, 1985, by Robert M. Gates, chairman, National Intelligence Council, and deputy director for intelligence, Central Intelligence Agency, and Lawrence K. Gershwin, national intelligence officer for Strategic Programs, National Intelligence Council, p. 5.

34. George C. Wilson, "US Says Soviet Erects 3 Radars, Apparently for Antimissile Use," *International Herald Tribune,* December 13-14, 1986, p. 6.

35. Mark E. Miller, *Soviet Strategic Power and Doctrine: The Quest for Superiority* (Bethesda, Md.: Advanced International Studies Institute, 1982), p. 244.

36. Paul Nitze, cited in *New York Times,* July 12, 1985, p. 6; and Paul Nitze, *SDI: The Soviet Program,* Current Policy no. 717 (Washington, D.C.: Bureau of Public Affairs, U.S. Department of State, June 28, 1985), p. 2.

37. *Aviation Week and Space Technology,* January 16, 1984, p. 16; and U.S. Department of Defense, *Soviet Military Power 1985,* in n. 28, p. 44.

38. Harold Brown, *Department of Defense Annual Report Fiscal Year 1979* (Washington, D.C.: Government Printing Office, 1978), p. 124.

39. U.S. Department of Defense, *Soviet Military Power 1985,* in n. 28, p. 48.

40. Gates and Gershwin, *Soviet Strategic Force Developments,* in no. 33, pp. 6-7.

41. Sayre Stevens, "Ballistic Missile Defense in the Soviet Union," *Current History,* vol. 84 (October 1985), p. 316.

42. James A. Schear, "Arms Control Treaty Compliance: Buildup to a Breakdown?" *International Security,* vol. 10 (Fall 1985), p. 160.

43. Roger P. Main, "The USSR and Laser Weaponry: The View from Outside," *Defense Systems Review,* vol. 3 (no. 3, 1985), p. 72. The fact that Soviet BMD kill mechanisms are believed to be predominantly nuclear at present raises several important questions—as does the potential vulnerability of Soviet BMD radars to nuclear effects. The Soviets probably intend to defend their radars, to use low-yield nuclear warheads of special designs, and to address nuclear effects such as blackout in various ways; but these issues cannot be treated concisely. For background, see Stevens, "The Soviet BMD Program," in n. 17, and Stephen Weiner, "Systems and Technology," in Ashton B. Carter and David N. Schwartz, eds., *Ballistic Missile Defense* (Washington, D.C.: Brookings Institution, 1984). The chief of staff of the French Armed Forces, General Jeannou Lacaze, recently indicated that the Soviets may be developing nonnuclear kill BMD capability in their advanced surface-to-air missiles (Lacaze, "L'avenir de la défense française," *Défense Nationale,* July 1985, p. 23).

44. This interpretation of Soviet military doctrine is influenced by works, some of which are unpublished, of John G. Hines, Philip A. Petersen, and Notra Trulock—among others, Notra Trulock's important study, "Weapons of Mass Destruction in Soviet Strategy," a paper presented at the conference on Soviet Military Strategy in Europe, sponsored jointly by the Boston Foreign Affairs Group and the Royal United Services Institute, Oxfordshire, England, September 24-25, 1984. On the basis of Soviet General Staff Academy lecture materials declassified by the U.S. government and other sources, Trulock throws new light on the Soviet interest in selectivity in nuclear employment.

45. *White Paper 1975/76,* in n. 8, p. 20.

46. Kevin Lewis, "BMD and US Limited Strategic Employment Policy," *Journal of Strategic Studies,* vol. 8 (June 1985), p. 140 (emphasis added).

47. While the controllability of nuclear escalation is unknown and scenario-dependent, the clear duty of the United States and NATO is to try to maximize the probability that any use of nuclear weapons necessitated by Soviet aggression remains as limited as possible. Selective use should therefore be recognizable as such, but no guarantees or confident predictions can be made as to the results of selective use.

48. Manfred Wörner, "SALT II: A European Perspective," *Strategic Review,* vol. 7 (Summer 1979), p. 13.

49. Uwe Nerlich, "Theater Nuclear Forces in Europe: Is NATO Running Out of Options?" *Washington Quarterly,* vol. 3 (Winter 1980), pp. 110, 116.

50. According to the President's Commission on Strategic Forces (the Scowcroft Commission), the Soviets ". . . now probably possess the necessary combination of ICBM numbers, reliability, accuracy and warhead yield to destroy almost all of the 1,047 U.S. ICBM silos, using only a portion of their own ICBM force. The U.S. ICBM force now deployed cannot inflict similar damage, even using the entire force." *Report of the President's Commission on Strategic Forces,* April 1983, p. 4.

51. Hans Rühle, "Die Zukunft der NATO," in Günther Wagenlehner, ed., *Die Kampagne gegen den NATO-Doppelbeschluss: Eine Bilanz* (Koblenz: Bernard und Graefe Verlag, 1985), pp. 197-98.

52. Testimony of John Gardner in U.S. House of Representatives, Committee on Armed Services, *Defense Department Authorization and Oversight, Hearings,* 98th Cong., 1st sess. (Washington, D.C.: U.S. Government Printing Office, 1983), Part 5, p. 269.

53. Major-General William E. Odom, "Trends in the Balance of Military Power Between East and West," in *The Conduct of East-West Relations in the 1980s, Part III,* Adelphi Paper no. 191 (London: International Institute for Strategic Studies, 1984), p. 21.

54. John G. Hines and Philip A. Petersen, *The Soviet Conventional Offensive in Europe,* DDB-2622-4-83 (Washington, D.C.: Defense Intelligence Agency, May 1983), p. vii. More readily accessible studies by Hines and Petersen, setting forth the same interpretation, are "The Conventional Offensive in Soviet Theater Strategy," *Orbis,* vol. 27 (Fall 1983), and "Military Power in Soviet Strategy Against NATO," *RUSI Journal,* vol. 128 (December 1983).

55. U.S. Department of Defense, *Soviet Military Power 1985,* in n. 28, p. 68.

56. Major Tyrus W. Cobb, "Tactical Air Defense: A Soviet-U.S. Net Assessment," *Air University Review,* vol. 30 (March-April 1979), p. 35.

57. U.S. Department of Defense, *Soviet Military Power 1985,* in n. 28, p. 50.

58. Ibid., p. 69.

59. Gates and Gershwin, *Soviet Strategic Force Development,* in n. 33, p. 5.

60. See the comments by General Bernard W. Rogers in *Air Force Magazine,* February 1985, pp. 20, 23, and Donald R. Cotter, "Potential Future Roles for Conventional and Nuclear Forces in Defense of Western Europe," in *Strengthening Conventional Deterrence in Europe: Proposals for the 1980s,* Report of the European Security Study (London: Macmillan, 1983), pp. 224, 238.

61. Philip A. Petersen and Major John R. Clark, "Soviet Air and Antiair Operations," *Air University Review,* March-April 1985, p. 51.

62. Lt. Col. Kerry L. Hines, "Soviet Short-Range Ballistic Missiles: Now a Conventional Deep Strike Mission," *International Defense Review,* December 1985, pp. 1912-13.

63. Dennis M. Gormley, "A New Dimension to Soviet Theater Strategy," *Orbis,* vol. 29 (Fall 1985), pp. 552-66.

64. U.S. Department of Defense, *Soviet Military Power 1985,* in n. 28, p. 48.

65. This should not be construed to imply any assumption that it would be simple to devise a nuclear deterrent for a Western European defense entity on the basis of the British and French forces. While it is widely conceded that reduced Western European dependence on U.S. nuclear guarantees would require greater Western European nuclear deterrent capability, the political obstacles to building such capability may be even more intractable than the economic and technical requirements. These political obstacles include the uncertain credibility of extending British and French deterrent guarantees to nonnuclear allies; understandable British and French reluctance to dilute national control mechanisms; the credibility uncertainties associated with a system of multiple "keys" and vetoes; the sensitivities attached to any West German involvement in control over nuclear weapons; possible Soviet exploitation of the Non-Proliferation Treaty to oppose the constitution of a Western European nuclear deterrent; and widespread Western European concerns that such a joint deterrent could somehow become a pretext for a reduction in the U.S. military presence in Europe.

66. D.J. Fewtrell, director of nuclear policy and security, Ministry of Defence, testimony in United Kingdom, House of Commons, *Sixth Report from the Defence Committee, Session 1984-85, The Trident Programme* (London: Her Majesty's Stationery Office, 1985), p. 49.

67. Paul Quilès, cited in *Le Monde,* November 13, 1985, p. 12. These warheads would evidently be more advanced than the TN-71 warheads scheduled to begin replacing the TN-70s on M-4 SLBMs in 1987. The TN-71 will have an improved yield-to-weight ratio, permitting the deployment of additional penetration aids; the warhead itself may also have a smaller radar cross section.

68. Commission d'Études sur les Armes Spatiales, *Rapport de synthèse présenté au ministre de la défense,* January 30, 1986, p. 11. This document is also known as the "Delpech report," since the commission was chaired by Jean François Delpech, director of research at the Centre National de la Recherche Scientifique.

69. Lacaze, "L'avenir de la défense française," in n. 43, pp. 23-24. For previous French policy on cruise missiles, see David S. Yost, *France's Deterrent Posture and Security in Europe: Part I, Capabilities and Doctrine,* Adelphi Paper no. 194 (London: International Institute for Strategic Studies, Winter 1984/1985), pp. 20-21, 28-29. If the French develop cruise missiles, they may not have the range, fuel efficiency, or accuracy of U.S. or Soviet ones. They might be more likely to resemble longer-range advanced versions of the Air-Sol Moyenne Portée (ASMP) standoff missile.

70. It should, of course, be recognized that increased nuclear force requirements occasioned by Soviet BMD would simply supplement other factors that have already encouraged cutbacks in conventional force levels. For a discussion of the French case, see David S. Yost, *France and Conventional Defense in Central Europe* (Boulder, Colo.: Westview Press, 1985), pp. 29-39, 77-86. Further adverse trends in the conventional force balance are not inevitable, however, and could be reversed with sufficient political will.

71. For a fuller discussion regarding France and BMD, see Yost, *France's Deterrent Posture,* in n. 69, pp. 23-26.

72. Hannes Adomeit, "The Political Rationale of Soviet Military Capabilities and Doctrine," in *Strengthening Conventional Deterrence in Europe: Proposals for the 1980s,* Report of the European Security Study (London: Macmillan, 1983), p. 95 (emphasis added).

73. Commission d'Études, *Rapport de synthèse,* in n. 68, pp. 12-13.

74. Stevens, "The Soviet BMD Program," in n. 17, pp. 217-18.

75. Organization of the Joint Chiefs of Staff, *United States Military Posture FY 1987* (Washington, D.C.: Government Printing Office, 1986), pp. 26-30. According to the OJCS, in contrast to the U.S. situation of no SAMs, 100 radars, and 300 interceptors, the USSR maintains some 9,400 SAM launchers, 10,000 radars, and 1,200 interceptors for strategic air defense. Another source attributes "nearly 12,000" SAM launchers to the USSR and notes that 2,800 fighter-interceptor aircraft in addition to the 1,200 dedicated fighters "would also be used in strategic defense missions." (This source also differs from the OJCS statement by attributing 118 strategic air defense radars to the U.S.) U.S. Under Secretary of Defense, Research and Engineering, *The FY 1987 Program for Research and Development* (Washington, D.C.: Government Printing Office, 1986), pp. III-15. As these differences regarding numbers of fighter aircraft suggest, counting rules vary concerning strategic and regional defense missions for such capabilities—a point that also applies to U.S. fighters. A U.S.-Soviet comparison obviously omits the air defense capabilities (and offensive strike capabilities) of third parties, notably those maintained by allies in Europe.

76. U.S. Department of Defense, *Soviet Military Power 1986,* in n. 20, p. 45.

77. *Aerospace Daily,* December 31, 1985, p. 306.

78. *Strategic Survey 1985–1986* (London: International nstitute for Strategic Studies, 1986), p. 46.

79. *Aerospace Daily,* December 31, 1985, p. 306, and Gormley, "A New Dimension," in n. 63, p. 568.

80. *Strategic Survey 1985–1986,* in n. 78, p. 47.

81. See François Heisbourg, "De la SDI à la défense aérienne élargie: quelles réponses de l'Europe?" *L'Armement,* March 1986, pp. 45-50; and Jeffrey M. Lenorovitz, "Aerospatiale Studies Missile System to Counter Tactical Soviet Threat," *Aviation Week and Space Technology,* April 21, 1986, pp. 75, 77.

82. The Soviet decision to approve the ABM Treaty may well have been motivated by several strategic purposes quite at variance with endorsement of a principle of mutual vulnerability: for example, (a) obtaining ceilings on U.S. ICBM and SLBM launchers inferior to those allowed the USSR in the SALT I Interim Agreement on Strategic Offensive Arms; (b) leaving U.S. ICBMs and other hardened targets unprotected so that Soviet counterforce targeting objectives could be pursued, if necessary, with fewer impediments; (c) slowing down U.S. BMD research and development efforts; (d) gaining time for Soviet BMD technology to catch up with that of the United States; and (e) funding Soviet BMD activities at less cost than such efforts would require if the U.S. were competing on a more intensive basis. The fact that Soviet BMD capabilities of that era were not likely to be as effective in protecting the USSR against U.S. multiple-warhead ICBMs as Soviet counterforce attacks against those missiles was probably the decisive consideration, not any approbation of mutual vulnerability as a desirable state of affairs.

83. Gates and Gershwin, *Soviet Strategic Force Developments,* in n. 33, p. 6.

84. Stevens, "The Soviet BMD Program," in n. 17, p. 217.

85. Lt. Gen. William E. Odom, "The Implications of Active Defense of NATO for Soviet Military Strategy," paper delivered at the European-American Institute for Security Research Workshop, Washington, D.C., November 1984.

86. Main, "The USSR and Laser Weaponry," in n. 43, p. 75.

87. As the Office of Technology Assessment observes, "There can be no assurance that the Soviets would actually behave as we think they should." Office of Technology Assessment, *Ballistic Missile Defense Technologies,* in n. 5, p. 34.

88. United Kingdom, House of Commons, *Third Report from the Defence Committee, Defence Commitments and Resources and the Defence Estimates 1985–1986,* vol. 1 (London: Her Majesty's Stationery Office, 1985), p. x.

89. *Report of the President's Commission on Strategic Forces,* April 1983, p. 12.

90. *Defense Against Ballistic Missiles: An Assessment of Technologies and Policy Implications* (Washington, D.C.: Department of Defense, April 1984), p. 22 (emphasis in original).

91. Stephen M. Meyer, "Soviet Strategic Programmes and the US SDI," *Survival,* vol. 27 (November/December 1985), p. 283 (emphasis in original).

92. Ibid., p. 284.

93. Lt. Col. Hines, "Soviet Short-Range Ballistic Missiles," in n. 62, p. 1914.

94. Gormley, "A New Dimension," in n. 63, p. 567.

95. Basic issues of ATBM technological feasibility are discussed in David S. Yost, "Ballistic Missile Defense and the Atlantic Alliance," *International Security,* vol. 7 (Fall 1982), pp. 157-63.

96. Stevens, "The Soviet BMD Program," in n. 17, p. 216.

97. According to an *Izvestia* editorial, "It is also clear to every unbiased person that the Soviet Union's air defense system bears no relation to ABM defense." *Izvestia* of January 25, 1985, in *Foreign Broadcast Information Service—Soviet Union* [hereafter *FBIS-SU*] Daily Report, January 25, 1985, p. AA5.

98. Even if the Soviets agreed that U.S. ATBM systems were allowed under the ABM Treaty, geographical asymmetries would favor the USSR. A Soviet ATBM, whether capable of ICBM and SLBM RV interceptions or not, could defend Soviet as well as allied territory. U.S. ATBM systems in Western Europe would defend U.S. forces and allies, but not the U.S. homeland.

99. An example is Wjatscheslaw Daschitschew, "Der sowjetische Standpunkt zu SDI," in Hans-Joachim Veen and Peter R. Weilemann, eds., *Standpunkte zu SDI in West und Ost* (Sankt Augustin bei Bonn, West Germany: Konrad-Adenauer-Stiftung, 1985), p. 34. Daschitschew described the SA-X-12 as simply an "air defense missile," however (p. 39).

100. T.K. Jones testimony in U.S. House of Representatives, Committee on Armed Services, *Department of Defense Authorization and Oversight, Hearings,* 98th Cong., 1st sess. (Washington, D.C.: Government Printing Office, 1983), part 5, p. 242.

101. Office of Technology Assessment, *Ballistic Missile Defense Technologies,* in n. 5, p. 270.

102. For background on this point, see Gerard Smith, *Doubletalk: The Story of the First Strategic Arms Limitation Talks* (New York: Doubleday and Co., 1980), pp. 91-93.

103. See the Tass dispatch of March 15, 1983, by Vladimir Bogachev, "The ABM Treaty and Stability," in *FBIS-SU* Daily Report, March 16, 1983, pp. AA4-AA5.

104. Indeed, West German Defense Minister Manfred Wörner holds that it is "not politically viable" for NATO to increase its INF deployments to overwhelm Soviet ATBM and air defenses. Wörner, "A Missile Defense for NATO Europe," *Strategic Review,* vol. 14 (Winter 1986), p. 16.

105. President's Commission on Strategic Forces, in n. 89, p. 12.

106. Paul Nitze, *The Objectives of Arms Control,* Current Policy no. 677 (Washington, D.C.: Bureau of Public Affairs, U.S. Department of State, March 28, 1985), p. 5.

107. Andrew W. Marshall, "Arms Competitions: The Status of Analysis," in Uwe Nerlich, ed., *The Western Panacea: Constraining Soviet Power Through Negotiation,* vol. II of *Soviet Power and Western Negotiating Policies* (Cambridge, Mass.: Ballinger Publishing Company, 1983), p. 3.

108. Ibid., p. 7.

6

The Implications of SDI for the Independent Nuclear Forces of Europe

Trevor Taylor

President Reagan's SDI, a U.S. military program in which its friends are at least as interested as its enemies, is distinguished by its range of implications for the United States' allies. In this chapter, the focus will be on the relationship of SDI to the viability, role, structure, and importance of the independent nuclear forces of Western Europe. Of necessity, the analysis is subject to a number of qualifications.

First, it is clearly problematic to analyze the implications of a phenomenon whose nature remains unclear, although definitely multifaceted. Despite its public emergence over three years ago, SDI is still characterized by considerable uncertainty. Thus SDI could be the start of a long-term U.S. effort to build comprehensive active defensive systems against all delivery methods for nuclear weapons, or it could be a bargaining chip to be abandoned in exchange for reductions in superpower intercontinental ballistic missile (ICBM) forces. It could be the start of a U.S. effort to defend missile silos and other military targets against nuclear attack, or it could be a prudent hedge of research effort (involving no deployment and little "development") to ensure that the USSR does not build any major lead in the ballistic missile defense (BMD) field. It could lead to the conclusion that invulnerable, cost-effective defenses against ballistic missiles cannot be built, especially once offensive countermeasures such as missile hardening are taken into account; yet, the process leading to this conclusion could result in the generation of many technological advances that would be useful in civil and conventional military industry. SDI could result in a leaky roof over only the United States or some protection too for Western Europe against a range of aerospace threats. The attitude of future U.S. administrations and Congresses toward SDI is obviously a major unknown. Of primary importance, it is a U.S. program to which the shape of the Soviet response is also still unknown.

The second qualification has to do with the comparative treatment of the U.K. and France in this chapter. They are similar enough to be considered together, but the differences between them ought not to be totally disregarded.

France stresses the independence of its deterrent and relies mainly on its own technologies, whereas the U.K. buys missiles from the United States and earmarks its forces for assignment to NATO in wartime. France has made a sustained effort to generate an explicit strategic rationale, whereas Britain places more emphasis on straightforward capabilities, particularly the capacity to destroy Moscow. The U.K. relies on a single invulnerable and advanced system for its deterrent, whereas France has a mixture of slightly less sophisticated delivery vehicles, two of which are somewhat vulnerable to first strike attack. Yet these differences are less important than the similarities. Both France and the U.K. see their forces as making a contribution to the defense of Europe as a whole, if only by increasing levels of uncertainty for the USSR. Both deterrents would have to be rethought in order to make much sense in a Western Europe that lacked a firm commitment from the United States. Both the U.K. and France need an effective major strike capability to achieve their fundamental deterrent purpose, and they have as yet accepted no need for a strategic nuclear warfighting capability. Finally, both countries have already had to face up to increased Soviet strategic defenses. The U.K. has explicitly addressed and evaluated the Soviet BMD threat through its Chevaline and Trident programs, and France has developed a MIRVed (multiple independently targetable reentry vehicle) missile and a standoff nuclear bomb in recent years.

Third, all students of defense and politics are accustomed to dealing with the possibility that an official speaker or writer may not be being especially truthful. Yet, in the field of BMD, where there is so little that is unambiguous about the efforts, capabilities, and motives of all the parties involved, this is a particular problem. So many groups and individuals have a stake in SDI that judgment has constantly to be used to evaluate the worth of any assertion about it.

The last qualification concerns the implications of SDI for both formal British and French policy and for many of the issues under debate which will influence the future shape of that policy. It is important, however, to distinguish the implications, which cover the various forms of pressure that SDI could exert, from the impact of SDI, which deals with the consequences it could generate. The impact of SDI will depend on how it interacts with the many other factors and problems that determine the shape of British and French nuclear policies. The U.K. Ministry of Defense currently recognizes that SDI has many implications but tends to emphasize that it has so far had little impact on British decisions.

The role of this chapter is to survey implications and to consider whether and where they will have a substantive impact. A series of questions will be presented and discussed.

To What Extent Is SDI an Attack upon the Conceptual and Moral Basis of British and French Policy?

President Reagan's speech of 23 March 1983,[1] which attacked the long-term reliance on nuclear weapons and on the targeting of populations as the basis for security policy, contradicted the defense arguments of the current governments in the U.K. and France. These see nuclear weapons as the central element in their countries' defenses and allocate funds accordingly. The U.K. is currently procuring the Trident D5 missile from the United States and is building its own submarines and warheads for the system. The total cost of the package will be at least $9.869 billion at 1985/6 prices,[2] a sum which will constitute for a period of several years in the late 1980s through the early 1990s around 11 percent of the British new equipment budget, at a conservative estimate. The Social Democratic Party claims that Trident will account for 30 percent of new-equipment spending by 1990.[3] Despite opposition, especially at the end of the 1950s and in the early 1960s from the U.K. Campaign for Nuclear Disarmament, British governmental determination to be a nuclear power has wavered little since the postwar Labour Government decided on the development of a British nuclear bomb. Reliance was placed first on British-developed bombers for a nuclear delivery system against the USSR and then on submarine-based Polaris missiles bought from the United States. Although formally the U.K. government likes to present the Polaris effort as inexpensive to run (at about 1.5 percent of the total defense budget), the overall costs of the U.K.'s nuclear program are clearly considerable, perhaps 5 percent on average of the total defense budget.[4] The government spent around $1 billion on the Chevaline warhead system alone from the late 1970s.[5]

France, which conducted its first nuclear test in 1960, spends more extensively on its nuclear forces. Its nuclear forces took 22 percent of planned-equipment spending in 1980, and they currently take around 30 percent. Nuclear R&D has been taking a declining share of this since 1981.[6] In the 1984-1988 period, France planned to spend 31.68 percent of its equipment budget on nuclear forces, with about six-sevenths of this going to strategic forces.[7] Including an estimate for the operating budgets of such forces, France spends perhaps 20 percent of its total defense budget on the nuclear sector. Although France has deployed long-based ballistic missiles on the Plateau d'Albion and will keep in service eighteen Mirage IVs with 100-kilometer-range standoff nuclear missiles until the 1992-1994 period,[8] like Britain it relies for deterrence mainly on nuclear submarines carrying submarine-launched ballistic missiles (SLBMs). Six such submarines are deployed, a seventh (an improved version) is being planned for 1994, and France's latest missile, the six-warheaded M.4, is being introduced. The planned Mirage 2000N force, equipped with standoff missiles, was described in the 1983 Loi de Progamma-tion, along with the Pluton and Hades missiles, under tactical systems designed to issue a final warning to the USSR that France was about to use its strategic nuclear forces.

These weapons are not acquired by the U.K. and France solely because of the national prestige and grandeur which they are felt to impart. Strategic nuclear forces are seen as being necessary for national defense and as therefore morally acceptable. "French defense policy," said the former Defense Minister Paul Quilès, "is based on the nuclear deterrent."[9] The U.K. government, which sees that there is no way of buying more deterrence of a Soviet attack than Trident will bring using $10 billion, judges similarly. The British government shares Phil Williams's view that "given a chance, Moscow would probably prefer the United Kingdom to abandon Trident, rather than simply cut conventional forces."[10]

In his March 1983 speech, President Reagan sought to take the moral high ground from the peace movement, which was arguing that nuclear weapons in general and Mutual Assured Destruction in particular were undesirable and immoral, but in doing so he confronted the views of the governments in London and Paris, which argue for the inevitable continued existence of nuclear weapons and the need for nuclear deterrence. In these capitals (and elsewhere in Europe) the view is firmly held that NATO will need a nuclear option at least until some way can be accepted of offsetting the USSR's conventional-force advantages in Europe, based on demography, geography, and culture. U.K. Foreign Secretary Sir Geoffrey Howe put it clearly in a speech in March 1986:

> The threat of retaliation, to punish aggression, is essential. The would-be aggressor must be as conscious of the prospect of punishment as of the risk of failure. In face of the geographical handicap and the present imbalance in conventional military strength, a purely conventional defense of Western Europe cannot achieve this. That is why, for the foreseeable future, the nuclear contribution to our defense is essential to effective deterrence of the threat of war.[11]

Prime Minister Thatcher defended the U.K. deterrent in March 1986 and used the expression "pie in the sky" to refer to the suggestion that the world might be rid of nuclear weapons while the knowledge existed to make them.[12]

Does SDI Threaten to Erode the Viability of the Independent Deterrents in Western Europe?

The March 23 speech threatened to lead to U.S. and subsequent Soviet actions that would improve ballistic missile defenses to the point where the U.K. and

France would not be able to deploy systems capable of inflicting appropriate damage on the USSR. There are clearly officials in the U.K. and France who hold such fears and who have expressed them in private.[13]

First, however, it is important to distinguish the implications of SDI from the implications of what the USSR was doing anyway. The USSR has been making a major research effort in the BMD field for some years, well before the announcement of SDI. The U.K. is inclined to concur with the estimates of the Soviet effort to be found in the U.S. official publications *Soviet Military Power* and *Soviet Strategic Defense Programs* (where Secretaries Weinberger and Shultz describe SDI as "a prudent and necessary response to the ongoing extensive Soviet anti-ballistic missile effort."[14] Although the U.K. is opposed to an arms race in space, it is aware of Soviet antisatellite programs and beam-weapons research and accepts that SDI did not stimulate the first Soviet efforts in the BMD field. Soviet BMD efforts have to a degree been independent of what the United States has done and, given the resources that the USSR is already devoting to defensive measures, it is by no means certain that the USSR will greatly expand its BMD efforts as a result of SDI. Indeed, a case can be made that the USSR may have to divert resources to the offence to ensure that its forces remain able to penetrate any envisaged U.S. defenses.

If it is assumed that SDI will promote further Soviet BMD efforts, the possibility must be recognized that a future slowdown in U.S. BMD research should cause the USSR also to relax its efforts. While it now seems unlikely that SDI will simply fade away, BMD advocates in the United States will have to fight harder in the future for funds, because (a) any future administration is likely to be somewhat less committed than that of President Reagan; (b) funding squeezes on defense seem likely to increase; and (c) technological progress may be less than currently hoped for. It is perceived in the U.K. and France that the United States will at most go ahead with active defenses for military targets, defenses that rely heavily on ground-based interceptors using information obtained in part from space. While the U.K. and France would regret the weakening of arms control, which the end of the ABM Treaty would probably entail, if the USSR followed the United States and defended military targets, the needed capability of the U.K. and France to hit primarily civil targets would not be greatly affected.

The U.K. and France recognize the extent of Soviet BMD efforts—efforts that obviously could be further stimulated by SDI, despite the USSR's resource problems. Yet they also anticipate that extant Soviet BMD capabilities are limited, and they forecast that these capabilities will not increase to the point of reaching a different order of magnitude in the next twenty-five years, especially given the planned improvements in European offensive forces. Paul Quilès, returning from a U.S. visit concerning SDI, said in connection with BMD that science might be able to advance by a series of rapid steps but not through miracles. As Lawrence Freedman put it, "The offense-defense duel is not about to swing in favor of the defense".[15] Technological assertions from ambitious scientists as to what is feasible in the BMD field have to be placed in the context of a current NATO inability to field an effective Identity Friend or Foe (IFF) system and of U.S. difficulties in developing an antiaircraft tank, the DIVAD system. Moreover, the USSR is clearly at a technological disadvantage vis-à-vis the United States in most areas. Also, deterrence rests in the final analysis on Soviet perceptions, both of the nature of the threat and of the efficacy of its defenses. States operating weapons tend to be more aware of their flaws than states facing them, and this is likely to be especially the case with BMD systems, where there would be limited opportunities for their realistic testing.

Another consideration is that the central deterrent roles of both independent European forces are relatively undemanding. The U.K. and France fundamentally need to be able to launch a successful major retaliatory strike once having received a substantial Soviet attack. The basic deterrent role of British and French nuclear forces is to induce the USSR not to devastate the territory of these two Western European countries. The British and French forces send a message to Moscow that should such devastation occur, the USSR too would suffer inordinate damage. Both countries rely heavily on a small number of submarines which would reveal their positions by firing a single missile, and with Polaris, the U.K. can be sure only of having one boat at sea at any one time, although a second boat is always in a state of high readiness.

Regardless of SDI, a weakness of the British and French deterrents is, of course, their difficulty in trying to deter with any credibility a very limited nuclear attack on their territory, one which causes major damage but does not destroy the society as a whole. I will return to this problem later, in the section on the possible role of antitactical missiles (ATMs), but it should be noted here that despite some debate, France still doctrinally rejects the idea of nuclear-war fighting, even at the tactical level. It is opposed to "flexible response," although it holds that the demonstration use of its final-warning tactical systems, its prestrategic forces, could induce the USSR to end a war; and, with the planned deployment of the Air-Sol Moyenne Portée (ASMP) weapon, or air-to-surface medium-range missile, on the Mirage 2000 and Super Etendard aircraft, and with the development of Hades, it will increase its capacity for nuclear strikes against Eastern Europe rather than the USSR itself.[16] In the U.K., the announcement of the decision to procure first the Trident C.4 and then instead the D.5 provoked something of a debate concerning the envisaged plans for the additional warheads and their increased accuracy compared with Polaris. Were there not too many warheads for a minimum counter-city deterrent, would all missiles be fired at once, and would some warheads not be aimed at military targets? However, this debate was quieted by the government's commitment to sixteen missiles per boat, with eight warheads per missile, as opposed to the maximum possible of twenty-four missiles each with fourteen warheads, and by the publicity given to Soviet missile-defense efforts, which raised the possibility that many U.K. warheads might not get through.

In the future, of course, concepts of British and French deterrence could change in such a way as to put more demanding requirements on their systems. For instance, the U.K. and France might wish their forces to serve as the basis for a European deterrent, a specific issue addressed in greater detail later in this chapter. Moreover, the moral acceptability of a counter-city deterrent might decline markedly within the U.K. and France. Robert Gessert, a U.S. defense analyst and active Christian, in supporting some of the views of the U.S. Catholic bishops, has observed that the "intentional destruction of cities even in retaliation is a morally inadmissible use of nuclear weapons."[17] While it would currently appear unlikely, this sort of argument could come to find much increased favor in the U.K. and France. These possibilities, however, represent political rather than SDI-related technological threats to the British and French deterrents. Overall, the basic argument remains that for an independent deterrent, neither the U.K. nor France needs the strategic counterforce capabilities that appear most susceptible to the BMD techniques likely to be available in the next twenty-five years.

While it can be expected that SDI/BMD research will lead to increased antisatellite (ASAT) capabilities on the part of both the USSR and the United States, it remains the case that neither the British nor the French deterrents are reliant on satellites to carry out their basic retaliatory mission against urban targets for which no great accuracy is required.

Both the U.K. and France are wary about saying precisely what damage they currently feel they must be able to inflict to get the deterrent effect they want. The U.K. 1981 defense White Paper spoke of the U.K.'s need to be able to pose "a convincing threat—of inflicting, on key aspects of Soviet power, damage which any state leadership would regard as out of all proportions to any likely gains from aggression against us." Another favored expression is that the U.K. should be "able to hold at risk critical elements of Soviet state power."[18] This is widely interpreted to mean that the U.K. needs at least to be able to destroy Moscow.[19] Since the late 1970s, France too has put more emphasis on destroying the Soviet economy and administration, "the vital works" of the Soviet state, rather than just its people.[20] A somewhat different approach was taken by David Hobbs, who examined the size of past and present U.K. nuclear forces to estimate the hidden requirement determining them, and who also analyzed U.K. forces as a proportion of relevant Soviet offensive forces. He concluded that the U.K. needed at most a force of seventy to ninety individually targetable "arriving warheads," although a force of thirty-two such warheads would be an adequate minimum.[21] To a degree, British and French aims of deterrence through destruction of the Soviet state seem to have been generated by the increased capabilities that Chevaline, Trident, and the M.4 have made available, rather than by recognition that just destroying tens of cities would not work. While some French experts argue today that France should be able to destroy between 100 and 150 Soviet cities, between 1964 and 1971 France relied for its deterrent on a force of just five dozen Mirage IVs.[22] The deterrent effect of British and French forces depends on what is unacceptable to the USSR with the strategic and industrial strength of the United States remaining intact. In the event of Soviet passive defenses providing protection to key Soviet officials and the theoretical survival of the Soviet state, British and French deterrence could still rest on the damage to be inflicted on the economy and the population.[23]

It is in the light of this that the Trident D5 procurement and the M.4 program should be summarized. Beginning in the late 1990s the U.K. will deploy four submarines, each armed with sixteen missiles. The U.K. will always have one boat on station, with a second being either at sea or in a state of high readiness. The USSR would virtually have to strike out of the blue to prevent a second British boat from getting to sea, and, should a crisis build up over a period of weeks, it would be possible to get a third boat out of short refit and into service. Nevertheless, the U.K. formally asserts that its "deterrent force rests and will continue to rest on the ability to maintain only one submarine on patrol at all times."[24] The U.K. has indicated that it will put a maximum of eight warheads on each D5 missile. Thus the minimum U.K. nuclear force on station would consist of 128 warheads. Assuming that the submarine would not be destroyed before it could fire and that 80 percent of fired missiles would work properly, the USSR would be faced with producing an active defense against a force of 102 warheads, using missiles in which there would be room for chaff and other decoys.

In addition, the U.K. could, if necessary, take further measures to strengthen its Trident deterrent, although most measures would be costly.[25] It could speed up refit schedules and change crew arrangements so that two boats were always at sea. It could procure a fifth submarine with missiles, which would certainly give it a constant two-boat presence. Missiles could be fired on depressed trajectories. The U.K. would not feel bound by its unilateral commitment to a maximum of eight warheads a missile should the USSR break the terms of the ABM Treaty and deploy additional ABM defenses. Trident missiles could carry fourteen warheads, giving a minimum two-boat U.K. strike force of $16 \times 14 \times 2 \times 0.8 = 599$ warheads. In general, despite the BMD issue, the U.K. government has sought to play down the number of warheads available with Trident in order to suppress criticism that the Trident procurement represents an escalation of the arms race, but there is no doubt that Trident does provide a substantially increased potential. Also, the U.K. could apply to Trident the technology it has developed under the Chevaline program. Precisely what this involves has been kept secret so as to minimize

the chances of the USSR finding a counter, but it certainly deals with maneu-
verable and perhaps hardened warheads (they are not, however, individually
targeted).

It is calculations like these which have made the U.K. government confident that Trident will be a viable deterrent at least for the next twenty to
twenty-five years. Undoubtedly, some officials in the U.K. and France have
been concerned that the end of the ABM Treaty would damage their national
deterrents,[26] but the time scale in which this could occur appears to be
extended. The then Defense Minister Heseltine told the House of Commons
in July 1985 that "our view is that within the lifetime foreseen for the Trident
missile, the defenses of the Soviet Union would not be adequate to remove its
deterrent capability."[27] The House of Commons Defence Committee, having
shown some concern the year before, reported in May 1985:

> After our discussions with representatives of the U.S. Administration in March
> and April this year we were left in no doubt that the new era of strategic
> defenses that has been advocated is unlikely to arrive while Trident is in
> service—which suggests that the current excitement is being generated
> about a project unlikely to reach fruition before 2020; meanwhile we note
> the confidence of Ministry of Defence that the improved Chevaline front end
> of the existing Polaris force will be capable of penetrating the Soviet defenses
> around Moscow which are currently being upgraded.[28]

British officials accept that they cannot absolutely predict the efficacy of
Trident as a deterrent for much beyond the end of the first decade of the next
century—there is too much technological uncertainty. In some ways this is an
uncomfortable message, since the last U.K. Trident submarine may not come
into service until very late in the 1990s and the government sometimes likes
to speak of Trident as having a thirty-year life. But on the other hand, there are
never any certainties in this realm, and the U.K. government is confident that
of all the strategic nuclear systems in Western arsenals, the Trident is the most
reliable prospect.

France, relying mainly on its own M.4 SLBM, with 6 warheads per missile
and deployed on a planned force of seven submarines, each carrying sixteen
missiles, is clearly also not in a desperate position. Assuming that three submarines can be kept at sea at any one time, that they can avoid destruction before
firing, and that 80 percent of the missiles work properly, this gives a basic
French strike force of 230 warheads. This is to omit consideration of the more
vulnerable French land-based ballistic missile force and French aircraft with
standoff missiles. France also plans improvements to its deterrent. It intends to
fit 9 warheads to the French SLBM in the 1990s. Since SDI, Paul Quilès and
Jacques Chevallier of the Commissariat à l'Energie Atomique have spoken of
making French warheads smaller and harder to detect on radar. Ideas for

blinding radars, presumably through explosions in space, and for depressed trajectories are being considered. The French governmental Delpech Study reported in January 1986 on the technical possibilities for BMD. It listed areas of research for France which should enable it to ensure that its missiles would get through. These areas included missile hardening; shorter propulsion phase times; "dividing the missile into independent sub-missiles"; improving the coordination of launches; the use of flat trajectories; the reduction of radar surfaces; the generation of electromagnetic and infrared decoys; improved radar jamming; and, possibly, antisatellite weapons. It ruled out the possibility of an impervious shield and argued:

> Over the next quarter of a century the clearest result of extensive research efforts engaged in by the Soviets and the Americans, if they culminate in success, would be to force the powers, which want to remain provided with an effective strategic nuclear capability, to modify the composition and modes of utilization of their forces and pursue modernization and hardening operations of considerable, though not unbearable, cost.
>
> Over a much longer period of time, the hypothetical realization of a sufficiently effective and not very vulnerable system could have strategic consequences for France, but this eventuality is remote and uncertain and a satisfactory modification of our strategic forces is not at all excluded.[29]

Thus France, too, has concluded that it will have a viable deterrent for the technologically forseeable future.

How Could SDI Affect the Erosion of Domestic Support in the U.K. and France for the National Nuclear Deterrents, in Light of the Debates About the Morality and Costs of Nuclear Weapons?

Difficulties in this area are more apparent in the U.K., where, in addition to such problems as recruiting suitable personnel for British nuclear weapons research and keeping going an aging Polaris fleet until Trident is ready, there is substantial political opposition to British nuclear weapons. Both opposition parties (Labour and the Liberal-Social Democrat Alliance) are opposed to Trident in particular. In the event of their election, possibly in 1987 or 1988, they are committed to cancellation of the Trident deal. The Labour Party has a comprehensive antinuclear policy on moral grounds and reflects many of the views of the unilateralist movement in the country as a whole, led by the Campaign for Nuclear Disarmament. Opposition to Trident in the Social Democratic Party (SDP) in particular is based on its cost as well as its perceived excessive capability, and there are some elements even in the Conservative Party who oppose it on cost grounds. Although a clear majority of British public opinion continues to favor the maintenance of an independent British nuclear deterrent,[30] and although it might be expected that the views of either political grouping would change once it exchanged opposition for power and responsibility, the stance of British political parties does suggest that Trident is under more immediate threat from U.K. politics than it is from SDI. In one way, SDI, by highlighting the capabilities and potential of Soviet BMD, has strengthened the case for Trident, whose effectiveness against possible countermeasures is least in question. On the other hand, by indicating that the future of nuclear weapons may be limited and that the threat of retaliatory destruction is becoming unacceptable, SDI threatens to undermine public support for nuclear forces. As a Western European Union Assembly Report put it, "If the idea spreads that the future depends on defensive weapons and that in the long run offensive weapons are destined to be relegated to the arsenal of obsolescent weapons, it is liable to become increasingly difficult to make an already hesitant public opinion accept the financial and other efforts necessary for the maintenance and development of nuclear weapons."[31]

Significantly, the moral impact of SDI as an attack on nuclear weapons has been diminished by U.S.-government acceptance that nuclear deterrence will be around for decades yet and that the United States needs to modernize its offensive strategic systems. Moreover, although for domestic political reasons the highest levels of the Reagan administration are not yet ready to cease their claims about a comprehensive defense that would make nuclear weapons obsolete, it is increasingly recognized by the United States that, at most, only partial defenses are feasible. Paul Quilès has observed that the medium-term character of SDI is that it could lead to the deployment of partial defenses for U.S. military targets, while its long-term nature as a potential comprehensive defense serves mainly to generate support for BMD work in general.[32]

In part because it has not offered a real prospect of removing the possibility of nuclear war, SDI has found few supporters in Western Europe who back it on moral grounds, although some U.K. Tories are ready to support it without explicit consideration of its effect on the U.K. deterrent.[33] The antinuclear/ unilateral disarmament movement has rejected SDI on the grounds that it will stimulate an arms race and as a ridiculous route to the removal of nuclear weapons compared with the direct method of disarmament.[34] The antinuclear movement in the U.K. has been little affected by SDI for better or for worse, with Trident and the cruise missile sites at Greenham Common and Molesworth being much more immediate concerns. In France the antinuclear movement has been of minimal political significance, since the conversion of President Mitterrand and the Socialist Party to support of the French deterrent. Although the original antinuclear message underpinning SDI threatened to make it harder to mobilize public support for independent nuclear forces in the U.K. and France, no such consequence has yet occurred.

It must be recognized, however, that in the longer term, that is, beyond 1995 or so, when the U.K. and France will be considering successors to their existing, if improved, deterrents, the domestic constituency in favor of national nuclear deterrents might shrink to a minority should Soviet defensive capabilities appear to have improved to the point that the two smaller European powers might have to spend very large sums to acquire systems to penetrate them. One reason why the U.K. majority in favor of a national deterrent has held up so far is that the U.K. force has been comparatively cheap to date, thanks to purchases from the United States.

However, for some years the U.K. and France have faced the problems of improved Soviet defenses making their delivery systems vulnerable. That is why they moved from aircraft to single-warheaded missiles and then to Chevaline and the M.4. It must also be remembered that BMD is only one technological threat among others to the Western European deterrents. In particular, a major breakthrough in antisubmarine warfare (ASW) would pose a fundamental challenge. Neil Kinnock, the U.K. Labour Party leader, has said that Polaris may already be vulnerable, and David Owen of the SDP believes that Polaris submarines may be too noisy by the end of the 1990s.[35] French submarines, although improved, are generally thought to be somewhat noisier than their U.K. equivalents. France is also in a slightly worse position than the U.K. in that the M.4 missile has a shorter range (over 4,400 km) than Trident (11,000 km) and perhaps even Polaris (4,600 km). Thus, France's submarines would have to fire from a smaller sea area.

In brief, while Soviet BMD capabilities could conceivably help to erode domestic opinion in favor of the British and French deterrents, so could other Soviet technological developments. These are considerations with which the U.K. and France have to live, although there are measures that they can take to offset them. For instance, France could well come to appreciate the benefits of moving away from a purely national effort for the development and acquisition of delivery systems. This issue is discussed in more detail later.

Almost certainly, however, Soviet BMD measures, stimulated to some degree by SDI, will generate even starker choices for the U.K. and France about the conventional forces to be foregone in order to fund the nuclear sector. Even without the problems that an enhanced Soviet BMD program would present, the British and French governments are currently looking at shortfalls in their defense budgets and commitments. If demands for more nuclear forces, cruise missiles, and antitactical ballistic missiles (ATBMs) get added in, either defense budgets will have to be much increased (not a likely development) or something will have to give. Since in an SDI-dominated future the need for conventional forces in Europe could well be greater than it is even today, a consequence could be that the capability of the U.K. and France to act outside the NATO area could decline still further.

Given the Existence of SDI, Should the U.K. and France Seek to Participate in Its Programs?

The U.K. has responded to this question with an enthusiastic yes. France, at least when it had both a Socialist government and a Socialist president, said that it would not participate as a government, since it disapproved of SDI. It would not, however, prevent French firms, including government-owned companies, from seeking SDI contracts, and in January 1986 it turned toward encouraging French firms to take part.[36] Considering the need to preserve the viability of national deterrents, prudence would suggest that a positive readiness to participate would be wise. The more a country is involved with SDI work, the better off it will be in terms of its scientific knowledge to judge the strengths and weaknesses of BMD technologies. The more it knows about BMD defenses, the better able it will be to devise counters to them. Basically, France's initial posture of noncooperation with SDI made sense only on the basis that such a posture would encourage others who disliked SDI to come out into the open and that the combined pressure of all SDI opponents would lead the United States to give it up. Not surprisingly, given that SDI represents a U.S. assertion of its right to seek to defend the lives of its citizenry, the United States to date has shown little sign of being influenced by external opinion as to whether or not it should press on with BMD work. The United States seems more likely to be swayed by those who support SDI in principle, as a research program, than by those who oppose it outright.

Could European ATBM Strengthen the British and French Deterrents?

One consequence already of SDI has been to raise the question of the extent to which Western Europe could be defended against ballistic missile attack. German Defense Minister Wörner has suggested missile defense for Europe, and from the beginning the United States has suggested that Western Europe should be covered by BMD systems. The issue of extended air defense (EAD) has established itself on the European agenda.[37]

To date there have been few public indications of commitment from European governments to extended air defense. The U.K. was initially wary of the divisive implication of two separate U.S. and European efforts in NATO with respect to BMD. Yet its officials are interested in what antitactical missiles (ATMs) could do, not least for the defense of the U.K. In France, Giscard d'Estaing has advocated ATMs and improved air defense for Europe through a partnership with the United States.[38] Governmental reticence reflects in part uncertainty as to where necessary funding can be found and in part the current discussions about which specific projects should be involved. The United States is encouraging consideration of a Patriot derivative as the initial system for European defense against theater ballistic missiles (TBMs), while Europeans, led by the French with their Aster project, are more interested in developing a replacement for the medium-range Homing All-the-Way Killer (Hawk) surface-to-air missile (SAM) with ATM capabilities.[39]

A salient question is whether the national nuclear deterrents of Europe could benefit from enjoying protection from extended air defense. Two arguments suggest that they could. First, nuclear installations, including command and control centers, could be given some measure of protection to increase the certainty that a retaliatory response would be forthcoming, although some defenses would have to be based in or very near cities. As former French Defense Minister Charles Hernu has said, France could defend the Plateau d'Albion (thus weakening the need for a mobile French land-based missile).[40] The Taverny and Houilles command centers would also be candidates for protection.[41] Both the U.K. and France could protect their submarine bases, perhaps with the consequence that in the early stages of war an additional submarine might be got to sea. In other words, deterrence could be strengthened by increasing the reliability of U.K. and French retaliatory capability.

It could be strengthened also in terms of credibility. A British or French threat to launch nuclear weapons against the USSR makes some kind of sense in the event of either the U.K. or France having been devastated. While critics would say that such devastation would not actually benefit the U.K. or France should they have suffered so much damage, the more salient point for the USSR is that it will not actually cost the U.K. or France much either: they will have nothing left to lose. More problematic, however, is a scenario in which the U.K. or France has been subjected to a small number of selected nuclear strikes against military targets, causing, say, 2 or 3 million dead. In those circumstances, the USSR might expect that the U.K. or France would not choose to use retaliatory nuclear forces en masse. This sort of scenario has led some to suggest that the U.K. and France need a capability for limited retaliation.[42] While acknowledging that any decision to use nuclear weapons would be very difficult, it is clear that a decision on retaliation after limited provocation would be particularly hard. However, the presence of an extended-air-defense capability would mean that there would be a chance of destroying a minimal Soviet attacking force. This would press the USSR either to use a much larger striking force or not to use nuclear weapons at all. The more the U.K. and France are damaged, the more credible becomes their threat to retaliate and the more deterrence is strengthened. As David Yost put it, "Obliging the U.S.S.R. to launch a broad attack is seen as a virtue" in France.[43] In short, extended air defense in the U.K. and France would make harder the execution of "surgical" strikes against these states which would damage their will and ability to fight but would not justify the release of retaliatory nuclear forces.

This is not to conclude that the U.K. and France will become rapid converts to ideas about extended air defense, if only because of the problem of cost. The two governments are having enough trouble taking on their existing missions without adding new ones to the list, especially when extended air defense shows every sign of being tremendously expensive. The Patriot system, at $11 billion, is an indicator of what even present generation systems can cost.[44]

Extended air defense, which would have implications for the degree of French participation in alliance activities, would be a matter for all the countries of Western Europe, not just the U.K. and France. However, since these two countries know the most about launchers and warheads, they could expect to play a leading part in any European discussions about just what is or is not technologically feasible.

What Does SDI Imply for Anglo-French Nuclear Cooperation?

Over time, SDI may well generate pressures for the U.K. and France to work more closely together on nuclear matters. To date, cooperation in this field has been virtually nonexistent, although France would probably have liked the U.K. to consider purchase of its M.4 missile instead of Trident, and the U.K.'s SDP leader David Owen is the most prominent among those who have argued for Anglo-French nuclear cooperation.[45]

The case for equipment collaboration is at least qualified. On the one hand, there is the argument that the U.K. and France, in the face of improving Soviet defenses, should seek to work primarily with the United States as the world's most technologically advanced country. This is the basic argument that justified the U.K. Trident purchase. As argued previously, effective nuclear retaliatory forces are likely to become even more expensive, and political support for them could be eroded as a result. The best way to keep down costs is to buy from or at least collaborate with the United States. In this context, the U.K. and France might find it worthwhile to coordinate their needs so as to get a better deal than they would obtain as separate governments.

On the other hand, there is the argument that the United States could well become less interested in and committed to Europe. Then much would depend on whether it would remain willing to help the U.K. and France with delivery systems. It might decide to do so on the grounds that the two European states could then defend themselves without additional U.S. help. This would represent a kind of nuclear version of the Nixon Doctrine, with France perhaps buying some Pershing IIs or a future equivalent.[46] But another possibility is that the United States would become reluctant to transfer key technology to the U.K. and France. To ensure against this, the U.K. and France could work together on research and development issues. David Owen and John Roper are among those who have suggested that the two countries could work to produce a collaborative cruise missile,[47] using guidance information provided, if necessary, by European satellites.

Even in the short term, the U.K. and France could quietly recognize the benefits of working together on targeting and deployment schedules, to try to ensure, for instance, that there is normally a total of five submarines from both countries at sea at any one time and never less than four. The attitudinal and bureaucratic obstacles to Anglo-French nuclear cooperation, however, must be recognized as substantial. The British are used to dealing with the Americans and the French are accustomed to doing things on their own. But this should not be allowed to disguise the fact that nuclear collaboration in Europe might begin to make more sense as the costs of national efforts rise still further. Significantly, the governments in both the U.K. and France have perhaps come to appreciate rather more a common interest in their both having an effective deterrent. Neither country today would relish the prospect of being the only nuclear power in Western Europe, and awareness of this possibility might help to lubricate any future efforts toward cooperation.

How Might SDI Affect the Roles and Importance of the European Deterrents?

In the U.K., the Liberal-Social Democrat Alliance is finding appeal in the idea of a British deterrent devoted to the defense of Europe. Franco-German cooperation, for its part, had a considerable nuclear dimension in 1985 and 1986, with France stressing its deterrent's contribution to European defense and agreeing to consult Bonn, to the extent possible in the circumstances, on any use of its nuclear weapons against German territory.[48] There is an established, if not particularly fruitful, debate in France about the extent to which its nuclear weapons could provide an area of extended sanctuary in war which would include Germany.

These are political developments that reflect a positive European preference for less reliance on the U.S. deterrent. But other points suggest that in any case the U.S. deterrent may be less available or credible as a consequence of SDI. One line of argument is that effective extended air defenses in the Warsaw Pact, generated in part in response to SDI, will take away the NATO option of selected nuclear strikes against military targets. NATO will lose the ability to escalate in small steps, and thus the credibility of flexible response will disappear. The USSR could come to hope that it would be allowed to occupy and/or destroy Western Europe without having to accept damage from U.S. strategic forces. Another perspective, although rejected by the Reagan administration, is that the United States, once protected by a defensive bubble, would lose interest in the defense of Europe. This sort of view is reinforced by European perceptions that the U.S. population is moving from the eastern seaboard to the South and West and is thus becoming less oriented toward Europe and more toward the Pacific and Latin America. The view of the Reagan administration, on the other hand, is that a United States enjoying some degree of protection will be more ready rather than less ready to fight for Europe.

These strategic points, however, neglect the political strains that would affect NATO should active defenses permit the United States to benefit from greater protection than its European allies. On arms control, East-West relations, and out-of-area issues, the views held by the countries of Western Europe are already often different from those held in the United States. This is in part because the United States and Western Europe already carry different burdens of risk. In the event of even a conventional war (let alone a limited nuclear war) with the Warsaw Pact, the United States would not suffer massive damage, whereas its European allies would. The sorts of risk that seem reasonable to people sitting in Washington therefore tend to look unreasonable to decision makers in Bonn, London, or Paris. Should the United States acquire an additional measure of protection besides the one already provided by geography, increased strains in NATO could be predicted as transatlantic allies sought to achieve a common line on crises and on potentially dangerous situations around the world. Together these arguments point to SDI as potentially decoupling and to the conclusion that in the future, the British and French deterrents either might have a more explicit coupling role or might need to become the basis of a Western European deterrent system independent of the United States.

British and French nuclear forces are already recognized in the alliance, in particular in the 1974 Ottawa Declaration, as having an implicit coupling role.[49] A major question attached to strengthening such a role of the British and French deterrents is how they could do this if their own territories had not been extensively damaged by nuclear weapons, even though those of their allies, including Germany, had been. Logically, it would be West German nuclear force that could play a coupling role most easily, although the political barriers to such a development are clearly insurmountable at this time.

Currently, the conventional wisdom of the alliance is that Europe cannot stand alone and that it needs the U.S. nuclear guarantee. Yet the possibility of a complete U.S. withdrawal from the defense of Europe is surely conceivable in the kind of time scale that effective BMD defenses involve. This draws attention to the possibility of independent European defense building on British and French nuclear forces, a possibility not ruled out by the USSR.[50] Again, however, a central problem is to find a credible means of providing a nuclear guarantee for West Germany. This problem cannot be solved, it would appear, without giving West Germany itself control over nuclear weapons. If the presence of increased superpower ballistic missile defenses does lead to U.S. decoupling from Europe, will West Germany have to look to other means for security, with the broad choice being to seek accommodation with the East or to cooperate even more closely with the U.K. and France?

Conclusion

The questions discussed herein represent only a selection among those which can be asked about SDI and the European deterrents. Nothing was said, for instance, about arms control and disarmament, although it is conceivable that SDI could lead to greater U.S.-Soviet progress in this area. While in many ways the British and French would prefer this, it is also likely that arms control progress would soon lead to pressures for the U.K. and France to cut the size of their "minimum deterrents" (which have expanded in warhead size in the past twenty years, in part because of improved Soviet defenses). Reducing the size of the European deterrents is not easy to arrange when the number of systems on station is somewhere between half and a quarter of the total number possessed and when the number of warheads is comparatively large but the number of launch platforms small.

Clearly, the central question concerns the future technological viability of the British and French deterrents. Their viability seems assured for the next twenty years or so, regardless of Soviet efforts or the future of the ABM Treaty. The limitations of terminal defense in the face of an attack on one target from perhaps dozens of warheads and decoys are predominant in that time scale. Should the ABM Treaty survive, the technological viability of the Western European deterrents would be that much more assured. In the long term, by stimulating Soviet BMD to some degree, SDI threatens the U.K. and French national deterrents because it makes it less likely either that they will be able to penetrate and/or that the British and French publics will be ready to pay the required price. This leads to the view that the U.K. and France ought to make efforts to acquire knowledge about BMD and how to counter it through participation in SDI work and that they ought to consider whether collaboration between themselves might help to lower the costs of future delivery systems. It also prompts the suggestion that the U.K. and France ought to continue with and even increase their consultations with their allies in Europe on the value of the European deterrents, despite the conventional forces that have to be foregone in order to pay for them. In burden-sharing debates with the United States, the U.K. and France will not want to see other European allies arguing that too much money is being spent on national nuclear forces in Europe in comparison with the deterrent benefit that is gained. In general, the less solid appears the U.S. commitment to Europe, the higher the sums that most Western Europeans would be ready to see devoted to the British and French deterrents.

Yet much of this could provoke a rejoinder that in international politics the long term is of little real relevance. Politicians and bureaucrats, for their own reasons, tend to be much more concerned with short-term problems, and, in the time scale of twenty-five to thirty years, many other factors could prove more influential than SDI. At least three other salient possibilities could have an enormous influence on the significance of an increased superpower BMD effort. One is that Western Europe will increasingly have to fend for its own defense without the United States. Another is that there will be sufficient advance in arms control and East-West relations for the U.K. and France to feel much less threatened by the USSR. A third is that there will be unambiguous and significant progress in antisubmarine warfare. SDI must always be seen in the context of the many other factors and problems that shape British and French policy.

Nevertheless, SDI is obviously of major importance. As a concluding point, it is suggested that not only can the U.K. and France be treated together, but the implications that really count regarding SDI are those which affect Western Europe as a whole: How will SDI affect U.S. efforts in terms of conventional forces? What effect will it have on East-West relations overall? What will limited BMD capabilities, especially if they use boost-phase interception and therefore provide area defense, do for strategic and crisis stability? What will SDI do for comparative rates of technological advance in the United States and Western Europe? What would a costly U.S. BMD system do for the United States' readiness and financial capacity to defend Europe? In all these and other questions the U.K. and France have a major interest, but it is one they share with their nonnuclear allies in the rest of Western Europe.

Notes

1. United States Information Service (London), 24 March 1983.
2. *Guardian* (London), 12 March 1986.
3. Social Democratic Party, "Defence and Disarmament: Peace and Security," *Policy Document* No. 9, London.
4. R.P. Smith, J. Fontanel, and A. Humm, "Managing the Cost of Defence: A Comparison of the British and French Experience," *Public Money,* March 1986. See also House of Commons, *Third Report* from the Defence Committee, *Defence Commitments and Resources and the Defence Estimates 1985–6,* Vol. II, Session 1984-5, (London: HMSO, 23 May 1985), Doc. 37-II, p. 159. See also M. Chalmers, *Paying for Defence* (London, Pluto Press), 1985, p. 162; House of Commons, *Sixth Report* from the Defence Committee, *The Trident Programme*, Session 19845, (London, HMSO), 10 July 1985, Doc. 479, Annex A, p. xxvi.

5. *Third Report* from the Defence Committee, p. 163.

6. F. Tiberghien, "L'Effort de Dé*fense Depuis 1981,"* *Défense Nationale,* Nov. 1985, p. 48; *Financial Times,* 16 December 1985.

7. Ministère de la Défense, *La Programmation Militaire 1984–8,* Dossier d'Information, No. 72, Paris, October 1983, p. 6.

8. *Le Monde,* 6 May 1986, and David Yost, "France's Deterrent Posture and Security in Europe, Part 1: Capabilities and Doctrine," *Adelphi Paper* No. 194 (London: International Institute for Strategic Studies), Winter 1984/5, p. 19.

9. Interview in *Jane's Defence Weekly,* 8 March 1986, p. 411. President Mitterrand put it more dramatically in 1982: "For a quarter of a century now France's defence has rested on this type of weapon. . . . If it disappeared, nothing would remain of my country's means of defence." Quoted in Yost, "France's Deterrent Posture," p. 3.

10. "Meeting Alliance and National Needs," in J. Roper, ed., *The Future of British Defence Policy* (London: Gower, 1985), p. 20. Interestingly, in this forward-looking discussion by a range of U.K. analysts, there was no concern shown about the USSR possibly offsetting the U.K. deterrent through BMD.

11. Speech to the Foreign Press Association, 17 March 1986, text from Foreign and Commonwealth Office. See also Paul Quilès interview, *Jane's Defence Weekly,* 8 March 1986, p. 411.

12. *Times* (London), 28 March 1986.

13. N.C. Brown, *The Strategic Defense Initiative and European Security: A Conference Report* (Santa Monica, Calif.: Rand Corporation, 1985), p. 19; P. Gallis, M.M. Lowenthal, and M.S. Smith, *The Strategic Defense Initiative and United States Alliance Strategy* (Washington: Library of Congress, Congressional Research Service), 1 February 1985, p. 31; "France's Deterrent Posture, Yost, p. 24; North Atlantic Assembly, *Interim Report* of the Special Committee on Nuclear Strategy and Arms Control, John Cartwright (Rapporteur), October 1985, p. 16; North Atlantic Assembly Military Committee, *General Report on the Future of Arms Control: Compliance and Verification Issues,* Sir Geoffrey Johnson Smith (Rapporteur), October 1985, p. 25.

14. U.S. Departments of Defense and State, *Soviet Strategic Defense Programs* (Washington, D.C.: GPO, Oct. 1985), p. 4; U.S. Department of Defense, *Soviet Military Power,* (Washington, D.C.: GPO, 5th ed., 1986).

15. For Paul Quilès's comment, see his *Le Monde* interview, 18 December 1985; for Lawrence Freedman's view, see his "The 'Star Wars' Debate: The Western Alliance and Strategic Defence: Part II," in *New Technology and Western Security Policy: Part III, Adelphi Paper* No. 199 (London: IISS, 1985), p. 45. Former U.S. Secretary of Defense Harold Brown broadly agrees. He wrote, "Both the United States and the Soviet Union will be able to undertake successful counter-measures against any system intended to defend urban-industrial centres and populations—however many the layers of defence." "The Strategic Defense Initiative: Defensive Systems and the Strategic Debate," *Survival,* March/April 1985, Vol. 27, No. 2, p. 58. However, Yost, in "France's Deterrent Posture," p. 26, doubts France's national capability to maintain an offensive advantage, at least with regard to high-value targets.

16. *Le Monde,* 18 December 1985.

17. Robert Gessert, "NATO and 'First Use,'" in R. English, ed., *Ethics and Nuclear Arms* (Washington: Ethics and Public Policy Center, 1985), p. 100. For a discussion of the counterforce targeting issue for France, see Yost, "France's Deterrent Posture," p. 41ff.

18. *Statement on the Defence Estimates 1981* (London: HMSO, Cmnd. 8212-1, April 1981), p. 12; Howe speech to the Foreign Press Association.

19. L. Freedman, *Britain and Nuclear Weapons* (London: Macmillan, 1980), pp. 47-61.

20. Yost, "France's Deterrent Posture, p. 15.

21. David Hobbs, "Alternatives to Trident," *ASIDES* (Aberdeen Studies in Defence Economics), No. 25, Summer 1983, pp. 5-12.

22. Yost, "France's Deterrent Posture," p. 28.

23. See Freedman, *Britain and Nuclear Weapons,* for U.K. consideration of the prospective destruction of nine Soviet cities as an adequate U.K. deterrent capability.

24. *Statement on the Defence Estimates 1985* (London: HMSO, Cmnd. 9430-1), Vol. 1, p. 7.

25. For a discussion of U.K. counters to Soviet BMD, see John Roper, "The British Nuclear Deterrent and New Developments in Ballistic Missile Defence," *The World Today,* May 1985, pp. 93-94.

26. Brown, *The Strategic Defense Initiative.*

27. Weekly *Hansard* Issue 1359, Oral Answers Col. 170, 2 July 1985.

28. House of Commons, *Third Report* from the Defence Committee, Vol. 1, pp. x-xi.

29. Commission d'Etudes sur les Armes Spatiales, *Rapport de Synthèse presenté au Ministre de la Défense,* 30 January 1986, translated by the U.S. Congressional Research Service, pp. 11-12. See also the *Times* (London), 14 November 1985; *Financial Times,* 13 November 1985; Paul Quilès's interview in *Le Monde,* 18 December 1985; and the *Financial Times,* 15 October 1985. Even Colin Gray, an advocate of SDI, accepts that British and French warheads would be able to "leak through" Soviet defenses by "the end of the century, and probably beyond." See Colin Gray, "A Case for Strategic Defence," *Survival,* Vol. 27, No. 2, p. 54.

30. In a British Social Attitudes poll, 73 percent of those questioned felt that the U.K. should keep its nuclear weapons until others had been persuaded to reduce theirs, and 56 percent felt that British nuclear weapons made the world a safer place. See Michael Jones in the *Sunday Times,* 12 January 1986. For a wider study of poll data, again broadly supportive of the U.K. deterrent, see Henry Stanhope in the *Times* (London), 13 December 1985. Pro-Trident sentiment as such is less strong, and a Gallup poll commissioned by the Campaign for Nuclear Disarmament found a majority against Trident. See the *Times* (London), 10 October 1985.

31. "WEU and the Strategic Defense Initiative—the European Pillar of the Atlantic Alliance," Assembly of the WEU Doc. 1034, 5 November 1985, p. 10.

32. *Le Monde,* 18 December 1985.

33. D.J. Smith, "Why 'Yes' to SDI," *A Bow Paper,* London.

34. See E.P. Thompson, ed., *Star Wars* (London: Penguin Special, 1985).

35. *Jane's Defence Weekly,* 15 March 1986, pp. 472-73. See Wayland Kennet in the *Times* (London), 26 February 1986, for an assertion that U.S. ASW capabilities are already strategically significant.

36. *Financial Times,* 8 January 1986 and 4 February 1986; *Guardian,* 25 January 1986.

37. See T. Enders, *Missile Defense as Part of an Extended NATO Air Defense* (Bonn: Sozialwissenschaftliches Forschungsinstitut Konrad-Adenauer-Stiftung), 1986.

38. J. Fenske, "France and the Strategic Defence Initiative: speeding up or putting on the brakes," *International Affairs,* Vol. 62, No. 2, Spring 1986, p. 242.

39. *Le Monde,* 19 June 1986; F. Heisbourg, "De la SDI à la Défense aérienne élargie: Quelles réponses de l'Europe," *L'Armement,* No. 2, March 1986.

40. Charles Hernu, "L'avenir de la Dissuasion," *Le Monde,* 9 April 1986.

41. See Yost, "France's Deterrent Posture," pp. 26, 35, and 39.

42. Discussed in ibid., p. 35; Hobbs, *op.cit.,* pp. 9-10; B. George and J. Marcus, "French Security Policy," *Washington Quarterly,* Fall 1984, Vol. 7, No. 4, p. 155.

43. Yost, "France's Deterrent Posture," p. 20.

44. Freedman, "The 'Star Wars' Debate," p. 43.

45. David Owen, "Anglo-French Nuclear Cooperation," *The World Today,* August/September 1985, pp. 158-61.

46. This is one of the ideas of Pierre Lellouche, whose views are summarized and critically analyzed in David Yost's "Radical Change in French Defence Policy: a Review Essay," in *Survival,* Jan./Feb. 1986, Vol. 28, No. 1, pp. 53-68. The essay covers Lellouche's book, *L'avenir de la guerre* (Paris: Mazarine, 1985).

47. See previous note and John Roper, "The British Nuclear Deterrent," p. 94.

48. *Times* (London), 17 July 1986; *Le Monde,* 7 May 1986 and 2-3 March 1986.

49. Prime Minister Margaret Thatcher recognized the coupling role of British nuclear weapons, which she called "last resort things," in an interview in the *Times* (London), 28 March 1986.

50. R.F. Laird, "Soviet Perspectives on French Security Policy," *Survival,* March/April 1985, Vol. 27, No. 2, p. 71.

7

SDI and European Security: A View from France

Pierre Lellouche

Looking back at the development of the past several years, since President Reagan's famous Star Wars speech of March 23, 1983, one is struck by the profound change that seems to have taken place in the debate on SDI within the Western Alliance.

Both the tone and the focus of the arguments appear to have altered. Issues that were prominent early on in the public debate—that is, the *strategic* implications of SDI for "coupling" and for NATO's "flexible response" doctrine, and the need to protect the ABM Treaty—have apparently disappeared from the public agenda. At the same time, a healthy narrowing down of the issues has also taken place: the initial and highly surrealistic discussion about a "postnuclear world" has now been succeeded by a much more sober understanding about what SDI is supposed to achieve. No longer is anyone seriously debating the merits of leak-proof astrodomes that the United States would generously offer both to its NATO allies and to the USSR. And even Ronald Reagan himself has toned down somewhat his early antinuclear rhetoric. The emerging consensus within the West is that nuclear weapons are here to stay at least through the first decades of the next century, even though strategic defenses may be introduced into the picture, modifying somewhat but not replacing nuclear deterrence.

Given this background, the current debate is mainly about technology, and no longer about strategy. The focus of alliance discussions has shifted to the difficult question of European access to the U.S. research program, as well as to the potential applications of SDI-related projects for future air defense requirements in Europe. Under pressure from industry both in Europe and in the United States and from some pro-SDI political-military circles in the United States (whose constituents correctly see this as a useful tactic to diffuse Europe's lingering opposition to SDI), a new debate has emerged in Europe around such concepts as antitactical ballistic missiles (ATBMs), extended air defense and the so-called European Defense Initiative (EDI).

Meanwhile, the tone of the whole SDI debate—which tended to be quite acrimonious earlier on (recall, for instance, Sir Geoffrey Howe's reference to a

"Maginot Line in space" and Secretary of Defense Caspar Weinberger's dicta-
torial sixty-day deadline for European participation in SDI)—has now been
replaced by a much quieter atmosphere. At present, industries on both sides
of the Atlantic conduct their business discreetly, while governments keep a
polite silence on the wider political and strategic issues on which they in fact
continue to disagree. In short, today's situation could be compared to a
temporary truce: the "big" strategic issues are in effect frozen—at least until
the technological horizon clears up, allowing deployment decisions to be
made or not made (presumably by the end of the decade); while in the
interim, an attempt is made on the part of the various governments and firms
involved to work out satisfactory cooperative relationships on the technology
front.

SDI and "Alliance Management"

There are obviously good reasons, from the perspective of "alliance management," to explain and even support such an evolution. Given domestic political realities on both sides of the Atlantic, NATO can scarcely afford, on the
heels of a very divisive intermediate-range nuclear forces (INF) controversy,
another *grand débat* in which all of the highly sensitive—and unresolvable—
issues related to risk sharing and to the differences of vulnerabilities between
the two sides of the Atlantic would be once again reopened. This is all the
more so in the case of SDI, since a fundamental question remains as to what
kind of defense will be possible, at what cost, and in what time frame. Until
these questions are answered, continued transatlantic quarrel on SDI would
serve no one, except the USSR.

Second, with the resumption in early 1985 of arms-control talks between
the United States and the USSR, coupled (as was to be expected) with a quite
unprecedented Soviet propaganda offensive aimed primarily at the Europeans,[1] the Western allies simply do not have the option of fighting each other
publicly; they cannot afford to weaken the U.S. negotiating stand in Geneva,
incur the risk of a major anti-European backlash in the United States, and, in
the end, serve Soviet ambitions in Europe.

Finally, even if all the European governments had chosen to go the route
of open opposition to SDI, European industry would have had another point of
view: any industry manager knows that waiting until the "big" strategic arguments are resolved before getting on to new research investments is simply
out of the question. Once the United States has decided to mobilize its resources around a whole array of new technologies—whether or not this is
done under an SDI flag—the alternative for European high-technology firms is
either to join in or be sure to perish at some later stage.

The Evolution of the French Attitude

Perhaps the clearest illustration of these realities can be found in the evolution of the French attitude toward SDI.

Although President Mitterrand initially appeared to be quite fascinated by the prospects of Star Wars (so much so that in a speech given at The Hague on February 7, 1984, he called for Europe "to look beyond the nuclear era" and jointly develop a military capability in space), France's official reaction, expressed in Geneva at the United Nations Committee on Disarmament (UNCD) on June 12, 1984, was clearly negative. France proposed "a ban, for a renewable five-year period, on the deployment—on the ground, in the atmosphere or in space—of guided-energy weapons systems, capable of destroying ballistic missiles or satellites at very long range and, as a corollary, a ban on the corresponding tests."[2] The French proposal also included a very strict limitation on antisatellite (ASAT) weapons and contained a line of arguments on the antiballistic missile (ABM) question which was embarrassingly close to the Soviet line, especially since the French proposal was made public two weeks before Mitterand's visit to Moscow.

Yet, having said no to SDI, the French government soon realized that it had backed itself into a corner: clearly, the United States was not going to drop its program just because its allies didn't like it. Even if it were to do so, France would still be left with potential Soviet defenses; the magnitude of existing Soviet defenses was suddenly highlighted by the SDI debate. Keeping a high profile of attack against the U.S. program was hardly tenable politically, given the resumption of U.S.-Soviet arms-control talks in early 1985 and the fact that France needed more than ever the total support of its American ally in order to reject repeated Soviet demands to constrain the *Force Nucléaire Stratégique* (FNS) as part of an intermediate-range nuclear forces (INF) deal. One can hardly be siding with the Soviets on the SDI issue and hope at the same time that the United States would continue to stick with France on the INF front. With ABM, ASAT, and space research likely to continue—and be accelerated in the future—France had no other option but to increase its own technological effort. The no in Geneva in 1984 and the further official no the following year in response to the idea of government-to-government cooperation with the United States left the whole technological side of the issue totally unresolved.

Given these realities, France gradually moved to a more pragmatic attitude based on a clear-cut distinction between the strategic and technological sides of the SDI issue.

On the strategic side, France maintained its opposition in principle, seeing SDI as (a) basically "destabilizing" for European security as a whole and for the arms competition between the superpowers;[3] (b) dangerously demobilizing in its implications for Western public opinion: the French saw Reagan's antinuclear rhetoric as an ex post facto justification of the European peace movement and as something that could further undermine what was left of Western consensus on deterrence after the Euromissile battle.[4] Implicit in this critique was a very real fear that Reagan's rhetoric could also threaten French domestic consensus on the national deterrent—something quite unacceptable to any French government;[5] (c) but of limited impact militarily, to the extent that SDI in no way implied the extinction of nuclear weapons. Given the uncertainty and the enormous difficulty of the technology (particularly for boost-phase interception), along with the large number of countermeasures that can be devised to defeat any comprehensive defense, SDI in all likelihood cannot be expected to replace nuclear deterrence. What is far more likely in the foreseeable future (that is, in the next three decades) is that SDI will lead to a far more complex combination of both offensive and defensive weapons but not to the outright replacement of nuclear deterrence. This would mean that the FNS itself would not be threatened at least until the year 2015 to 2020.[6]

A major implication followed from this: France's priority should be—in addition to maintaining domestic French, and beyond that, European, consensus on deterrence by countering Reagan's rhetoric—to mobilize its technological resources to make sure that its FNS would retain its credibility in the face of a rapidly changing technological environment.[7]

This is precisely where the strategic aspect of SDI encounters the other side of the coin, namely, technology. After having tried in early 1985 a European and "peaceful" route to cooperation in high technology (Eureka), France realized that it too had no alternative but to go for direct cooperation with the United States. Pressure from industry, combined with a lack of commitment by both the U.K. and the Federal Republic of Germany (F.R.G.) to invest in Eureka, led once again to a pragmatic adjustment: in the fall of 1985, Prime Minister Laurent Fabius and the new defense minister, Paul Quilès, announced that France's opposition to SDI and the absence of government-to-government cooperation with the United States on technology in no way precluded French firms from entering directly into cooperative deals with their U.S. counterparts or even with the Pentagon itself.[8] From that moment on, France found itself in the somewhat bizarre position (its critics would call it hypocritical) of opposing SDI in principle while letting its firms—including the nationalized ones—run to Washington to secure contracts.

Interestingly enough, the establishment of the Chirac government following the March 16, 1986, legislative elections has brought no basic change in this pattern. Contrary to expectations, especially from outside of France, that a right-wing government would adopt a more "positive" attitude toward SDI, the Chirac government has remained extremely careful on the whole subject of SDI, insisting instead on France's continued commitment to nuclear deterrence[9] (a commitment made even stronger by Chirac's apparent commitment to build the S-X mobile ballistic missile).[10] The only difference here is one of style, not substance. Chirac and his defense minister, André Giraud, have refrained from openly criticizing SDI the way the previous government had done.[11] The more careful tone adopted by the United States over the past few months on the whole issue of the future of nuclear deterrence may have been the determining factor in the general improvement of the dialogue. As to technology cooperation, the new French government, despite statements made before the election by some right-wing leaders,[12] shows no sign of following the British or German route of government-to-government agreements with the United States. Instead, what we do have is a continuation of the same policy: French firms, if they so choose, may enter into deals with the Strategic Defense Initiative Organization (SDIO) or with U.S. firms without being hindered by the politics of SDI. Ironically, French industry executives, far from feeling penalized by the absence of inter-governmental agreements, find this situation much more satisfactory than that of their British and German colleagues.

The Attitude of Other Alliance Partners

Leaving aside the question of national style, the evolution of French attitudes with respect to SDI is in fact remarkably similar, in substance, to that of the other major European players. As usual in such sensitive alliance matters, what the French have done—notably in the June 1984 document presented to the UNCD—was to articulate openly what the other Europeans think but dare not say to the Americans quite so bluntly.

Yet, even if the F.R.G., the U.K., and Italy have been on the whole rather more forthcoming than France toward SDI (despite a string of highly critical public statements by senior British and German officials earlier on), it is evident that major disagreements remain with the United States on a whole series of issues, ranging from the security implications of SDI for NATO strategy to technology and economics.

On the strategic front, for instance, both the U.K. and the F.R.G. officially support SDI as a legitimate, prudent hedge against Soviet ABM programs. And yet, neither the British nor the German government is ready to live with the logical consequences of their "support," namely, to support the U.S. refusal to deal on SDI at the Geneva table and (even less) to support the U.S. desire to test such weapons and perhaps even to modify the ABM Treaty if and when necessary. On the contrary, London and Bonn—like Paris—are on record as favoring a deal on SDI in exchange for deep cuts in offensive weapons, and all three strenuously oppose any modification of the ABM regime. The same basic ambiguity exists on the technological front: the British first (in late 1985), followed by the Germans (in early 1986), concluded government-to-government agreements with the United States designed presumably to define the rules of the game for technology cooperation on SDI projects. And yet, while it is clear that the United States obtained what it wanted with these agreements (namely, to demonstrate to the world—and to the U.S. Congress in particular—that Europe was fully on the American side on SDI), the same can hardly be said to be true for either Bonn or London. According to various sources—and according to the text of the U.S.-German agreement that was recently leaked to the German press—none of the conditions for technology sharing put forth by the Europeans were accepted by the United States. The agreements reportedly contain only vague principles but no clear obligation on the part of the United States to guarantee its allies a wide access to the results of SDI. Indeed, it is the contrary outcome that would have been surprising: the long track record of U.S.-European cooperation on high technology (be it on civil nuclear energy, space, or armaments) suggests that U.S. firms, when they get into cooperative deals, rarely practice philanthropy and instead drive very hard bargains indeed. Margaret Thatcher's hope to secure for the U.K. a whole slice of the SDI cake (up to an amount of $1.5 billion), and West German Chancellor Helmut Kohl's expectation that German industry would have access, across the board, to the whole array of SDI-related results, were equally naive. To the extent that there will be allied cooperation on SDI, it will be based instead—as was the case in the past—on a series of cooperative arrangements in the areas where European technology and know-how is actually needed by the United States, either because it is superior or cheaper. Moreover, only in those areas can one expect a two-way street on technology sharing, and even then under strict legal constraints imposed by U.S. firms (licensing) and the U.S. government (secrecy, no transfer rules). Given these realities, it is not surprising that French firms do not feel particularly penalized, as compared to their European competitors, by the absence of a government-to-government agreement between Paris and Washington.[13]

A Modus Vivendi—for the Time Being

For the time being, at least, the complex modus vivendi that has come to exist between the Western allies on the SDI issue has been on the whole rather positive, particularly for the United States. Not only has the Reagan administration managed to neutralize what was initially a strong European public opposition to its plan, but it has even succeeded in turning this opposition into a supportive attitude—at least in declaratory terms, a useful asset indeed before both the Congress and the Soviets (at the arms-control table).

In return, the Europeans have obtained two important points:

1. A modification of the Reagan rhetoric in a direction less damaging to public consensus on defense (ironically, however, it is SDI and Reagan's earlier promise to do away with nuclear weapons which seem to have helped in making many Europeans—including those who fought against the Pershings—rediscover the merits of nuclear deterrence).

2. The inclusion in U.S. policy of certain key limitations vis-à-vis the future of SDI, namely, the notions that the ABM Treaty should continue to be respected and that any deployment decision would require prior negotiations with the Soviets. One can argue, of course, that both of these conditions were in any case inevitable: abiding with the ABM Treaty would probably have been necessary anyway in order to secure continued congressional funding of SDI; as to prior negotiations with the Soviets, these are inevitable if one is to prevent massive Soviet countermeasures with respect to a nascent SDI deployment program (this has been recognized by the Reagan administration itself, as reflected in Paul Nitze's criteria for the so-called "transition phase"). On the whole however, one cannot discount the role played by the Europeans in turning these two key conditions into official U.S. policy.

On the negative side of the SDI issue the Europeans have given further proof of their chronic inability to "get their act together" on a subject of immediate importance to their own safety and economic integrity. The failure to come up with even a minimum common political platform among the key European capitals (even though they all shared the same fears and views of SDI) and the even poorer show of European unity on the technological front (with the de facto failure of Eureka) are indeed quite depressing. Politically and technologically fragmented, such a Europe is condemned to further dependence on the United States rather than less, and to more complaints, rather than the kind of positive actions that would be required to influence U.S. and NATO policy in a direction consistent with European interests.

All this means that the modus vivendi we now have between the Western allies should be seen as fragile and only temporary. For the purposes of this chapter, the essential point is that the larger issues related to strategy—that is, the future role of nuclear weapons in European security and the continued validity of flexible response in an offense/defense world, involve fundamentally different security interests on the part of the allies and that these show no sign of being resolved at any time soon.

Three years after President Reagan's March 23, 1983, speech, one has yet to hear a single convincing argument as to why an SDI world would be better for European security and NATO.[14] The notion sometimes advanced by U.S. SDI advocates that an invulnerable United States (as in the 1950s) would better be able to guarantee the safety of a vulnerable Europe simply does not fly. Since any ABM deployment on the U.S. side would inevitably be matched by the Soviets, the result will not be a "fully inaccessible U.S. facing an unprotected USSR, but two protected superpowers."[15] That in itself may not be a bad thing, at least as far as U.S. and Soviet security are concerned. Indeed, it may very well be that reducing the vulnerability of U.S. retaliatory forces to Soviet potential first strikes may contribute to enhancing deterrence between the superpowers and thus reduce the risk of direct "out of the blue" attacks from one super-power against the other. But the price for reducing such a minimal risk would most probably be a new spiral in the strategic arms race, both in terms of offensive and defensive weapons (a point that was strongly made by the French government in its June 1984 proposal to the Geneva Committee on Disarmament). Moreover, even if one assumes that the strategic defenses may reinforce stability between the two superpowers themselves, the same logic does not hold true for Europe.

For in Europe, the primary condition for U.S. extended deterrence—given parity at the strageic level—is that the U.S. president be given a wide array of selective employment options, allowing for both escalation control and early war termination. Short of that, extended deterrence would be tantamount to suicide, something which is neither acceptable to Americans (be they liberals like McNamara or conservatives like Kissinger) nor credible to the Soviets. In this connection, one should always bear in mind that under current NATO doctrine and force posture, it is the U.S. president who is supposed to take the historic responsibility of initiating the use of nuclear weapons. Thus, if one assumes (as most Europeans do) that we would have ABM on both sides and not just in the United States then the logic of strategic defenses would be to reduce drastically the chances for selective first use of nuclear weapons—at least for those weapons targeted against the territory of the USSR. In order to penetrate Soviet defenses, any attack against military assets would have to be drastically increased, thus making the likelihood of such first use even less probable than it is today. The one exception would be the use of short-range battlefield weapons targeted at Soviet assets in Eastern Europe, but the result of that would be to limit the war to Europe only, leading in fact to the very decoupling that the deployment of the Pershings and Cruises was precisely aimed at remedying.[16] Ironically, then, the logic of SDI advocates who argue that the United States should move away from mutual assured destruction (MAD) and "killing innocents" and go instead for increased selectivity, actu-ally turns against its authors: the end result of ABM deployments on both sides would in fact be to kill selectivity and turn back the clock to the era of massive counter-city strikes.[17] In such a world, the risk of substrategic wars, both conventional and short-range nuclear, would be increased and would be channeled directly to the various peripheral regions—and of course to Europe, while the U.S. strategic arsenal would lose even the residual relevance it has today for non-U.S. contingencies.

In short, then, as far as European security as a whole is concerned, the reintroduction of strategic defenses in the nuclear equation between the superpowers is clearly not a positive prospect. It threatens to undermine what is left of the credibility of U.S. first use of nuclear weapons, and it will also necessarily translate into much fewer resources being devoted to NATO, as more and more funds will be directed to SDI deployments.[18] Another consequence will be to force both European nuclear powers (the U.K. and France) to devote more funds and efforts toward maintaining the credibility of their own national deterrents, leading in the case of France in particular to further cuts in the conventional forces that are needed in central Europe.

Wrong Assumption in Europe

Like it or not, these wider security considerations, which for the moment have been quietly swept under the carpet, are bound to affect the future evolution of intra-alliance relations as SDI ceases to be "pure" research (which it is not in fact) and increasingly moves on to the development and deployment stages. Implicit in the current stage of the transatlantic SDI relationship are, it seems to me, a couple of wrong assumptions implicitly made on both sides of the Atlantic.

The first assumption flows from a sensible proposition but arrives at a wrong implication. The sensible proposition analyzed earlier in this chapter is that since we don't know what kind of defenses SDI will eventually lead to, there is no point in having today a sterile and divisive strategic debate within the alliance. The wrong implication is that sometime in the next five years or so there will be a clear-cut point at which technological findings will be such as to permit a fully informed deployment decision and an analysis by the alliance of its implications for NATO strategy. Implicit in this reasoning is a European secret hope that either SDI will fail to bring cost-effective defenses, in which case there will be no change required to NATO's current flexible response posture, or that even if some defenses are possible, the alliance will in due time find the means to adjust to them.

The point, however, is that in reality there won't be one clear-cut decision point or one clear-cut deployment decision but a far more complex flux of mini-decisions, spread over time. This is so because we are dealing not with one single technological development but with a whole range of different fields of technology, each with a different time scale (whether one looks at electronics, ground-based conventional BMD, or space-based directed-energy segments). Moreover, in every case, there won't be a clear-cut jump between "pure" research and deployment, but more likely a whole series of "in between" phases, notably testing. And since testing will inevitably at one point or another call into question the continued existence of the ABM Treaty, at least under its present form, then it is quite likely that the alliance will have to face up to the larger security and arms-control implications of SDI *before* deployment decisions will actually be made. For the moment, Europeans in general—including European governments—have remained aloof from the U.S. debate about whether the United States should adopt a "restrictive" or a "broad" interpretation of the ABM Treaty. Yet this issue is bound to spill over into alliance politics sooner than governments tend to think.

A second assumption—which, interestingly enough, is precisely aimed at overcoming the difficulties stemming from the first assumption—is that the best way to secure a continued alliance consensus on SDI is to launch an equivalent defensive program for NATO, specifically tailored to the Europeans' needs. Whether it is called ATBMs, EDI (European Defense Initiative), or Extended Air Defense, such a program would have a whole series of advantages:

It would create a political commitment in Europe for defenses, thereby reinforcing U.S. policy.

It would create a strong constituency in European (and U.S.) industry, thereby reinforcing the whole SDI program.

It would help prepare NATO for future military requirements (notably against the threat of conventionally armed short- and medium-range missiles).

It would allow unlimited testing of ABM-relevant technologies, to the extent that the ABM Treaty applies only to the interception of intercontinental missiles.

Over the last year or so, the idea of a mini-European SDI has gathered strength both in the United States and in Europe (including in Germany and France itself),[19] fueled by active lobbying efforts from industry. And it has just recently been proclaimed as a substantial element of the overall SDI effort by Secretary Weinberger.[20] The amazing thing about this whole trend, however, is that it has not been accompanied by even a minimum of strategic thinking about what ATBMs would do for European security. The assumption is that since the United States does SDI and the Soviets also have an active ABM program, then Europe should do it, too. But for what purposes and at what costs? How does one prevent the Soviets, for instance, from saturating a theater BMD in Europe? And assuming that a mobile BMD can be devised to overcome that particular difficulty, how mobile would it be, given the size of European territory, and who would buy it, given the stained state of all European defense budgets? Finally, if both NATO and the Warsaw pact go for such theater BMD, what would happen to NATO's latest Follow-On forces Attack (FOFA) doctrine and the stress being put on deep interdiction through ballistic conventional missiles?

Thus, while there is certainly an argument that favors Europe keeping a close technological watch on defense-related technological developments, the strategic and economic rationale of a full-fledged ATBM program (as compared, in particular, to buying more effective offensive weapons to penetrate future Soviet defenses) is far from being convincing at this stage. This implies, in turn, that using ATBMs as a means to sustain alliance cohesion to SDI may not be, over the long run, as promising a strategy as some like to think.

SDI and Arms Control

Adding to these unresolved political and security difficulties within the alliance is, of course, the complicated arms-control game played in Geneva since January 1985.

If, as the Reagan administration claims, it is true that SDI forced the Soviets to return to Geneva, Geneva is also the place where the Soviets will do their utmost to slow down SDI and to exploit diverging security interests among the Western allies. What is equally true—and worrisome for European and alliance security interests—is that the Reagan SDI rhetoric about doing away with nuclear weapons has provided the Soviets with a golden propaganda tool. Since Gorbachev's proposal of January 15, 1986, what we have had is a rather amazing escalation of propaganda diplomacy, focusing precisely on the theme of denuclearization, the worst possible idea in terms of European stability.

As to the substance, I can see no chance whatsoever for an agreement, simply because the history of arms-control talks suggests that agreements generally require two basic conditions, neither of which is met in this case: first, a situation of parity between the two sides, and second, an agreement on the basic rules of the deterrence game.

Clearly, the possible reintroduction of defenses into the strategic equation through technologies that remain to be defined and tested imposes a huge question mark on the kind of deterrence equation that will apply between the superpowers by the turn of the century. In the absence of an agreement on the rules of the game—which can only come either from a political decision on both sides or, more likely, from an assessment of the feasibility and cost-effectiveness of new defensive technologies—I can hardly see what Washington and Moscow can agree on, since they themselves do not know what their strategic relationship will look like in the coming decade.

This means that far from making possible any serious reduction in offensive arms (since neither side will have the absolute certainty that the other will not come to a series of technological breakthroughs in the next five, ten, or fifteen years which could be rapidly translated into an effective ABM shield of some kind), this situation of complete uncertainty on the defensive side will most likely incur a further accerleration of the offensive buildup, first by the USSR and later by the United States. Hence the total impasse in Geneva, with each side wanting exactly the opposite of what the other seeks: the Soviets want a deal now preventing any defensive arms, in exchange for what they promise will later be deep cuts in offensive arms; the United States wants the opposite: deep cuts now on the offensive side, and no constraints on defense.

In the aftermath of the 1985 Reagan-Gorbachev summit, an attempt was made (particularly in the exchange of letters between Gorbachev and Reagan in June and July 1986) to bridge this fundamental gap by linking a reduction of offensive arms to a time clause to be applied to defensive-arms deployments. According to what is known of the so-called "grand compromise" formula, Gorbachev initially proposed in June 1986 to trade a 30 percent cut in strategic offensive arms—with the U.S. forward-based systems (FBS) not included in the count—in exchange for a fifteen-to-twenty-year commitment by the United States to remain within the constraints of the ABM Treaty. While "research" on defensive arms would have been authorized (as it is in the ABM Treaty), the proposal would have, in effect, frozen any SDI testing, development, and, of course, deployments, for the duration of the agreement. In reply, Reagan proposed to agree to a postponement of *deployments* by seven and a half years (half of Gorbachev's proposal) but insisted on America's freedom to continue, in the interim, both research and developments (including testing).

Not surprisingly, the grand compromise ended in a deadlock, since it failed to resolve the basic questions raised earlier, namely, parity and the relationship between offense and defense. For the Europeans, the persistence of such an impasse on strategic offensive and defensive arms has raised and will continue to raise a number of extremely sensitive issues. The main difficulty here is not just, as we have seen earlier, that most European governments would rather see the superpowers reduce offensive arms and consolidate the ABM Treaty (which is widely considered in Europe to be good both for European public opinion and for the stability of the security equation), but also that in the absence of a deal on central strategic arms, both superpowers may be tempted to trade a little too lightly on European security interests.

The catch here, of course, is the link, imbedded in the Geneva talks themselves, between strategic nuclear and space arms, on the one hand, and medium-range nuclear weapons based in Europe (and Asia) on the other. From the very beginning of the so-called Nuclear and Space Talks (NST) in January 1985, the Soviets have been extremely persistent in trying to use this link to play U.S. strategic interests against the strategic interests of their allies, and vice versa. During the first year of the talks (from the January 1985 Shultz-Gromyko meeting in Geneva to October of that same year), the Soviets, in an effort to rally the Western Europeans against SDI, insisted that there would not be any deal on the Euromissiles as long as SDI was not settled. When this failed to scare the Europeans—particularly after the U.K. and Germany not only softened their public criticism of the U.S. initiative but even began preparing government-to-government agreements with the United States on technology transfers—the Soviets abruptly changed their tactics. Knowing from the time of the first Reagan-Gorbachev summit in November 1985 that the U.S. president was personally committed to his program and that as long as Reagan was president, at least, there would be very little chance of seeing an SDI settlement in Geneva satisfactory to Soviet interests, the Kremlin began pushing the United States in the direction of a separate deal on Europe. Their calculus was simple and accurate: given that it was still premature to try to win the SDI battle now, at least one could try using Reagan's domestic problems to score some decisive points on the European front. The key Soviet objective here was the withdrawal of U.S. INF forces from Europe as a major step toward the gradual expulsion of the United States from Europe. The shift in Soviet arms-control priorities from SDI to Europe and INF actually began in October 1985, with the Mitterrand-Gorbachev summit in Paris, where it was rumored for the first time that the Soviets might be willing to agree to decouple INF from SDI. There were more rumors on the same subject in November 1985, during the first Reagan-Gorbachev summit, but the official announcement came on February 6, 1986, when Mikhail Gorbachev informed Senator Edward M. Kennedy that the USSR was no longer insisting on an SDI ban as a prior condition for a settlement on the INF situation.

Another key element in the shift had come two weeks earlier, in the spectacular announcement of Gorbachev's January 15 plan "to rid the world of all nuclear weapons by the turn of the century." When stripped of its rhetoric, the only really new part of the plan was that the Soviets were now ready to accept a "zero-zero" formula on INF in Europe, a major shift from their earlier position (until then, the Soviets had insisted on keeping at least as many SS-20s as the aggregate number of French and British warheads). The Soviet shift from SDI to INF was met with a sigh of relief in the United States.

With its attention entirely focused on how not to bargain on SDI at the negotiating table, the Reagan administration had tried from the very beginning (notably during the Shultz-Gromyko meeting of January 1985) to decouple the INF affair from the strategic "table," and, within the latter, to further decouple progress in offensive-arms reduction from discussions on defensive arms. With respect to the INF affair, the great American nightmare was to see the Soviets rally the European allies against SDI after convincing them that the continued deadlock on INF was due only to U.S. "intransigence" in refusing to negotiate on SDI. This fear of seeing SDI made the hostage of INF—and therefore a subject on which the allies would have to be constantly consulted and convinced—explains why President Reagan was so eager to support

Gorbachev's suggestion (circulated in October 1985 in Paris) for direct nuclear talks between Moscow and the two European nuclear powers as a solution to the never-ending French and British inclusion issue; and it also explains why in February 1986 the Reagan administration was keen to accept the Soviet offer of a separate INF deal at zero-zero. By that time, another consideration had come to reinforce this general attitude, namely, the need for the Reagan administration to diffuse mounting domestic pressures against its own strategic programs (on such items as ASAT, the test ban, and, of course, SDI), by producing at least some concrete evidence of progress on the Geneva front in time for Reagan's second summit with Gorbachev in late 1986. Of all three "tables" in Geneva, INF was the obvious candidate, given the U.S. refusal to accept any limitation on SDI (which in turn meant a deadlock on offensive arms as well).

The Soviets, of course, knew of these U.S. preoccupations and obviously calculated their "concessions" for maximum impact: the decoupling between SDI and INF came as a divine surprise in Washington, especially as no U.S. sacrifice of any kind was requested by the Soviet side in order to achieve an INF deal. Not only did the Soviets recognize, at least implicitly, the legitimacy of U.S. INF deployments in Europe, but they even dropped the demand for U.S. "compensation" for French and British systems. The only thing the Soviets now demanded from the United States involved the forces of its allies (a no-transfer commitment and a freeze on French and British systems), but no unequal limits whatsoever on U.S. forces. A very tempting offer indeed, and one should not be surprised if the United States came close to being tempted, at least initially.

To its dismay, however, the Reagan administration found, upon sending emissaries to Europe in the course of preparing the U.S. answer to Gorbachev's plan, that the Europeans, who had wavered so long during the predeployment years, now wanted to keep the Pershings and GLCMs and generally opposed any thought of a zero option. No longer facing domestic opposition against the NATO missiles, and fearing the political and military implications of their possible withdrawal, the European began to suspect that the Reagan administration was perhaps ready to "sell the Euromissiles in exchange for keeping their SDI." An unfair suspicion perhaps, but one that reflected quite accurately the change of attitude that had taken place since the end of 1983. Throughout the INF battle, it was the United States which was accused in Europe of negotiating in bad faith and blocking the chances for any agreement, while in the United States, the Europeans were considered ready to sign just about any deal in order not to deploy. By February 1986, the whole scene had been turned upside down: *Newsweek,* for the first time in a very, very long time, wrote about the allies' "hard line" on arms control, while the Europeans, very much in the same way as during the "gray era" debate of the mid-1970s, began to suspect that the United States could perhaps sacrifice allied interests at the Geneva table in order to salvage those strategic programs that the United States saw as vital to its own interests.[21]

The trouble, however, is that while the U.S. temporarily yielded to the European reaction by rejecting Gorbachev's zero-zero offer, the respite did not last more than a few months. By the fall of 1986, after the grand compromise had failed to break the deadlock on strategic and space issues, INF emerged once again as a prime candidate for *the* one and only deal that could be had during the second Reagan-Gorbachev summit, scheduled for the end of that year.

Zero-zero being out, the United States tried to get the Soviets to accept an interim deal at a level around four hundred warheads. The Soviets, however, still maintained their preference for zero and offered one more "concession" by agreeing to leave out at least temporarily the issue of French and British forces from an *interim* accord. The result was that by September 1986, even though many details remained to be worked out (particularly with respect to the duration and verification of the agreement, and to the number of SS-20s allowed in Asia), the United States finally agreed to bring down the number of its INF in Europe to one hundred warheads, only in the framework of an interim agreement.

Although on the surface an agreement at such a low level could be presented as a "good" deal for the West (since it would impose proportionally deeper cuts on the Soviets, who now have nearly 800 SS-20 warheads, than on NATO, whose total number of Pershing and Cruise was to be 572), it was clear that such a deal would *not* be in Europe's interest. In the first place, a lowering of the SS-20 threat would be of little military value as long as the several hundreds of other shorter-range INF—such as the SS-21, 22 and 23— were not eliminated in the same manner. For the latter can easily inflict the same kind of damage (and political blackmail) on Europe as the SS-20.

Second, and more important, one has to ask what effect a withdrawal of most NATO INF would have on the entire military and political rationale of the original INF of December 1979: namely, the perceived need in Europe to adjust flexible response to the new era of strategic parity. Wasn't, after all, what Helmut Schmidt, in his famous International Institute for Strategic Studies (IISS) speech in 1977, had called the "neutralization" of the superpowers' strategic arsenals what made it imperative for the alliance to have long-range nuclear assets based in Europe, capable of reaching Soviet territory in a reliable fashion so as to "recouple" the European theater to continental U.S. defense? Although the case for INF modernization was predominantly— and erroneously—argued to the public in reference to a single Soviet weapon system, the strategic rationale for NATO INF deployment is, in fact, much broader than the SS-20 issue. It was and remains founded on the evolution of the overall nuclear balance between the two superpowers.

With this in mind, it is by no means evident that 100 INF warheads only (that is to say, if the Soviets accept a "mix" of some 36 Pershings and sixteen batteries of 4 GLCMs each) would be sufficient to ensure the coupling that was sought in the first place, especially if the Soviets are allowed to keep all or most of their short-range INF. For the longer term, and depending on the duration of such an "interim" deal, the Europeans are bound to ask themselves whether this INF withdrawal is not another major step—after Montebello and NATO's gradual shift toward the "conventionalization" of its doctrine—toward a de facto U.S. nuclear disengagement from Europe, leading at some future date to its conventional disengagement as well.

But even leaving these long-term military issues aside, European governments are also bound to face, in the event of a massive INF withdrawal, the political consequences of such a decision by the United States. Wouldn't such a move validate ex post facto the arguments of those sectors of the European left, in particular, who opposed NATO's INF decision in 1979-1983 on the ground that it was only a dangerous political game with no military value at all? That the missiles, in short, were not necessary in the first place?

The additional difficulty here is that NATO had committed itself in advance to accept such a withdrawal, including the possibility of a zero-zero formula in the event the Soviets did the same. Hence this dilemma: the Europeans can hardly refuse a deep reduction in INF, which they have been insisting upon since 1979; and yet accepting a massive withdrawal of Pershing and cruise is bound to reopen the still unresolved issue of what flexible response really is about in an age of parity and what kinds of weapons it really requires. One does not need to dwell on the political consequences of such a situation; the danger is that the latent nuclear debate in Europe will once again be argued at the very time when the center of gravity of the security debate in Europe and in the European left (particularly in the U.K. and the F.R.G.) is clearly moving toward unilateral denuclearization.

Another issue that is bound to be raised once again is that of the French and British forces, even though these would be temporarily left out of an interim agreement. With respect to the United States, the Soviets—as noted earlier—have been clever enough to drop their contention of U.S. compensation for their allies' nuclear forces. So long as the Soviets maintained that particular demand, the United States had a strong *national* (as opposed to alliance) interest in rejecting any deal constructed on that basis. That interest today has been removed, and the only argument that the United States can offer from now on is that it cannot negotiate on behalf of other countries. The problem, however, is that this argument may not be held forever by the United States and that it is weak on several counts. First, it is weak on its merits: to be sure, the United States cannot negotiate for the French and the British, but the Soviets can readily answer that they have already offered Paris and London direct talks precisely to deal with that problem but that both countries turned down the offer. If Paris, London, and now Washington refuse to negotiate, who is to blame? Second, it remains to be seen how long the current U.S. reply will be viewed as a convincing argument by those in Europe, as well as in the United States, who see some justice in the Soviet contention.

Already during the summer 1986 negotiations between the two super-powers, the United States reportedly came very close to accepting the inclusion of French and British forces in the INF balance, leading to strong protests, particularly from Prime Minister Thatcher. Clearly, the issue will be reopened by Moscow as soon as the talks move to a final INF (zero-zero) deal in the aftermath of an interim agreement. Regretfully, a growing number of people—including political leaders and opinion makers—do agree with Moscow that French and British weapons "are not on the moon," and that they are targeted against the USSR. Moreover, the increasingly publicized growth planned for the two European forces (at about twelve hundred warheads by the late 1990s) makes them no longer irrelevant to the total nuclear balance (particularly if both superpowers agree to come down to six hundred warheads). Thus, the risk of increased political pressure from *within* the alliance, leading perhaps to the marginalization of France and the U.K., is quite real. In fact, the danger of these two countries being seen by European public opinion in general as the sole obstacle to an "ideal" INF agreement is all the more serious given the apparently "minor" sacrifices that the Soviets seem to require from Paris and London.[22]

All this adds up to quite a formidable offensive against France and the U.K., as well as European and alliance cohesion, at the very time when both European nuclear powers have no other options (given the strategic-defense race in particular), but to keep on and even to accelerate their current modernization plans.

This is precisely where the INF issue, which the Soviets so "generously" offered the United States to decouple from SDI, merges once again with the defensive problem and the highly sensitive issue of the ABM Treaty's future, this time, however, through non-superpower forces. Quite clearly, for both Paris and London, a freeze today will mean the extinction tomorrow of the two forces, at a time when both superpowers will continue to keep thousands of atomic warheads and will go on developing their arsenals.

Not surprisingly, therefore, in their negative replies (dated March 3 and March 10, respectively) to Gorbachev's January 15 plan, both Margaret Thatcher and François Mitterrand reportedly restated their conditions for their participation in nuclear negotiations. These include not only deep reductions of the superpowers' offensive arsenals but also a ban on improvement of defensive capabilities. Inevitably, this second condition puts both the French and British governments in line with the Soviet crusade against SDI, at the very time when both countries need, more than ever, the support of their U.S. ally on the inclusion issue. There also is a precarious balance, indeed, that may not be maintained for very long.

In short, what we now have, through the mechanism of arms control, is an even more complex equation, linking not only offensive and defensive *strategic* weapons (that was always the case since the SALT I agreements) but also the whole question of offensive/defensive strategic weapons to INF and Third Country forces allied to the United States. At some point, the United States will have to choose between its own national interests as it perceives them (that is, with or without a need to deploy ABM systems) and those of the French and British forces, whose future relevance will obviously be contingent on the kind of defensive environment they will have to face. Obviously, none of the highly complex and sensitive issues discussed herein are likely to find a clear-cut solution in the future. Neither clever arms-control fixes nor a European ATBM program is likely to resolve the issue.

What is needed, instead, above and beyond skillful alliance management, is an effort by the Europeans themselves to prepare for a not-so-remote future when they will have to live not just with strategic parity and Soviet superiority on their continent but with the reintroduction of some strategic defenses on both sides and a gradual U.S. nuclear disengagement from Europe. It is highly debatable whether flexible response, as we have known it, will survive such an evolution. It is now up to the Europeans to prepare for such a future and to plan for their joint defense accordingly.

Notes

1. Gorbachev's January 15, 1986, proposal for "the complete elimination of nuclear weapons" by the turn of the century is analyzed in the last section of the chapter. It should also be noted that this offer was followed by a half-dozen proposals mainly targeted at the Europeans, including, in particular, deep reductions on conventional and tactical nuclear weapons in Europe, a ban on chemical weapons, the creation of nuclear-free zones in Europe, and the dissolution of the two military alliances.

2. See the French Statement to Conference on Disarmament (excerpts), June 12, 1984, in *Survival,* Vol. XXVI, No. 5 (September/October 1984), p. 236.

3. This was restated recently by François Mitterrand himself in his book *Reflexions sur la Politique Etrangère de la France* (Paris: Fayard, 1986).

4. The clearest official presentation of this argument can be found in Defense Minister Paul Quilès's interview in *Le Monde,* December 8, 1985. Also illustrative of the French exasperation with the early U.S. rhetoric on SDI is the remark by Claude Cheysson (former foreign minister) that was reported in *Liberation,* May 3, 1985: "We have made a major effort to convince the Germans to deploy Pershings in the face of Soviet SS-20. A few months go by, and now they are told that in any case the missiles are obsolete and that they will become rapidly useless. In other words, this encourages neutralist sentiment and those in Germany who say 'No nukes in our home.'"

5. See, for instance, the comment of Raymond Barre reported in *l'Express,* May 31-June 6, 1985: "European countries must at all cost prevent their public opinions

from believing that a new type of defense, which would permit the renunciation of nuclear deterrence, is within reach. European security has rested and will rest for a long time on nuclear deterrence."

6. Mitterrand (during the launching of the new submarine-launched ballistic missile (SLBM), *l'Inflexible,* on May 25, 1985): "Deterrence is based on nuclear submarines and it has many long years before it . . . In my opinion, strategy will necessarily be spatial during the next century, but we will have to wait many decades before it becomes operational. The 'link' between both strategies may well take a half century, and as for myself, I am accountable for one part of that half century." A detailed forecast of the impact on SDI-related technologies on the French nuclear force as seen by a chief weapon planner (now a key adviser to Defense Minister André Giraud) is set forth in a paper by Jacques Chevallier entitled "Nouvelles technologies et Force Nucléaire Stratégique" (unpublished), written in November 1985. Chevallier sees eventual deployment of ground-based BMD in the United States by 1990-1992, and possibly space-based boost-phase interceptors around 2015 at the earliest.

7. As early as November 1984, Defense Minister Hernu announced an additional 550 million francs in the 1985 defense budget for R&D work aimed at improving the penetration of French warheads. The move was presented as a "preventive measure" against defensive developments by the two superpowers.

8. See the Quilès article in *Le Monde,* January 25, 1986.

9. Chirac's inauguration speech to the National Assembly read in part (*Le Monde,* April 11, 1986): "Technological progress is leading to the emergence of defensive systems utilizing space. Their birth will not upset for many years to come, and may never upset, the fundamental basis of nuclear deterrence. Our American allies are actively working on this project, and important changes may thereby occur in the world balance, in the dialogue between the two great powers, as in the defense of Europe. We must watch this evolution carefully, as well as the technological gaps that may result therefrom, proceed to the necessary adaptations and avoid missing the opportunities to strengthen European solidarity in this field as well." It should be noted that Chirac stressed the same views in his speech to the Institut des Hautes Études de Défense Nationale (IHEDN) in early September 1986.

10. This is one important difference with the previous Socialist government, which had dropped the S-X from the five-year defense Program Law (1983-1988) and wanted to postpone a decision on new nuclear-delivery vehicles until more was known on the potential for new defensive technologies.

11. *Le Monde,* May 23, 1986.

12. Most such statements, however, rarely mentioned French-U.S. technological cooperation as such but insisted on French participation in the framework of a "European cooperation" (that is, with the F.R.G. and the U.K.) with the United States. See Giscard d'Estaing in *Le Monde,* December 4, 1985, and Raymond Barre in *Politique Internationale* (Fall 1985). As to the common Rassemblement Pour La Republique-Union Pour La Démocratie Française (RPR-UDF) platform drafted before the March elections, it read: "The opposition favors a participation (by France) with the U.S. SDI, in connection with Britain and Germany."

13. The successful sale by Thomson CSF of the Rita Communication System to the U.S. Army in 1985, despite direct political pressures by Margaret Thatcher on behalf of

a competing British system, is often quoted by French industry in support of this view.

14. See Pierre Lellouche, *L'Avenir de la Guerre* (Paris: Mazarine 1985).

15. See Pascal Boniface and François Heisbourg, *La Puce, les Hommes et la Bombe* (Paris: Hachette, 1985).

16. Lellouche, *L'Avenir de la Guerre.*

17. Ironically, the point was made quite candidly to the author by George Keyworth, Reagan's scientific adviser, in a March 1985 interview. Keyworth spoke of giving back the superpowers' strategic forces their original role of pure retribution—instead of the war-fighting role they had now acquired. With SDI, he added, these forces will become like the French *force de frappe.*

18. To the displeasure of the Reagan administration, this point was made publicly by the SACEUR (Supreme Allied Commander, Europe) himself (General Rogers) in a February 1986 presentation at the Institut Français des Relations Internationales (IFRI.)

19. Following statements made by the German defense minister, Manfred Wörner, the Elysée began moving in that direction in January 1986.

20. See *International Herald Tribune,* April 26, 1986.

21. *Newsweek,* March 3, 1986.

22. See, for instance, the *Pravda* editorial dated February 4, 1986, "The European aspect of the Soviet nuclear disarmament plan." See also the *Novosti* reply to my *Newsweek* column dealing with the French and British question, in *Newsweek,* February 3 and March 10, 1986.

8

SDI and NATO: The Case of the Federal Republic of Germany

Ernst-Otto Czempiel

The European Reaction to SDI

Western Europe's concern with SDI now focuses on economic cooperation between Western European and American industry, following the lead of the U.S. government, which has shifted its emphasis from the strategic and political implications of SDI to the technological and industrial ones. The main event in this respect has been the agreement, signed by the United States and the Federal Republic of Germany (F.R.G.) on March 27, 1986, concerning the exchange of technology and German participation in research. Owing to a news leak, the two agreements and the accompanying letters were published in West German magazines and newspapers in late April 1986. West Germany thus became the second European nation to conclude an official agreement with the United States in regard to SDI.

It is obvious that the public debate will now quickly return to the strategic and political implications of SDI. Although the German federal government has repeatedly stated that Germany's participation in SDI is limited to the technological and research-centered aspects of the project and that these must be seen as strictly separate from any form of development and deployment of SDI, it can be assumed that the implications posed by precisely these points will become the focus of interest in the coming debate. By continuously emphasizing these latter aspects, the USSR and the German Democratic Republic (G.D.R.) will certainly attempt to further influence the debate.

Although, with regard to this problem, it is very difficult to generalize about Western European attitudes, it is perhaps possible to isolate certain common points of view. NATO is facing the third wave of discussions. The first wave began in the late fifties and ended in 1967, when Western Europe accepted the American strategy of "flexible response" and NATO, at the same time, developed its two-track position toward the USSR, which combined détente and defense. The basic problem has been, and still is, the strategic and political relationship between the United States and Western Europe, particularly concerning the preparedness of the United States to become directly involved in the protection of Western Europe against a Soviet attack and/or the threat thereof. Although the strategy of flexible response has never been explained in sufficient detail, it has been accepted by Western Europeans as a feasible means of deterring the USSR and thereby guaranteeing their security. With the exception of France, which perceived a certain element of unreliability in the U.S. protection and which developed its own *force de frappe,* all other members of NATO accepted flexible response as a guarantee for the involvement of the United States.

The second wave of the discussions came in the early seventies and dealt with détente and, particularly, the SALT I agreements. Western Europeans now feared that cooperation between the two superpowers would diminish the value of Western Europe in American eyes. They particularly expressed the fear that the superpowers might use the ABM Treaty of 1972 to shield themselves against direct involvement in a European war. During the seventies, this fear diminished with the evolution of détente, which lowered the degree of tension and, thus, the chance of war in Central Europe.

In the late seventies, this situation changed, and the fears rose once again as the relationship between the United States and the USSR deteriorated to a stage of sharper confrontation. Given the development of a new strategy of war-fighting capabilities by the United States, the Europeans felt the anxiety that a European war could evolve which, because of a decoupled United States, could be confined to European soil. In this situation, West German Chancellor Helmut Schmidt articulated a European demand for the presence of American theater nuclear forces (TNF) in Western Europe as a counter-weight against the new Soviet SS-20.

The situation became blurred when the Reagan administration came to power and brought with it a confrontational rhetoric that seemed to endanger the regime of détente in Europe. What had been asked for as an assurance of enduring U.S. protection to some extent took on the color of a means of directly threatening the USSR within a much more confrontational context. American Pershing II and cruise missiles acquired a different meaning, and opposition to their deployment grew. Since the European governments had such a great interest in "coupling" the nuclear power of the United States to Western Europe, and since the USSR continued to increase the numbers of deployed SS-20, the deployment took place. In the wake of it, the USSR, in the autumn of 1983, left the arms-control negotiations in Geneva.

Given this situation, it was to be expected that President Reagan's announcement in early 1983, introducing his Strategic Defense Initiative, would rekindle European apprehensions about the strategy of the United States. When the United States would be able to shield itself against all Soviet retaliation, it would be far more tempted to decouple itself from any European troubles. Considering this aspect, the European protection gained by American TNF would be lost on account of SDI. European apprehension was heightened when members of the Reagan administration stated in public that "détente is dead" and Washington became reluctant to resume and to continue actively the arms-control discussions with the USSR. With détente weakened, the arms-control negotiations adjourned, and the individual protection of the United States promoted by SDI, Western European security was perceived as deteriorating rapidly. The European disappointment was all the greater as there had been no consultation prior to, nor clear-cut information after, the announcement of SDI. Two years after President Reagan's address, the United States still had not considered at all the possible consequences of SDI for Western Europe. And not before Secretary Weinberger's letter of March 26, 1985, had there been any official information given to Bonn by Washington.[1]

Two sets of questions raised in Western Europe can be distinguished. One deals with the physical problems involved in SDI, the other with the strategic consequences stemming from it. Within the first set, the main question concerns the technological feasibility of SDI and the enormous costs involved. Many Europeans think that the technological obstacles facing SDI are insurmountable and that the amount of money to be spent is intolerable. They emphasize that even if it might be possible to defend against large ballistic missiles attacks, it would probably be impossible to develop systems of defense against intermediate-range and, above all, tactical missiles.[2] Thus, with the United States completely protected, Western Europe would be left vulnerable.

Important objections, however, are also directed against SDI as a strategy. In the eyes of Europeans, it would damage arms control, particularly the ABM Treaty, which until now has kept the arms race from being extended into space. Seen in its final perspective, SDI would eliminate deterrence, which until now has served peace and stability between East and West in Europe. Finally, in light of a distinct element of U.S. superiority involved in SDI, the program would damage détente and diminish all prospects of further arms-control agreements.

Given these arguments, it is no wonder that a research team of the Congressional Research Service reviewing Western European attitudes toward SDI in early 1985 came to the conclusion that in Western Europe there are "a variety of viewpoints with the overwhelming preponderance of opinion negative towards the systems that the Strategic Defense Initiative could ultimately produce."[3]

The F.R.G. shared all of these viewpoints, more or less, stressing particularly the necessity of including antitactical missiles (ATMs) and the reduction of conventional armaments and troops in Central Europe. As the only major Western European power without nuclear capabilities of its own, the F.R.G. is particularly sensitive to all tendencies toward decoupling on the part of the United States and to the possibility of any limited war in Europe. The F.R.G. is afraid of the transitory phase between the end of the antiballistic missile

(ABM) regime and the completion of SDI, in both the strategic and the regional realms.

The political implications of SDI are no less important for the F.R.G. Owing to its geopolitical position, its special relationship with the G.D.R., and its interest in good and improving political and economic relations with the USSR, the Federal Republic is bound to have a vested interest in détente. At least for Bonn, there is validity in what former Secretary of State Kissinger stated years ago: "There is no alternative to détente." Even if Bonn does not take seriously the threat by the USSR and the G.D.R. that West Germany's acceptance of SDI would necessarily hurt *Ostpolitik,* Bonn must be unwilling to pay for SDI with a deterioration of relations toward the G.D.R. and Eastern Europe.

If this interest stems from sheer reason of state, it is augmented by domestic considerations. The internal consensus within the F.R.G. has suffered considerably under the strains of the TNF deployment. Public opinion reacted actively against Washington's confrontational rhetoric. It was compared unfavorably with the many proposals for a moratorium on nuclear tests, a comprehensive test ban (CTB), and, very recently, a reduction in conventional armaments, flowing almost incessantly from the new leadership in Moscow. This Soviet campaign is directed particularly against West Germany and certainly has not been unsuccessful. Because of its particular exposure to the East, the lack of a long tradition as a nation-state, and a feeling of insecurity, the F.R.G. has reacted much more nervously to SDI than its Western neighbors, who are also opposed to this initiative. In June 1984, France submitted a proposal to the UN Disarmament Commission to foreclose all testing and deployment of Ballistic Missile Defense (BMD). President Mitterrand urged the two superpowers to abandon all plans for weapons in space. The U.K. was more cautious, but Prime Minister Thatcher nevertheless criticized the SDI program at the end of 1984 leading to a new arms race.[4] Afterward, both countries shifted their position without any domestic strains to a more open and pragmatic approach, which permitted the U.K. to conclude an agreement with the U.S. and French industry to cooperate actively with American corporations. Italy joined in this approach, the moderate conditions of which were outlined by Prime Minister Thatcher during her visit to Washington in February 1985.[5] But in the Federal Republic a prolonged and excited debate developed, with the government wavering between divergent positions.[6]

In summary, there appears to be a reluctant and diffuse readiness in the F.R.G., as in Western Europe generally, to go along with SDI as long as it remains a research program and is not translated into development and deployment without prior consultation. Europeans are interested in the continuation of the strategy of deterrence by flexible response, along with efforts to lower the tension by successful control and reduction of arms.

Western Europe is particularly upset because of the possible consequences of SDI for security. It would be endangered substantially if a complete BMD shield around the United States (and the USSR) would neutralize the protective nuclear power of the United States. Conventional war would then be possible again in Central Europe. The reverse argument that the United States would be more ready to intervene in Europe because it need not fear a Soviet retaliation against the American continent does not have much value here, because of the preceding two debates which revealed a structural U.S. interest in avoiding any direct confrontation with the Soviets in Central Europe. Furthermore, with a complete SDI, the French and British nuclear forces would have lost their capability to deter the USSR and to serve as an automatic link to the strategic nuclear weapons of the United States.

The situtation would be somewhat different if SDI would finally be reduced to point defenses. This could perhaps definitively close the "window of vulnerability" and therefore strengthen the strategy of deterrence. Although it would still neutralize U.S. strategic forces, it would leave the French and the British nuclear countervalue capabilities unharmed. Thus, a European deterrent would remain. Whether it would be sufficent to counter the SS-20 remains open, since the strategy of flexible response would have suffered substantially. The F.R.G., in any case, would still face the SS 22-23 and the conventional superiority of the USSR. For those reasons, Western Europe certainly would prefer a world without SDI, although it knows very well that technological progress has made missile defenses an unavoidable element of the strategies of the future.

The Europeans obviously hope that the technological obstacles will finally render SDI obsolete and free them from the necessity of having to dissociate themselves openly from the United States. The Reagan administration obviously hopes that technological breakthroughs, the investment of vast amounts of money, and the perspective of regaining superiority over the USSR will finally lead the Europeans to accept SDI and its strategic consequences.

All outcomes will affect NATO. If the Western Europeans decide to accept the U.S. program and to go along with it, the old continent might remain safe, but NATO will become a regional appendix to the U.S. strategy toward the USSR. If the Europeans make up their minds and wills to do more for their own security, to form the famous European pillar of the Atlantic Community, NATO again will not remain the same. The construction of the alliance has obviously reflected an international phenomenon, called the East-West conflict, which has dominated the international system from 1947 to the late seventies and has given way to a new international constellation with a new bilateral U.S.-Soviet conflict at its top. NATO will most certainly have a future, as it is useful for the United States and necessary for the Western Europeans. However, it will be a new future, not a prolongation of the old one.

In the summer of 1986, all these problems were veiled, because the Reagan administration had shifted the emphasis from the strategic to the scientific prospect of SDI and to the technological benefits that might result. Since both are of great interest to the Europeans and, particularly, to the West Germans, the discussion in 1985 and 1986 concentrated upon those aspects.

SDI and German Opinion

West German attitudes toward SDI range from total opposition to reluctant acceptance. It is no overstatement to say that the negative positions prevail and that they can be found in public opinion, in the political parties, and also in the governing conservative-liberal coalition.

Public opinion, of course, is unspecific. It has no clear-cut attitude toward SDI. Important movements of public opinion have taken place recently, however. Within the three and a half years between June 1982 and January 1986, the percentage of West Germans preferring to cooperate with the United States instead of the USSR shrunk from 52 to 32 percent. The tendency toward a policy of "equidistance" rose from 39 to 54 percent. These tendencies were particularly strong among Germans under age thirty. In 1982, 70 percent of them supported German membership in NATO; by 1986 this rate had fallen to only 52 percent. Support for unilateral disarmament rose among this age group from 44 to 55 percent.

The percentage of those arguing in favor of stronger cooperation with the USSR remained constant at an insignificant 1 to 2 percent.[7] The trend, therefore, must not be interpreted as mounting support for the position of the USSR but as a stronger criticism of the policies of the Reagan administration. There is no pro-Soviet consensus within the F.R.G., but it has become obvious that the long-standing pro-American consensus has suffered since the early eighties.

There are several reasons for this shift, but the discussion about the deployment of U.S. TNFs and about SDI certainly have contributed to it. The interest in détente and arms reduction is widespread in West German society, which is very much opposed to any program such as SDI which would lead to an arms buildup and to a deterioration of détente.

Even the official position of the Federal Republic has been cautious and ambiguous. The Kohl government supported SDI, but only as a research program, the results of which had to be discussed with the allies and with the USSR. Kohl placed SDI into the context of the current NATO strategy, thus neutralizing, or at least diminishing, its possible long-term strategic consequences. If SDI would not meet these conditions, the Federal Republic would not support it.

This support was never meant to include the active participation of the Federal Republic, which declined any financial and political contribution beyond the official, condition-ridden declarations. On the other hand, Bonn never explained why, under these circumstances, Germany was ready to sign a U.S.-German agreement at all. It was certainly not necessary for the participation of German industry in SDI. Bonn usually answered that the agreement would guarantee an equal exchange of technological know-how and that German corporations had asked for it.[8] It is nevertheless safe to assume that the interest of the U.S. side in obtaining the support of the German government for SDI, if only indirectly, has played an important role in the history of these agreements.

The first official formulation of West Germany's position toward SDI came with Kohl's statement at the Wehrkundetagung in February 1985.[9] In a lengthy speech, Kohl put SDI into the regime of arms control. He stated explicitly that SDI and its possible Soviet counterpart should be included in the expected talks in Geneva and that cooperative solutions should be sought. He reaffirmed the ABM Treaty and interpreted "strategic stability" in a manner that contradicted the position of the Reagan administration. For Kohl, strategic stability implies the conservation of a second-strike capability for both sides, abandonment of the aim of superiority, and the maintenance of the strategy of flexible response. Couched in friendly and neutral language, Kohl declined all long-term goals that the Reagan administration pursued with SDI.

Six weeks later, after a meeting of the German Security Council in Bonn, the government went even further in an official statement.[10] Referring to the resumption of U.S.-Soviet arms-control talks in Geneva, the government emphasized the ongoing validity of the Harmel concept of NATO, with its two elements of constructive dialogue and comprehensive defense. Bonn again underlined the value of the strategy of flexible response for NATO and mentioned, once more, that all weapons systems should be included in the arms-control discussions in Geneva.

In his official declaration of April 18, 1985, before the German parliament,[11] Kohl for the first time officially endorsed the SDI research program "in principle." He remained cautious, however. He mentioned that the goal of his government is to secure peace with less weapons and he stressed anew the politico-strategic conditions on which the German support of SDI was predicated. Flexible response must remain intact as long as no alternative can be found; the security of Europe must not be decoupled from the security of the United States, and there must be no zones of different security within NATO. Although only in passing, he also mentioned a completely different alternative: the drastic reduction of offensive weapons. This could reduce the need for defensive weapons in space, or at least the numbers of such weapons that might be needed.

During the summer of 1985, the reluctance of the German government grew. Secret analysis by the government's intelligence service pointed to the numerous technological obstacles facing the inclusion of Western Europe into the protection of SDI.[12] Accordingly, the position of the government hardened in the summer of 1985. It even put in doubt the possibility of an intergovernmental agreement regulating industrial cooperation.[13] When, during the second half of 1985, the Reagan administration altered its position and presented SDI predominantly as a technological research program with immense implications for the civilian economy, the situation of the government was somewhat improved.[14] For the time being, the politico-military and strategic aspects of SDI could be put on the back burner. As it turned out, the improvement was not a very big one. Looked at in detail, U.S.-German cooperation in the field of SDI did not promise very many spinoffs for German industry. Several German government delegations went to the United States to explore what could be gained by the German participants in view of the restrictions built into the ABM Treaty, U.S. trade legislation, and the general attitude of Congress toward protectionism. Particular German apprehensions were based upon the prescriptions of the Export Administration Regulations (EAR) and the International Traffic in Arms Regulations (ITAR).[15] The *Frankfurter Allgemeine Zeitung* called attention to the restrictiveness of U.S. policies.[16] Nevertheless, there were calculations that despite these restrictions, European corporations might receive contracts in the value of between $30 and $300 million, but by no means in the $3 billion range mentioned by the U.S. government.[17] In August 1986, the German doubts had been sharpened considerably in view of a tendency in the U.S. Congress to restrict further the farming out of contracts to European industries.

On December 18, 1985, the government decided to come to certain agreements with the United States. In order to underline the economic character of these agreements, Bonn had them signed by the minister of economics, Martin Bangemann. On March 27, 1986, Bangemann signed two agreements that also included a number of letters between the two sides. The terms were disclosed by the newspaper *Express* and the magazine *Der Spiegel*.[18]

One of the two agreements deals with bilateral cooperation between the United States and the Federal Republic in the fields of industry, science, technology, and security. It is not a treaty, only a declaration of political obligations. Its value lies in strengthening U.S.-German bilateralism. The second document regulates U.S.-German cooperation with regard to SDI. Mentioning many points that are obvious in themselves, the political meaning of this agreement is in limiting the transfer of technology to the East. It is safe to state that with these agreements, Bonn fell in line behind the SDI program of the Reagan administration, however reluctantly, and emphasized U.S.-German bilateralism instead of a closer European, particularly German-French, cooperation.

Within the governing Christian Democratic Union/Christian Social Union-Free Democratic Party (CDU/CSU-FDP) coalition, there was no great consensus regarding the agreement. Minister of Foreign Affairs Hans-Dietrich Genscher denied its necessity in toto; he would have preferred a French-like position giving German industries a free hand but declining the formal inter-governmental agreement.[19] This would have retained all of the economic benefits—should there be any—for German industry, without bringing the German government into a formal relationship with SDI, thereby avoiding its implicit politico-strategic implications. Genscher repeatedly pointed out that the agreement organized technological cooperation only, that political and strategic questions could not be dealt with bilaterally but belonged within the framework of NATO. In contrast, Minister of Defense Wörner emphasized the military nature of SDI, which should not be reduced to a program of transfer-ring technology only.[20] Ministerpräsident Franz Josef Strauss stressed the mil-itary aspects of SDI even more strongly.[21] He underlined its strategic necessity and urged the government to give it unlimited support. While the FDP and the liberal wing of the CDU put more weight on the purely economic character of the agreement, the conservative faction of the CDU and the right-wing CSU interpreted it as supporting the new strategy developed behind SDI.

Thus, the agreements of March 27, 1986, have been highly controversial, even within the governing coalition. The notorious infighting between Strauss and Genscher grew considerably, and the division within the CDU, between the *Stahlhelm*-wing and the more liberal group, deepened. It is interesting to note that the right wing of the governing coalition is obviously prepared to accept SDI in spite of its negative, or at least uncertain, effects for West Germany's security. The right would reestablish security by supplementing SDI with a European Theater Ballistic Missiles Defenses, referred to in Ger-many as the *Europaische Verteidigungsinitiative* (EVI, or, in translation, Euro-pean Defense Initiative). Nobody knows whether such a defense will ever be possible, because the technological problems are greater than in the case of SDI. But the right is not disturbed by technology; its aim is politics. This wing supports SDI because it sharpens the confrontation with the USSR and weak-ens détente and arms control.

Given the serious doubts within NATO about SDI and its consequences for East-West stability and for the strategy and cohesion of the alliance, the position of this right wing should not be interpreted as particularly pro-American. On the contrary, it is a German national position that attempts to use the confrontational elements involved in SDI to influence West German public opinion against any kind of understanding and arrangement with the East. One has to remember that in the sixties Strauss was the leader of the Gaullist faction in German politics and that he has never been a convinced Atlanticist. He supports the policies of the Reagan administration because they fit his own political convictions, not because they necessarily strengthen the cohesion of NATO. In the same way as President Reagan and his administration put unilateralism and recognition of U.S. national interest ahead of consultation and consensus building within NATO, Strauss, mirroring Reagan, favors national unilateralism. The identical, or similar, ideological position produces similar political options. As the Reagan administration is ready to leave the Harmel consensus of 1967, so is Strauss and the right wing of the CDU/CSU.

This is certainly not true for the center-CDU, which attempts to please Reagan without following him in all respects. It is absolutely untrue for the FDP, which, within the governing coalition, tries to continue the traditional two-track policy of détente and defense, to promote arms-control discussions, and to foster stronger European cooperation within NATO. This position is certainly critical of SDI and the hard-liners in the Reagan administration. For just these reasons, this position is explicitly pro-United States and pro-NATO. As mentioned previously, NATO still is directed by the Harmel formula. This liberal wing of the governing coalition was successful in stimulating the government at least to come out openly in favor of accepting, as a serious step, the Gorbachev proposal of the spring of 1986 regarding arms control, including the reduction of conventional forces.

For the broad liberal wing, research on BMD is perhaps unavoidable, because technological progress continues and the USSR has, for a long time, promoted its own research in this field. However, the supreme goal remains the reduction of tension and of arms in order to facilitate stability and cooperation. According to this view, the mix between offensive and defensive strategic weapons can be crucially influenced by reducing offensive weapons. SDI, therefore, has to become a central element of the arms-control deliberations in Geneva instead of being kept outside of them. If tactical and Euro-strategic weapons could be eliminated, there would be no need for theater ballistic missile defense (TBMD). The conventional superiority of the USSR would, however, remain to be dealt with. There are, furthermore, several other obstacles to a successful arms-control agreement. The main point, however, is that the liberal wing of the governing coalition, and particularly the FDP, is trying to keep alive all relevant East-West conferences—Mutual and Balanced Force Reduction (MBFR), Conference on Security and Cooperation in Europe (CSCE), and Conference on Disarmament in Europe (CDE)—and to integrate SDI within this cooperative East-West context. Not without some caveats can it be said that this liberal wing within the governing coalition is skeptical toward SDI, because it is in favor of the traditional position of NATO. It looks to arms control, not missile defense, in order to establish security in Europe.[22]

The majority within the Social Democratic Party (SPD) agrees, more or less, with the liberal position. In regard to SDI, the necessity of arms control and détente, and the timeliness of a stronger European cooperation in NATO to balance U.S. weight, the SPD is still on common ground with Minister of Foreign Affairs Genscher and the position of many of his followers. In the field of *Ostpolitik* and arms control, the social-liberal coalition is pretty much intact.

As the official opposition party, the SPD is not only free but bound to articulate its criticism. The party argued quite vigorously against the U.S.-German agreements. Already on December 4, 1985, the SPD *Bundestagsfraktion* produced two resolutions, declining German participation in SDI[23] and rejecting the development of a European defense system against theater ballistic missiles (EVI).[24] Majority Leader Hans-Jochen Vogel said that the party, after its possible return to power, would cancel the agreements. Against them, the SPD argued that German participation could be interpreted as political support for SDI, which would be politically, militarily, and strategically detrimental for East-West relations and could damage the credibility of the Western Alliance. Neither SDI nor EVI could help against Soviet short-range nuclear forces (SNF) and short-range intermediate nuclear forces (SRINF). They would only accelerate the nuclear arms race in Europe. The SPD favors a conventional air defense, though,[25] and instead of SDI the party prefers European cooperation in European Research Coordination Agency (Eureka), which, as a civilian program, could successfully face the technological challenge posed by the United States and Japan.

As far as the strategic consequences of SDI are concerned, the SPD, much more than the CDU, fears that the program will create zones of different security.[26] With the two superpowers shielded against strategic attacks, conventional war in Europe could become possible again, a concern that is also shared by the *generalinspekteur* of the Bundeswehr, Wolfgang Altenburg. In any kind of war in Europe, even a minor one, the Federal Republic would suffer most and immediately.

In the eyes of the SPD, SDI appears to be driving a wedge into the alliance insofar as it abandons the basis of the common defense. It could exchange second-strike capability for a (possible) first-strike capability. It invites the USSR to a new arms race, with defensive and offensive weapons that reach into space; and, finally, it would eliminate the last hope for substantial success in the Geneva arms control talks.[27]

So far, so good. This position of the SPD is shared by many Germans and by many members of the FDP and of the CDU alike. With regard to the strategies necessary for successful arms-control agreements, the SPD, however, goes much further than the positions of the CDU and FDP. The SPD would replace the strategy of deterrence with a "strategy of security-partnership, of common security."[28] Although it is still not quite clear what the "strategy of security-partnership" means in political detail, it is meant to be a cooperative undertaking engaging both West and East in the process of the reduction of armaments and tensions. It is certainly more in line with the old Harmel formula, but it enlarges the second element, that of cooperation and détente, considerably. It relies upon the basic assumption that given the devastating capabilities of modern-weapons technology and the action-reaction process in the arms buildup, real security cannot be won by unilaterally stepping up the arms race, only by bringing it down by mutual consent. Consequently, the SDP argues in favor of a restructuring of the defense posture by both sides, which could then facilitate arms control and arms reduction.

With regard to closer Western European cooperation in the field of BMD and space technologies, the SPD is as vague as the CDU. The party has already asked Western Europeans to invest more in the sphere of European basic research and civilian space travel than in the political and military program of SDI. The SPD comes out strongly in favor of Eureka. All of these projects are, as will be pointed out later, of a civilian, not of a military, nature. The platform of the SPD-Prasidium[29] for the party convention scheduled for August 1986 asked for a more independent role for the Western Europeans within NATO. However, it did not elaborate, but confined itself to this general remark. When this "Leitantrag" (or leading proposal) delineated the changes in NATO's strategy which the SPD is asking for, it did not mention any kind of closer cooperation of Western Europeans within the alliance.

There are some leading SPD officials who try to be more precise. Horst Ehmke has put forward the idea of stronger European self-reliance.[30] Norbert Gansel asked whether stronger Western European self-determination should take place within NATO, within the Western European Union (WEU), or via the WEU within NATO.[31] Within the party in general, however, there is as little detailed discussion of those problems as there is within the CDU.

This is true also for those on the left wing of the SPD, who argue in favor of following the example of France and leaving the organization of the alliance, but not the alliance itself. The *ministerpräsident* of the Saarland, Oskar Lafontaine, is the most important spokesman in this regard. Within the lower ranks of this wing, some can be found who would go even further and leave the Western Alliance to seek some neutral position for West Germany (and possibly the G.D.R.). These tendencies certainly have been enhanced by SDI. Their overall strength has not grown, however, and they have no answers for the complex political and strategic problems posed to the NATO countries by the further development of military technologies.

On this left fringe of the party, there is some overlap with the Greens. To put it differently: many left-wing neutralists who joined the peace movement now belong to the leadership of the Greens. Nevertheless, the party of the Greens is still an agglomeration of individuals and individual views, and it is very difficult to discover a clear-cut strategic policy. The party declaration called for the withdrawal of the F.R.G. from NATO and for offers of unilateral disarmament.

This position can be neglected within the overall party landscape of the F.R.G. The previously mentioned polls indicate, however, that some attitudes lying beneath these political demands are spreading throughout the West German population. In pushing SDI, the Reagan administration is contributing directly to this movement. These effects of SDI can be felt even within the ranks of the SPD. The party that had asked for U.S. TNF in 1979 decided to reject them in 1983, after four years of a new administration in Washington.

It is, of course, not very easy to delineate possible consequences for the future of the alliance. Some observations may be offered, however.

Short-Term and Long-Term Consequences

The discussion about technological cooperation between U.S. and German corporations is more or less closed. Cooperation is taking place, and the first American orders have been given to German corporations, particularly Messerschmidt-Bölkow-Blohm in Munich and Carl Zeiss in Wetzlar. The volume is in the range of $20 million, not very much but a beginning.[32] The discussion might be resumed if Congress restricts cooperation, as mentioned previously. Although the German terrorist group Red Army Faction (RAF), by murdering a leading director of Siemens in May 1986, tried to exploit and to stimulate the general interest of the German population in SDI and its possible consequences, the excitement was pretty much gone as of the summer of 1986. With the official confinement to scientific research and civilian cooperation, SDI has passed the first hurdle of acceptance.

Nobody in Germany can afford to forget, however, that SDI is not a civilian research program but a strategic one, with enormous consequences for the security of the F.R.G. and its position in the Atlantic Alliance. Everybody knows that the problems have only been postponed, that they will show up soon again and will continue to embarrass NATO for a long period, until a final decision can be taken. The F.R.G. remembers with shivers the painful discussions that took place in the four years between NATO's dual-track decision in 1979 and its first implementation in the autumn of 1983.

In the summer of 1986 German attention was focused upon the bilateral U.S.-Soviet arms-control dialogue. The Federal Republic watches with the greatest interest the possible outcomes for SDI. If it will not be integrated into a U.S.-Soviet arms-control compromise but pursued further as a full-fledged defense program, the discussion in the F.R.G. will be resumed and will deal exclusively with the strategic aspects. Several important elements of this discussion have already surfaced.

With the exception of the CSU and the right wing of the CDU, SDI generally is assessed as a new and very important sign of procedural, as well as substantive, unilateralism on the part of the United States. West Germany, along with Western Europe generally, learned anew that it is not asked before Washington imposes important decisions. It also learned that the substance of these decisions favors the American interest predominantly, if not exclusively. In the case of SDI, Western European interests had to be added to the unilateral American decisions later. It is still open to question whether they can and will be taken care of.

This experience affects the value of NATO. The existence of the alliance has not kept the Reagan administration from making important decisions alone and without prior consultation. This experience was repeated when the

Reagan administration attacked Libya against the advice of the Europeans. If SDI teaches anything, it is the readiness of the United States to "go it alone" and to leave it to the Europeans to follow suit. That the NATO alliance has been reduced to such a negligible value has been, perhaps, the most severe consequence of SDI for the short-term future of the alliance.

In the short term, the F.R.G. has only limited options. It can try to go along with the U.S. initiative and hope for the best. This is obviously the solution preferred by the governing coalition of the CDU/CSU and the FDP. It sees no possibility of stemming the tide and openly opposing the Reagan administration. Kohl had to give in and to sign the cooperative agreement that, in fact, brought the F.R.G. behind SDI. There is hope that the technological problems will keep SDI from fully developing and will, thus, reduce it to an improved point defense, which could be integrated into the existing strategy of mutual deterrence and would pose no severe problems with the USSR. It would, on the other hand, not solve all the security problems of the F.R.G., which, in order to deter the USSR, would have to look more and more to France and the U.K.

To go along with SDI means also to register the damage that is being done to East-West relations and to try to soften this damage. Therefore, the Kohl government is pushed toward the G.R.D., strengthening the "community of responsibility" accepted by both parts of Germany. *Ostpolitik* in a much more national sense will be the natural outcome of this development.

The second option open to the F.R.G. is to reject SDI and hope for the best. This option is preferred by the SPD. It means criticizing the government and regretting the damage being done to arms control and détente. It means accepting and enhancing public apprehensions against new arms races and using them as a steppingstone for a return to power. The hope is that at some future time SDI will have boiled down to a point defense and that German industry will have learned the hard way that the wall of U.S. protection in the fields of security and arms production is insurmountable. At the same time, the SPD can demonstrate the range of possibilities open to its strategy of common security. The *Nebenaussenpolitik* (literally, "near" foreign policy) leading to the proposal of a zone free of chemical weapons in Central Europe points in this direction.

Thus, in the short term, SDI will raise suspicions in the F.R.G. about the reliability of the United States as a protecting and cooperative partner and will encourage Bonn to pursue its policy of détente with the G.D.R. and the East. Since SDI belongs exclusively to the strategic relationship of the superpowers, the F.R.G. must be interested in evading its consequences for its *Ostpolitik*. In a certain sense this situation is similar to that of the seventies, when the U.S. policy of cooperation and détente led to a partial duopoly of the two super-powers, which was perceived by the smaller European powers as detrimental to their interests. This perception was not, and is not, completely unjustified. Any bilateral relationship between the United States and the USSR, whether cooperative or confrontational, must weaken the U.S. orientation toward its Western European partners. NATO suffers accordingly.

What will happen if SDI is kept in its full dimension as a space defense program, nobody within the two great German parties could have known in 1986. This is a matter for long-term speculation, given the five to fifteen years the two superpowers will probably have before they must decide whether to deploy "Star Wars" defenses. Already it is apparent that American unilateralism is a fact of political life which the smaller NATO members have to reckon with. To mention it does not mean to blame the Americans. As a superpower, the United States must maintain as broad as possible a freedom of action. This is the structural lesson SDI is teaching. In the past, the United States has more often than not concealed its unilateralism behind numerous discussions and consultations. With the power struggle between the United States and the USSR heightening, Washington is further tempted to give first priority to U.S. interests. The United States is still offering discussions and information to its allies. But the element of consultation is diminished. Sometimes, as in the case of SDI, there is even no information. This organizational-procedural development proves, once more, that NATO in its present structure is outmoded. It is, therefore, no surprise that the Europeans, when thinking about the long-term consequences of a fully developed SDI, also think about closer European cooperation within NATO. As the example of the European Community (EC) demonstrates, such a Europe speaking toward the United States with a single voice can balance the U.S. preponderance and construct a structural symmetry as a sound and enduring base for an indefinite relationship.[33] If the European states, accordingly, would form a "European pillar" in NATO, they could make the military relationship equally symmetrical and, within such a new structure of NATO, could implement the strategies they deem necessary for their defense. In this realm, SDI adds to a debate that is already traditional within NATO.

For the reasons mentioned previously, German (and European) discussions at present focus upon the research aspects of SDI. In 1985, France started an initiative for Eureka[34] which should mirror institutions like NASA.[35] Eureka, as an interstate agency, should cooperate with the technology programs of the EC, notably ESPRIT I and II. Bonn supported the idea but not the agency. Eureka now has only a small secretariat and is confined mainly to support the cooperation of private industry in the field of high technology, environment, and an infrastructure of information and communication.[36] Eureka now has nineteen member-states. Its third conference, in June 1986 in London, assembled forty European ministers of research and development. The EC is a member of Eureka, but there are bound to be several overlaps with the many technology programs of the EC itself. In 1985 the EC Council created the European Technology Community and in 1986 embedded it in a proposed Unified European Act. In a sense, Eureka, with its emphasis on the initiative of private business, must be seen as an alternative to the bureaucracy-led EC programs.[37] It is true that Eureka is predominantly oriented toward civilian technology. Since much of this technology has a dual capacity, though, Eureka has a certain relation to the military aspect of SDI. It is a weak one, however, and the Deutsche Gesellschaft für Auswärtige Politik published in summer 1986 a proposal for an outright European Space Program.[38] The more restrictive the transfer of U.S. technology to Western Europe becomes, the more attention activities of this kind are likely to attract.

As of the summer of 1986, the security problems posed by SDI had not been reflected, officially at least, in the discussions about stronger European military cooperation in NATO. This discussion received a new impulse from U.S. unilateral decisions relating to the neutron bomb and the Follow-On Forces Attack-(FOFA) and air-land battle concepts. In 1985, there was some immediate discussion about the European Defense Initiative aiming at missile defenses for Europe. This debate has been revived, and not only because of the shift to the research implications of SDI. More intensive European cooperation in military matters would bring with it many and far-reaching political and strategic consequences.

Certainly, European cooperation in defense matters has improved. There is the Eurogroup and the Independent European Program Group (IEPG). There is still the WEU, which could serve as a framework for a European defense. In addition, French-German military cooperation has improved in practice. But the main obstacles against a truly integrated European defense remain unchanged. They are the high value given to the notion of national independence, the fear of the role the F.R.G. could play in such a context, and the negative consequences that might emerge for the relations to the East.[39] For the Federal Republic, U.S. military—and political—protection is much more important and reliable than anything the British and French nuclear forces could provide.

This overall distribution of interests will not be changed by SDI, particularly since its future and real implications are open. It is obvious, as even the U.S. ambasssador to the F.R.G., Richard Burt, has pointed out, that in the very long run both Europe and the United States will benefit from a stronger European defense pillar.[40] It is equally obvious, however, that SDI has not yet produced the point of no return.

Notes

1. Address by Horst Teltschik to a colloquium of the Konrad Adenauer Foundation, printed in *Europa-Archiv* 40, 20, October 20, 1985, p. D 579. Teltschik is *Ministerialdirektor* in the Office of the Chancellor and main advisor to Chancellor Kohl in foreign-policy matters.

2. See, for example, Konrad Seitz, "SDI—die technologische Herausforderung für Europa, in *Europa-Archiv* 40, 13, October 7, 1985, p. 387. Dr. Seitz is chief of the planning staff in the Foreign Office.

3. Paul E. Gallis et al., *The Strategic Defense Initiative and United States Alliance Strategy* (Washington: Congressional Research Service, Report No. 85-48 F, February 1, 1985), p. 18.

4. John Tirman, ed., *The Fallacy of Star Wars—Why Space Weapons Can't Protect Us* (New York: Random House, 1985). Here used in the German edition: *SDI, Der Krieg im Weltraum,* (Scherz-Verlag, Bern 1985), pp. 240ff.

5. Statement by Sir Geoffrey Howe before the Royal Services Institute in London, March 15, 1985; German translation in *Europa-Archiv,* 40, 8, April 25, 1985, p. D 221.

6. For a sharp criticism of Bonn's attitude from a strict conservative point of view, see Uwe Nerlich, "Folgerungen aus SDI fur Strategie, "Rüstungskontrolle und Politik: Zum Entscheidungsbedarf der Bundersrepublik Deutschland," in *Europa-Archiv* 41, 4, February 25, 1986, pp. 89ff.

7. Elisabeth Noelle-Neumann, "Mit den Kindern im Meinungszwiespält," *Frankfurter Allgemeine Zeitung,* April 23, 1986, p. 11.

8. Address by Teltschik, September 30, 1985 (note 1), p. D 580. See also Hans Rühle et al., *Standpunkte zu SDI in Ost und West* (Bonn: Melle, Knoth, 1985).

9. Printed in *Europäische Wehrkunde* 34, 3, 1985, pp. 133-40.

10. Declaration of the Federal Government, March 27, 1985, in Presse und Informationsdienst der Bundesregierung, *Bulletin No. 35,* March 29, 1985.

11. Declaration of the Federal Government regarding the Strategic Defense Initiative, April 17, 1985, in *Bulletin No. 40,* April 19, 1985, pp. 341ff.

12. Quoted in *Handelsblatt,* May 24, 1985.

13. *Die Welt,* June 13, 1985, and *Generalanzeiger,* June 21, 1985.

14. Judith Miller, "European Allies Grudgingly Give Support to U.S. SDI Research," *International Herald Tribune,* January 15, 1986, p. 6.

15. See Hanns-D. Jacobsen, "Auswirkungen der amerikanischen Technologiekontrollpolitik auf die West-West-Beziehungen, in *Europa-Archiv* 41, 15, August 10, 1986, pp. 443ff.

16. "Weiterhin Unklarheit über die deutsche SDI-Beteiligung," *Frankfurter Allgemeine Zeitung,* May 8, 1985.

17. John Pike, "SDI Contracts: Will U.S. Allies Be Sold Short?" *International Herald Tribune,* June 16, 1986, p. 7.

18. *Express,* April 21, 1986; *Der Spiegel* 40, 17, April 21, 1986, pp. 27ff.

19. See, for example, "Widersprüche in den Darstellungen über SDI-Verhandlungen mit den USA," *Suddeutsche Zeitung,* March 22-23, 1986, p. 1.

20. *Frankfurter Allgemeine Zeitung,* March 3, 1986.

21. Ibid.

22. Konrad Seitz, "Die Zukunft von Sicherheit und Abrüstung in Europa," in *Europa-Archiv* 41, 5, March 10, 1986, pp. 119ff.

23. "Antrag der Fraktion der SPD: Keine Beteiligung am amerikanischen SDI-Program," *Deutscher Bundestag,* 10. Wahlperiode, Drucksache 10/4441, April 12, 1985.

24. "Antrag der Fraktion der SPD: Europäische Verteidiginginitiative zur Abwehr ballistischer Raketen, *ibid,* Drucksache 10/4440, December 4, 1985. For a general statement of the SPD-Bundestagsfraktion regarding the civilian and military use of space, see *Informationen der Sozialdemokratischen Bundestagsfraktion,* Ausgabe 678, April 9, 1986, passim.

25. Statement of Representative Gansel (SPD), in *Deutscher Bundestag,* Stenographischer Bericht, 185. Sitzung, October 13, 1985.

26. "SDI und die Interessen Europas," in *Politik, aktuelle Informationen der Sozialdemokratischen Partei Deutschlands,* No. 3, May 1985, p. 3.

27. Statement of the Prasidium of the Social Democratic Party of Germany, February 25, 1986, *Informationen for the Press,* p. 2.

28. Statement of Representative Dr. Ehmke (SPD), in *Deutscher Bundestag,* Stenographischer Bericht, 210. Sitzung, April 17, 1986, p. 16056.

29. "Entwurf für einen Leitantrag zur Friedens-und Sicherheitspolitik," submitted by the Präsidium of the SPD, April 7, 1986, p. 4.

30. Horst Ehmke, "Eine Politik zur Selbstbehauptung Europas; Überlegungen angesichts der Entfremdung zwischen Alter und Neuer Welt," in *Europa-Archiv* 7, 1984, pp. 195-204.

31. Gansel (note 25).

32. *International Herald Tribune,* August 7, 1986.

33. For an early analysis cf. E.-O. Czempiel, "Organizing the Euro-American System," in Czempiel and Dankwart A. Rustow, eds., *The Euro-American System— Economic and Political Relations between North America and Western Europe* (Frankfurt: Campus-Verlag, Boulder: Westview Press) 1976, pp. 206-33.

34. See the Documentation in *Europa-Archiv* 40, 22, November 24, 1985, pp. D 622ff.

35. Yves Boyer, "Raketenabwehr im Weltraum: Antwort auf eine moralische Frage oder Reform der Strategie: Eine Beurteilung aus französischer Sicht," in *Europa-Archiv* 40, 15, August 10, 1985, p. 473.

36. Heinz Riesenhuber, "Eureka als Element europäischer Technologiepolitik," in *Europa-Archiv* 41, 7, April 10, 1986, pp. 185ff. Dr. Riesenhuber is minister for research and technology.

37. See the special edition of *Das Parlament,* No. 33-34, August 1986, esp. pp. 1 and 12.

38. Forschungsinstitut der Deutschen Gesellschaft für Auswärtige Politik e.V., *Deutsche Weltraumpolitik an der Jahrhundertschwelle. Analyse und Vorschläge für die Zukunft* (Bonn 1986).

39. For an overview, see Peter Schmidt, "Europeanization of Defense: Prospects of Consensus," in *EIS Journal* No. 6/85, pp. 2ff.

40. Richard Burt, "Why America and Europe Clashed," in the *New York Times,* May 7, 1986, p. 27, and "Europe and the Alliance: Revising the Twin Pillar Concept," in *U.S. Policy Information and Texts* No. 26, February 25, 1986, pp. 1ff.

9

Civilian "Spillovers" from Military R&D Spending: The U.S. Experience Since World War II

Nathan Rosenberg

his chapter will examine R&D expenditures for military purposes in
the United States since the end of World War II. The purpose of this
examination is to provide the basis for an assessment of the benefits
that have flowed from these military R&D expenditures to the private civilian
economy and those that may be anticipated from SDI research.

It is important to recognize certain basic facts at the outset. The first is
that large *peacetime* R&D spending by the federal government for military
purposes was a distinctly novel intrusion into the American political and
economic scene. To be sure, it has been a dominating fact of life for the past
forty years, but it has no precedent in earlier U.S. history. Indeed, if we look at
the federal budget for 1940, the last peacetime year before the military
deluge, it turns out that federal R&D expenditures for the Department of
Agriculture actually exceeded those for the Department of Defense. In that
year, federal R&D expenditures for the Department of Agriculture amounted
to $29.1 million, compared to $26.4 million for the Department of Defense.

Second, the postwar period has witnessed a drastic change in the institu-
tional arrangements through which the federal government has financed R&D
activities of all kinds. In 1940, almost all federal R&D went to the support of
"in-house" research—that is, research that was actually performed within the
federal establishment by government civil servants: the National Bureau of
Standards, U.S. Department of Agriculture, or the Public Health Service, or by
state institutions financed by federal grants, as in the case of the agricultural
experiment stations. In the postwar period, by contrast, although the proportion has varied substantially over time, the vast majority of federal R&D funds,

This chapter originally was prepared for presentation at the Conference on Technical Coopera-
tion and International Competitiveness, April 2-4, 1986, Lucca, Italy. The author wishes to
acknowledge useful discussions with Karl Habermeier, Steve Keehn, David Mowery, and W.
Edward Steinmueller. Harvey Brooks made some especially valuable comments at a later stage.
Preparation of this chapter was supported by the Center for Economic Policy Research at Stanford
University.

about 75 percent in 1984, has been spent on activities performed by a number of different kinds of organizations within the private sector. Thus, while the federal government now plays a far larger overall role in the financial support of R&D activities than it did before World War II, the actual performance of R&D has been predominantly in the hands of private institutions.[1]

Third, it is important to realize just how large these postwar federal expenditures on military R&D have been. Although there have been some drastic swings in the share of defense R&D in the federal R&D budget, such expenditures have dominated the federal R&D budget for the past quarter century, falling below 50 percent of federal R&D obligations only in 1966 and 1979 (see table 9-1). Indeed, in 1960, defense R&D constituted no less than

Table 9-1
Federal Funds for R&D, by Major Budget Function, 1960-1986

Year	Total	Defense	All Other	Defense	All Other
		billion dollars		*percent*	
1960	$8	$6	$1	81	19
1961	9	7	2	77	23
1962	10	7	3	70	30
1963	12	8	5	62	38
1964	14	8	6	55	45
1965	15	7	7	50	50
1966	15	8	8	49	51
1967	17	9	8	52	48
1968	16	8	8	52	48
1969	16	8	7	53	47
1970	15	8	7	52	48
1971	16	8	7	52	48
1972	16	9	8	54	46
1973	17	9	8	54	46
1974	17	9	8	52	48
1975	19	10	9	51	49
1976	21	10	10	50	50
1977	23	12	12	51	49
1978	26	13	13	50	50
1979	28	14	14	49	51
1980	30	15	15	50	50
1981	33	18	15	56	44
1982	36	22	14	61	39
1983	38	25	14	64	36
1984	44	29	15	66	34
1985(Est.)	50	34	16	68	32
1986(Est.)	58	42	16	72	28

Source: *Science Indicators: The 1985 Report*, p. 226.

Note: Detail may not add to totals on account of rounding. Estimates given for 1986 may change significantly as the result of congressional action on agency budget requests. Data for 1960-1977 are shown in obligations; data for 1978-1983 are shown in budget authority.

81 percent of federal R&D funds. It declined sharply from that level (a decline that was offset by the growth in the space program) and hovered around the 50 percent level until the early 1980s, when it rose swiftly again. If expenditures on space-related activities and atomic energy are added to the defense budget, on the ground that they were strongly driven by defense-related justifications, these defense-related categories have totally dominated the federal R&D budget for the past thirty years. If we focus upon federal R&D funds that go specifically to *industrial* firms, it turns out that no less than 97 percent of such federal spending in 1982 came from the Department of Defense, the Department of Energy, and the National Aeronautics and Space Administration (NASA).

To calibrate these recent federal R&D expenditures in dollar terms, total federal R&D expenditures in 1984 amounted to $44 billion. Defense R&D spending, 70 percent of the total, amounted to $29 billion. Thus, any attempt to examine U.S. military R&D expenditures from the point of view of their economic benefits, as opposed to their contribution to national security, must not lose sight of the fact that the expenditures involved have been simply immense. In addition, as we will see, they are overwhelmingly for development. Furthermore, care must be exercised in distinguishing between defense and nondefense R&D expenditures when making international comparisons. Although the U.S. ratio of R&D expenditures to GNP has been higher than those of other member countries of the Organization for Economic Cooperation and Development (OECD) until recently, West Germany and Japan have had substantially higher ratios of *civilian* R&D expenditures to GNP for many years (see table 9-2).

Past Civilian Spillovers

It is not difficult to identify specific civilian technological systems that have realized substantial benefits from military R&D in the past forty years. At one time or another during this period, military and space R&D have made major contributions to commercial jet aircraft (including airframes, jet engines, and avionics), to computers, to semiconductors, to communications satellites, and to nuclear power.

Although it is relatively easy to identify specific technologies where military R&D has generated important civilian benefits, measuring the size of these benefits is far more difficult. This is so for a number of reasons. First is the fundamental measurement asymmetry that is common to all R&D activity. The costs of R&D are, at least at certain levels, reasonably easy to quantify because they are expressed in money terms in the budgets of specific agencies. On the other hand, the "output" of the R&D activity is diffuse and elusive.

Table 9-2
Estimated Nondefense R&D Expenditures as a Percentage of Gross National Product, by Country, 1971-1985[a]

Year	France[b]	West Germany	Japan	United Kingdom	United States
1971	1.46	2.03	1.84	NA	1.68
1972	1.50	2.08	1.84	1.50	1.63
1973	1.38	1.94	1.89	NA	1.62
1974	1.43	1.98	1.96	NA	1.69
1975	1.46	2.08	1.95	1.41	1.68
1976	1.44	2.01	1.94	NA	1.68
1977	1.44	2.01	1.92	NA	1.67
1978	1.41	2.10	1.98	1.51	1.69
1979	1.42	2.27	2.08	NA	1.75
1980	1.43	2.30	2.21	NA	1.86
1981	1.51	2.38	2.37	1.72	1.87
1982(Prel.)	1.63	2.48	2.46	NA	1.94
1983(Est.)	1.69	2.47	2.60	1.61	1.91
1984(Est.)	1.76	NA	NA	NA	1.86
1985(Est.)	NA	NA	NA	NA	1.89

Source: *Science Indicators: The 1985 Report*, p. 190.

Note: The latest data may be preliminary or estimates. The figures for West Germany increased in 1979 in part because of increased coverage of small and medium enterprises not surveyed in 1977. NA = not available.

[a]Gross expenditures for performance of R&D, including associated capital expenditures, except for the United States, where total capital expenditure data are not available. U.S. estimates for the period 1972-1980 show that the inclusion of capital expenditures would have an impact of less than one-tenth of 1 percent of the R&D GNP ratio.

[b]Gross domestic product.

It takes the form of knowledge for which there is no unambiguous measuring rod.

Second, one can only conjecture about the dimensions of the appropriate counterfactual world—in this case, about how the rate and direction of innovative activity would have differed in the *absence* of the military R&D. In most cases, surely, it is implausible to argue that in the absence of military R&D, certain civilian technologies would *never* have been developed. More commonly, the effect of military R&D was that the civilian technologies came on-line sooner than would otherwise have been the case. But how much sooner? And how large were the economic benefits that should be attributed to the faster realization of these technologies?

A further distinction needs to be made. The term "spillover" has recently come to serve as a catchall for economic benefits that originate in one sector (usually the military) and are transferred to another (usually the civilian). In fact, however, these benefits can take a number of different forms.

The jet engine was a specific piece of hardware which had its origins in military R&D during and after World War II. Eventually, after it had attained certain levels of reliability and maturity, it was transferred, with design modifications, to the civilian aircraft industry.

But spillovers may take a number of forms different from embodiment in specific pieces of hardware. To the extent that the military expenditures support basic research, the findings of such research are not yet incorporated in specific products of any kind. The high degree of uncertainty normally attached to basic research means that it is very difficult to predict the specific relevance of such knowledge for either the military or civilian sector. Thus, the potential civilian benefits of basic research are in a form very different from specific final products such as jet engines, computers, or communications satellites. In fact, in the case of truly basic research there is presumably no way of establishing, *from the research itself*, whether the sponsoring agency is military or civilian.

There are other, somewhat more subtle ways in which military R&D programs may generate benefits for the civilian sector. The common denominator is that the existence of military R&D programs may, at least in certain respects, reduce the cost or improve the capability for performing R&D in the civilian sector. For instance, if there are significant economies of scale at specific stages of the R&D process, military programs may generate cost reductions at such stages for civilian R&D. Large wind tunnels that are essential in generating design data for military aircraft are also used in determining optimal design for commercial aircraft. The same argument may hold for the use of supercomputers. Very expensive equipment for testing the performance of jet-engine prototypes for the military may also be used for testing new civilian jet engines. (The recent decision of the Japanese to enter into a joint project with Rolls Royce for the development of a new jet engine was motivated, at least in part, by the fact that Rolls Royce possesses highly expensive equipment for testing jet engines not available in Japan.)

The instances just cited, each of which has been important in the postwar period, represent cost reductions in R&D. They are quite separate from the possibility for sharing the use of manufacturing facilities for the actual production of a final product. Nevertheless, it is necessary to recognize that in the case of firms that produce goods for both the military and the civilian sectors, and also perform R&D, there may be benefits of more than one kind flowing to civilian production from military contracts.

As a closely related matter, the enormous amount of testing and evaluation, to which new weapons development eventually gives rise, provides another spinoff that may be of great significance. Such testing and evaluation has created a large market for laboratory instrumentation, much of it highly sophisticated. Thus, military R&D and procurement may have played a major role in introducing such instrumentation into production and industrial control for civilian markets, and into civilian R&D activities, much earlier than would have occurred in the absence of weapons development programs. Unfortunately, not much is known about scale economies and learning curves in the production of scientific instruments, but they may well be very large. Thus, it is possible that the military sector in effect subsidizes the development and production of scientific instrumentation to the larger economy—indeed to the world economy, since spinoffs of this kind are, in most cases, readily available to foreign purchasers.

An even less tangible but possibly very significant benefit flowing from military R&D is that the performance of R&D may be, itself, subject to certain important learning experiences. Indeed, there is no doubt that this is so. The difficult question, again, is how to measure their magnitude. R&D comprises a range of very different kinds of activities, but they all share the characteristic that skills are acquired in a cumulative way through experience in these activities themselves, as opposed to the learning of well-codified material in formal classroom situations. Military expenditures thus result in building up the capability of private industry for the performance of R&D through contracts that result in the more rapid movement downward along certain learning curves—in this case, learning how to perform successful R&D.

A Disaggregated View of Military R&D

In order to assess the civilian impact of military R&D, it is essential to disaggregate the overall numbers. As soon as this is done, some central facts become apparent. The most important is that defense R&D is strongly development oriented. Whereas federal nondefense R&D breaks down fairly evenly among the three components of basic research, applied research, and development, defense R&D consists overwhelmingly of Development expenditures. This is apparent in the figures for 1982, shown in table 9-3.

Table 9-3
1982 Federal R&D Expenditures
(% share)

	Defense[a]	Nondefense
Basic research	3.2	33.7
Applied research	11.0	35.3
Development	85.8	31.0
Total	100.0	100.0

Source: Congressional Budget Office, *Federal Support for R&D and Innovation*, April 1984, p. 53.

[a]Defense includes, in addition to expenditures of the Department of Defense, expenditures on military programs in the Department of Energy.

The largest items in the Department of Defense R&D budget, by far, involve the development of advanced weapons systems, the construction and testing of weapons prototypes, and so on. The costs of these activities are, unfortunately, gigantic. The other side of the coin is the small share of the Department of Defense's budget that goes to basic and applied research. Those shares are, by far, the smallest of any major government agency.

A further aspect closely related to this emphasis on Development is that defense R&D exhibits a high degree of industrial concentration. In fact, the concentration is in just two industry sectors. In 1981, more than half of federal funding for R&D went to aircraft and missiles (one sector), and almost a quarter went to electrical machinery. Thus, over 75 percent of total federal R&D went to these two industry sectors. Nonelectrical machines was a distant third, and motor vehicles and other transportation equipment were fourth (see table 9-4).

The aircraft and missiles sector not only absorbs a large fraction of the federal R&D budget; it is also the only major industry sector that provides substantially less than half of its R&D funding from internal sources (27 percent in 1981, up from 21 percent in 1971). In the case of electrical equipment, by contrast, although the federal contribution has been extremely large in dollar terms, it has represented a much smaller fraction of total R&D spending in the industry. In 1981, private funding accounted for 62 percent of industry R&D, and this represented a sizable increase over 1971, when that ratio was only 49 percent.

Thus, while military expenditures have indeed resulted in building up the R&D capability of private industry, the effects have been felt primarily in the design, testing, and manufacture of military hardware. This R&D spending has had certain distinct characteristics. It has been allocated overwhelmingly to development;[2] it has been directed toward categories of products for which the federal government was also, simultaneously, conducting large-scale procurement programs; and it has been marked by an extremely high degree of industrial concentration. Indeed, it is apparent that a large fraction of civilian spillovers, in the past, have been concentrated in civil aviation, computers, and telecommunications. More difficult questions, however, relate to secondary transmittals to other industries that are harder to trace. Much of the "output" of military R&D has been incorporated in improved products and processes that have been widely diffused throughout the economy. Military (and space) programs have played a major role in the development of new and improved materials with highly desirable performance characteristics (for example, light weight, high strength, durability, electrical conductivity, and so on). Capturing the full civilian benefits would thus involve an extensive tracing out of many small improvements in numerous sectors of the economy.

An even more difficult issue than tracing out the interindustry flow of technological improvements is establishing the precise content of the learning process in those sectors where military R&D is highly concentrated. There

Table 9-4
Company and Federal Funding of Industrial R&D for Selected Industries, 1971-1981

Industry	Total		Federal		Company[a]	
	1971	1981	1971	1981	1971	1981
	millions of current dollars					
Total	$18,320	$51,830	$7,666	$16,468	$10,654	$35,362
Chemicals and allied products	1,832	5,525	184	383	1,648	4,942
Industrial chemicals	1,009	2,553	159	367	850	2,186
Drugs and medicines and other chemicals	823	2,770[b]	25	20[b]	798	2,756
Petroleum refining and extraction	505	1,920[b]	17	140[b]	488	1,777
Rubber products	289	800[b]	69	190[b]	221	616
Primary metals	272	889	6	182	266	707
Ferrous metals and products	144	560[b]	2	140[b]	142	414
Nonferrous metals and products	128	330[b]	4	40[b]	124	293
Fabricated metal products	242	638	11	80	230	558
Nonelectrical machinery	1,860	6,800	315	739	1,545	6,061
Electrical machinery	4,389	10,466	2,258	3,962	2,131	6,502
Communication equipment and electronic components	2,731	6,396	1,479	2,167	1,252	4,228
Motor vehicles and other transportation equipment	1,768	5,089[b]	309	704[b]	1,461	4,381
Aircraft and missiles	4,881	11,702	3,864	8,501	1,017	3,201
Professional and scientific instruments	746	3,685	164	638	583	3,047
Scientific and mechanical measuring instruments	133	1,680[b]	14	400[b]	120	1,285
Optical, surgical, photographic, and other instruments	612	2,000[b]	150	240[b]	463	1,762
All other manufacturing industries	2,889	8,325[b]	395	963[b]	2,494	7,368
Nonmanufacturing industries	704	2,080[b]	452	880[b]	252	1,199

millions of constant 1972 dollars[c]

Total	$19,081	$26,511	$7,984	$8,423	$11,097	$18,087
Chemicals and allied products	1,908	2,724	192	196	1,716	2,528
Industrial chemicals	1,051	1,306	166	188	885	1,118
Drugs and medicines and other chemicals	857	1,410[b]	26	10[b]	831	1,410
Petroleum refining and extraction	526	980[b]	18	70[b]	508	909
Rubber products	301	410[b]	72	97[b]	230	315
Primary metals	283	455	6	93	277	362
Ferrous metals and products	150	290[b]	2	70[b]	148	212
Nonferrous metals and products	133	170[b]	4	20[b]	129	150
Fabricated metal products	252	326	11	41	240	285
Nonelectrical machinery	1,937	3,478	328	378	1,609	3,100
Electrical equipment	4,571	5,353	2,352	2,026	2,220	3,326
Communication equipment and electronic components	2,844	3,272	1,540	1,108	1,304	2,163
Motor vehicles and other transportation equipment	1,841	2,602[b]	322	360[b]	1,522	2,241
Aircraft and missiles	5,084	5,985	4,025	4,348	1,059	1,637
Professional and scientific instruments	777	1,885	171	326	607	1,558
Scientific and mechanical measuring instruments	139	860[b]	15	210[b]	125	657
Optical, surgical, photographic, and other instruments	637	1,020[b]	156	120[b]	482	901
All other manufacturing industries	3,009	4,260[b]	411	490[b]	2,598	3,769
Nonmanufacturing industries	733	1,060[b]	471	450[b]	262	613

Source: National Science Foundation, *Research and Development in Industry*, 1980 (NSF 82-317), pp. 11, 14, and 17, and National Science Foundation, preliminary data.

a Includes all sources other than the federal government.

b Estimated.

c GNP implicit price deflators used to convert current dollars to constant 1972 dollars.

is much evidence that what is "learned" by product designers and technical specialists in these sectors is an indifference to cost considerations in the pursuit of performance improvements in advanced weapons systems. Military (and space) programs have notoriously subordinated cost considerations in the attempt to tease out further improvements in performance—often incurring very high costs for very small or very dubious improvements, and even more often for improvements of a kind that have no conceivable relevance to civilian markets. Large-scale and well-financed military R&D programs may also have encouraged the "learning" of expensive and ultimately inefficient habits—for example, a predisposition to substitute large-scale experimentation and computation for rigorous thought. Such learning spillovers are in fact highly dysfunctional in nature and may systematically incapacitate skilled personnel for work in competitive consumer markets, where close attention to cost considerations is likely to be a matter of commercial life or death.

One needs to make a distinction here between cost considerations in the *performance* of R&D and the cost considerations that are incorporated in the *design* of the finished product—or "gold plating," as it is sometimes called. The purely economic impact of the gold plating of military hardware may be very large. But, in addition, the entire defense procurement system fails to provide incentives for R&D in the manufacturing *process* technology. Military suppliers have learned over the years that contracts are won on the basis of product performance (or hoped-for product performance), not on the basis of improved technologies that will make it possible to manufacture the product as a lower unit cost. Thus, the implicit ground rules in military procurement create a strong bias for contractors to search for product improvement and to neglect possibilities for cost reduction.[3]

Assessing the independent impact of military R&D spending is further complicated by a factor to which we have already referred: the role of federal procurement policies. Most military R&D has been directed at the development of products that were designed for eventual purchase by the military itself. Indeed, the allocation of military R&D expenditures may be taken as an excellent guide to military procurement intentions.

This point is fundamental to the evaluation of the American experience with respect to military R&D in the past forty years. The vast benefits that are sometimes perceived as flowing from military R&D are, in fact, the product of military R&D *plus* military procurement, often on a massive scale. The willingness of private industry to commit substantial resources to technological change in a particular sector has been dominated by the intense awareness of the possibility of large potential markets for military products of superior design and performance capability. Without the huge pull of defense procurement in such sectors as jet aircraft, integrated circuitry, and computers—especially in the critical early years of products development—the impact of military R&D spending by itself would have been far smaller.

The critical role of the procurement factor and the much more modest role of military R&D expenditures are strikingly apparent in the history of semiconductors. It is clear that the military services were always intensely aware of the potential military applications of semiconductors and followed such developments closely. Yet "followed" is the proper operative word. The major breakthroughs in semiconductors were achieved in the private sector with private funds, and not, in the most important instances, with military R&D support. Yet the people working in semiconductors were suffused with an awareness that military electronic equipment was plagued by complex circuitry, extensive reliance upon vacuum tubes, and serious operating difficulties connected with equipment unreliability. Thus, there was the continual lure, and the eventual reality, of vast procurement contracts.

The invention of the transistor at Bell Laboratories was achieved without government financial support but with an awareness of the large potential market within the telephone industry for a solid-state substitute for vacuum tubes. Although, with the discoveries of 1947-1948, Bell was well aware of a large military interest, its more immediate concern was to prevent that interest from translating into restrictions that would limit the civilian diffusion of the new technology. According to one authority, "There was substantial concern in early 1948 that disclosure of the transistor to the military prior to public announcement might lead to restriction of its use or its classification for national defense purposes. Thus, Bell did not disclose the invention to the military until one week prior to public announcement."[4]

During the 1950s, the military did indeed support a number of semiconductor R&D projects. As it happened, these projects, such as Tinkertoy and Micromodule, were not successful, and, in fact, none of the major technological breakthroughs of that period were directly supported by the military. Nevertheless, some of the most important breakthroughs, such as the silicon transistor and the integrated circuit, were undertaken with the needs of the military foremost in the minds of the successful inventors.[5]

The large procurement needs of the military and NASA, and the increasing concern with the importance of miniaturization, were vital in the early years of new product development in electronics. The Signal Corps was the largest military purchaser of semiconductors in the early- and mid-1950s. A major expansion in demand occurred in 1958 with the announcement by the U.S. Air Force of its intention to employ semiconductors in the guidance system of the Minuteman Missile. In 1962, NASA made public its intention to introduce integrated circuits into the guidance computer of the Apollo spacecraft. Soon after, the air force announced that the guidance system of the improved Minuteman intercontinental ballistic missile (ICBM) would make extensive use of integrated circuits.

From the mid-1950s to the late 1960s, purchases by the federal government (overwhelmingly the military and NASA) accounted for a very large, although declining share, of the output of semiconductor devices (see table 9-5). In the first year of integrated circuit production, the federal government purchased the entire $4 million of output (table 9-6). It remained the largest buyer for the first five years, although the government share declined rapidly. By the end of the 1960s, the rapidly growing computer industry displaced the military as the largest end-user market for integrated circuits.

Several conclusions can be drawn from the semiconductor experience in America:

1. The major innovations were not achieved on projects supported by military R&D.

2. Military R&D expenditures on possible alternative routes to miniaturization were largely spent "betting on the wrong horses."

Table 9-5
Government Purchases of Semiconductor Devices, 1955-1977

Year	Total Semiconductor Shipments (millions of dollars)	Shipments to Federal Government[a] (millions of dollars)	Government Share of Total Shipments (percent)
1955	40	15	38
1956	90	32	36
1957	151	54	36
1958	210	81	39
1959	396	180	45
1960	542	258	48
1961	565	222	39
1962	575	223	39
1963	610	211	35
1964	676	192	28
1965	884	247	28
1966	1123	298	27
1967	1107	303	27
1968	1159	294	25
1969	1457	247	17
1970	1337	275	21
1971	1519	193	13
1972	1912	228	12
1973	3458	201	6
1974	3916	344	9
1975	3001	239	8
1976	4968	480	10
1977	4583	536	12

Source: Richard C. Levin, "The Semiconductor Industry," in Richard R. Nelson, ed., *Government and Technical Progress* (New York: Pergamon Press, 1982), p. 60.

[a]Includes devices produced for Department of Defense, Atomic Energy Commission, Central Intelligence Agency, Federal Aviation Agency, and National Aeronautics and Space Administration equipment.

Table 9-6
Government Purchases of Integrated Circuits, 1962-1968

Year	Total Integrated Circuit Shipments (millions of dollars)	Shipments to Federal Government[a] (millions of dollars)	Government Share of Total Shipments (percent)
1962	4[b]	4[b]	100[b]
1963	16	15[b]	94[b]
1964	41	35[b]	85[b]
1965	79	57	72
1966	148	78	53
1967	228	98	43
1968	312	115	37

Source: Richard C. Levin, "The Semiconductor Industry," in Richard R. Nelson, ed., *Government and Technical Progress* (New York: Pergamon Press, 1982), p. 63.

[a]Includes circuits produced for Department of Defense, Atomic Energy Commission, Central Intelligence Agency, Federal Aviation Agency, and National Aeronautics and Space Administration.

[b]Estimated by Tilton (1971).

3. The procurement needs of the military provided a pervasive and well-understood presence that served as a powerful inducement to innovative activity on the part of private firms spending their own R&D money. Indeed, one may speculate that profits and overhead from military procurement contracts served as sources of financial support for company-funded R&D, which may, in turn, have generated more civilian spillover than R&D that was directly funded by the military.

Are Spillovers Increasing or Decreasing?

There is another aspect of the spillover issue that needs to be made explicit, because it is of central importance to the determination of policy. Granted that spillovers have, at certain times and in certain industries, been a significant economic phenomenon, are they as large today as they were twenty or thirty years ago, and are spillovers from the military to the civilian sector likely to be rising or falling in the years ahead?

There is in fact a perception that civilian benefits of military (and space) R&D expenditures in the 1980s are a great deal lower than was the case in the 1950s and 1960s, because military R&D has become concerned with an increasingly arcane and exotic set of needs of modern weapons systems. The needs of such systems involve qualities and performance characteristics that have no obvious extensive counterparts in civilian products. While the problems of measurement are substantial, some such transition does appear to have occurred with respect to the commercial aircraft industry, the industry that was probably the largest single beneficiary of military R&D in the postwar years.

Table 9-7 shows sources of aeronautical funding between 1945 and 1969. The dominance of the military is clear. The most rapid period of growth was in the years 1950-1954, reflecting the huge infusion of military funds during the Korean War. R&D expenditures rose from less than $600 million in 1950 to more than $2 billion in 1954. Seventy-eight percent of this increase was accounted for by increases in military-supported R&D. Throughout the entire period, even in the late 1960s, the defense portion of total R&D expenditures never fell below 65 percent. "Nonreimbursed expenditure," private industry's own direct contribution, never accounted for more than 25 percent of total R&D spending, and was less than 20 percent of the total for most of the 1945-1969 period.

The civilian benefits flowing from these military R&D expenditures were very large and had much to do with U.S. dominance of the commercial aircraft industry. The development of the first jet engine itself, going back into the years of World War II, was entirely financed by military expenditures. Further improvement in the power plant continued to be heavily financed by the military into the 1960s, reflecting the need for large military transports as well as for fighter planes capable of performing at very high supersonic speeds. Military spillovers probably culminated with the competition over the C-5A transport. It was out of that competition, when the air force in 1964 asked for engines with two or three times the thrust of existing power plants, that high-bypass ratio engines, which now power the wide-bodied commercial transports, were first developed. Fifty-five percent of the R&D costs for these turbofan engines were provided by the Department of Defense, while the Federal Aviation Administration (FAA) and NASA accounted for about 13 percent. Industry's expenditures were 32 percent of the total.

In addition to jet-engine spillovers, commercial jet aircraft also benefited substantially from military support of airframe development and production for purely military purposes. With the advent of jet aircraft, airframe makers were increasingly able to apply knowledge gained in military projects to commercial-aircraft design, tooling, and production. In some cases, similarities in airframe design were sufficiently great that development and tooling costs for commercial airframes were substantially reduced. One early jet prototype, the Boeing 367-80, gave birth to two major jet aircraft, one civilian and one military. One, the Boeing 707, America's first commercial jet, was the workhorse of the airline industry for an entire generation. The other, the KC-135, was a jet tanker that provided in-flight refueling for two strategic bombers, the B-47 and the B-52, that Boeing also sold to the air force. Thus, large development costs were successfully amortized over two separate aircraft.

Table 9-7
Sources of Aeronautical R&D Funds: Annual Expenditures in Millions of Dollars

	Defense					Federal Nondefense				Private Industry	
Fiscal Year	Air Force	Navy	Army	ARPA	Industry Reimbursed	NASA	FAA	SST (FAA)	AEC	Non-reimbursed	Total
1945	170	124			17	30	1			23	365
1946	188	209			21	37	1			28	484
1947	182	139			28	30	1			37	417
1948	141	186			35	42	2			48	434
1949	198	160	2		54	53	2			70	539
1950	245	112	4		80	52	8			91	592
1951	308	179	14		176	62	4		7	164	914
1952	558	217	21		295	113	3		11	277	1495
1953	878	241	29		366	76	3		21	339	1953
1954	996	265	36		363	55	1		24	343	2085
1955	941	249	40		343	47	1		27	320	1968
1956	958	243	50		353	51	1		49	353	2063
1957	1037	248	57		381	50	1		79	392	2243
1958	1135	266	74		360	45	15		73	356	2325
1959	1082	268	68		319	48	28		76	339	2228
1960	896	274	49		290	32	48		69	329	1987
1961	979	247	72		293	39	45		69	306	2050
1962	1011	214	88		301	44	53	11		304	2026
1963	1333	261	104		293	66	59	19		234	2419
1964	1290	250	101		298	84	38	18		304	2383
1965	1231	244	76	9	304	102	30	21		353	2370
1966	1268	257	98	23	367	110	31	112		445	2711
1967	1058	303	104	14	452	134	35	190		565	2855
1968	1138	243	131	11	481	171	35	63		673	2946
1969	779	461	134	2	457	216	36	94		609	2806

Source: David C. Mowery and Nathan Rosenberg, "The Commercial Aircraft Industry," in Richard R. Nelson, ed., *Government and Technical Progress* (New York: Pergamon Press, 1982), p. 134.

It is obvious that the spillover effects will be greatest when military and commercial design requirements closely resemble one another. As military aircraft moved into the world of supersonic speeds, however, they began to assume performance and associated cost charcteristics that were increasingly inappropriate for the cost-conscious world of commercial travel. The federal Supersonic Transport (SST) program represented an attempt to develop a supersonic transport. The program was motivated by the perceived threat to U.S. dominance of commercial aircraft sales embodied in the British-French Concorde. It was also intended to exploit the putative technological spillovers from the B-70 strategic bomber prototypes. Performance requirements were stipulated by the FAA, which paid scant attention to such considerations as seat-mile operating costs, ordinarily a central preoccupation with airlines when they dominated the design process. In the event, the original Boeing prototype design proved not to be feasible, and cost estimates escalated dramatically. At the same time, the project encountered growing opposition from environmental groups. Congress finally terminated the program in 1971.

Both the SST and Concorde experiences represented attempts to exploit military spillovers, in the form of improved technical performance capabilities, in commercial aircraft. Doing so, however, involved the suppression of normal commercial judgments and considerations. The American SST was never built, and only sixteen Concordes were constructed, after an extraordinary development effort costing several billions of dollars. The indiscriminate pursuit of military spillovers thus turned out to be a recipe for commercial disaster when optimal design requirements of the military and civilian sectors were sharply divergent.

The spillover from military to civilian aircraft has certainly declined over the past fifteen years, for the simple but compelling reason that there have been no substantial procurement programs for large military transports, and the technological requirements for fighter aircraft are drastically different from the needs of civilian aircraft. Indeed, the most conspicuous spillover in recent years has flowed from the civilian sector to the military. The largest purchase of military tankers is currently for the KC-10, a direct derivative of McDonnell-Douglas's wide-bodied commercial jet, the DC-10.

In retrospect, it seems plausible to argue that the whole thrust into supersonic technology, and not just its embodiment in specific designs, has resulted in very little civilian payoff. In fact, the shift by the military to supersonic performance may have diverted attention away from potential generic advances in subsonic aerodynamics—in such essential problem areas as boundary layer control, fuel efficiency, and the reduction of noise and pollution.

At the very least, it seems safe to assert that other important sectors may be found where the needs of the military and civilian sectors are sharply divergent and where the prospects for civilian spillover are correspondingly declining. In communications satellites, where spillovers from the military and NASA were once very significant, military priorities are now pushing in directions more remote from civilian needs. Thus, the civilian sector attaches a high priority to satellites placed in geosynchronous orbit. It needs satellites of a very complex and multipurpose nature to deal with a diverse range of civilian demands for voice, visual, and data transmission purposes. It requires satellites with lots of built-in power in order to redirect strong signals back to earth. The military, on the other hand, attaches great importance to covertness and therefore has very different requirements. The armed services want to develop random-orbit rather than geosynchronous satellites. They strongly prefer placing most of the equipment on the ground rather than in orbit. They want a technology that can detect weak signals of a kind that cannot readily be picked up by "the other side"—as when communicating with a far-flung submarine fleet. Currently, moreover, in remote sensing, military and civilian performance requirements have also been increasingly divergent. Military requirements have pushed in the direction of improvements in resolution beyond what has been commercially justifiable for most civilian applications. In addition, some of these remote-sensing technologies have been classified because of national security considerations.

The growing divergence between military and civilian needs is also apparent in the integrated circuit industry. The appropriation of sizable funding for the Very High Speed Integrated Circuits (VHSIC) program was partially justified on the ground that it would generate large commercial spillovers and thereby strengthen the U.S. position in an increasingly competitive industry. In fact, the program reinforces the perception that the two sectors confront increasingly divergent needs. The unique performance requirements of the military, whose products must perform reliably in highly hostile environments, has led to many costly design tradeoffs that are of little use or relevance to manufacturers of civilian products. As one observer has noted:

> Consumers have no expectation that their product will continue to work in temperatures over two hundred degrees Fahrenheit while being bathed in ionizing radiation. Military systems must continue operating in such environments. This has always caused military specifications to be higher and the resulting cost of production of military specifications components to exceed those of civilian components.[6]

Furthermore, the high priority attached by the military to rapid development and use of new components has led to design characteristics that are suboptimal in civilian markets; and the highly specialized nature of military components has led to the development of manufacturing processes for custom-designed (or semi-custom-designed) products of limited relevance to civilian semiconductor markets, which require manufacturing technologies emphasizing low-cost and high-volume production. The continuing military preoccupation with speed of performance, rather than cost reduction, and the increasingly exotic nature of electronic warfare in the future, strongly suggest increasing divergence between military and civilian semiconductor requirements in the years ahead. Programs such as VHSIC are most unlikely to serve as a panacea for the competitive difficulties of the U.S. semiconductor industry—which are located primarily in the area of manufacturing, not product design. As far as the flow of spillovers is concerned, it is likely that spillovers from the civilian to the military have, for some years now, exceeded the flow from the military to the civilian.

A wholly separate category of concerns deals with governmental controls, for reasons of national security, upon such spillovers as might otherwise find their way from the military to the civilian sphere. U.S.-government export restrictions in "dual use" technologies would seem to render additionally problematic, at the very least, the exploitation of civilian derivatives of military VHSIC technologies.[7]

The Strategic Defense Initiative

Many of the points raised so far apply directly to the evaluation of the civilian usefulness of the activities currently being carried out under the Strategic Defense Initiative.

SDI is important because it is expected to absorb a large fraction (over 30 percent) of new military research in the coming years, and because it will in all likelihood constitute a fairly large portion (over 10 percent) of the military R&D budget, and perhaps 5 percent of total R&D expenditures for the country as a whole (that is, federal and private R&D expenditures).

SDI at present is a fairly small program. Moreover, many of the details of the R&D projects that are being, or that will be, conducted under its auspices are either still cloaked in secrecy or even, as yet, of indefinite content. Thus, any attempt to assess the impact it will have on future technological developments necessarily contains a large speculative element.

In assessing the future civilian usefulness of SDI, a few basic points should be kept in mind. Clearly, expenditure on SDI is motivated primarily by military and strategic considerations. Its civilian benefits should be regarded as welcome, but incidental, side effects. However, for purposes of this discussion, one could pretend that SDI is mainly a federal R&D support program such as those administered by the National Science Foundation (NSF). One can then evaluate its usefulness to the civilian economy in the same way as one would evaluate any other program. One point emerges with great force when the problem is viewed from this perspective. SDI represents a highly inefficient way of organizing support for the civilian economy. It should be remembered that the economic justification for civilian R&D support programs is the need to overcome market failures, especially those which cause underinvestment in R&D—low appropriability and capital market imperfections are the two most important.

Much of the R&D under SDI is shrouded in secrecy. In this respect, it differs fundamentally from civilian R&D support programs. This secrecy will inevitably delay the wide diffusion throughout the economy of any new technologies that may be developed. For political reasons, it is likely that SDI will remain a bargaining chip in arms negotiations with the USSR for a long time to come. The need for secrecy is clearly far greater in the case of SDI than it was, for instance, in the case of jet transport or the Apollo program. The need for secrecy could therefore drastically reduce the civilian benefits that might otherwise be expected to flow from such a program.

More generally, consider the case of some universally useful basic research done under the auspices of SDI. If the results were kept completely secret, there would be wasteful duplication of this research by civilian investigators, both in the United States and abroad. If the results were released immediately, there might be high civilian benefits, but there would also be a conflict with security considerations. Finally, with respect to the portion of the research that might be undertaken by the civilian sector in the absence of the SDI program, one could conceive of the release of similar research findings by SDI at a similar pace. Under these circumstances, SDI research would, in effect, amount to a substitution of public research for private research, but probably at a higher cost as a result of the pressure for greater speed that is usually inherent in military programs.

While the goal of secrecy reduces the usefulness of SDI as a program of civilian R&D support, the substantial divergence between the needs of the civilian economy and the military goal of strategic defense provides a formidable array of concerns which casts further doubt on the efficacy of SDI as a program that will contribute to increasing the technological abilities of the civilian economy. This is a topic that has already been introduced in the previous section of this chapter.

Of course, useful serendipitous findings are always possible in any search or exploration process. But such possibilities in no way constitute an *economic* argument for research of the kind that will be supported by SDI. The case for serendipity is greatest at the basic research end of the spectrum, where eventual civilian usefulness is already established with near certainty. However, the great bulk of SDI expenditures appears to fall into neither of these categories. There is a basic research component, but it appears to be very small. The vast bulk of the funds appears to be devoted to downstream military hardware applications, as well as to achieving a high degree of survivability of that hardware under extreme circumstances.

It is difficult to evaluate the SDI program in precise financial terms, since its budget has been subjected to frequent revision within Congress as well as between Congress and the executive branch. For FY 1987 the Department of

Defense submitted an initial budget request of almost $5 billion; about $3.2 billion was appropriated.

In FY 1985 the SDI budget was $1.4 billion, broken down into six categories, as shown in table 9-8. It is not possible to classify expenditures neatly under each of these categories into their basic research, applied research, and development components. Furthermore, within each category, different facets of such technologies as lasers, cryogenics, and semiconductors are being simultaneously explored, with a variety of anticipated military applications. One may, however, make a number of specific observations.

A large share of the budget has been directed to the development of essentially conventional technology, namely, ground-based ballistic missile defense (BMD). This is a rather straightforward weapons development project, incorporating what is essentially off-the-shelf technology. No substantial breakthroughs are necessary, and most of the funds have been devoted to development, test, and evaluation (DT&E).

Another large sum is being spent on hypervelocity electromagnetic railguns. These are large devices that accelerate larger particles of matter in much the same way as a linear accelerator speeds up small particles. Conceptually and technologically, these are devices with little or no apparent applicability to civilian purposes. The sometimes-stated proposition that this technology will perhaps find an application to ground transportation is, to put it mildly, farfetched. It is highly unlikely at this time that even massive research would provide a useful civilian transport system at anything like a competitive cost.

Clearly, as these two major examples suggest, a good part of the SDI budget is being allocated to developing and testing technological systems with no immediate civilian usefulness.

Table 9-8
SDI Appropriations, FY 1985
(millions)

Sensors	$546
Directed energy	376
Kinetic energy	256
System analysis and battle management	99
Survivability, lethality, space power, and logistics	112
Management	11
Total	1,400

Source: Senate Hearings, *Department of Defense Appropriations, Fiscal Year 1986*, S. Hrg. 99-217, Pt. 2 (Washington, D.C.: G.P.O., 1986), p. 77. This volume also contains testimony that provides much valuable information about the SDI program. Another valuable source is Council on Economic Priorities (CEP), *The Strategic Defense Initiative: Costs, Contractors & Consequences* (New York: CEP, 1985).

The largest portion of SDI resources is being allocated to Surveillance, Acquisition, Tracking, and Kill Assessment (sensors). While it is, of course, possible to learn many useful things from research on sensor technology—for example, on such important subjects as cryogenics and optics—it is likely that it will prove necessary to devote the major portion of this budget to making these surveillance systems more survivable, since they will necessarily be based in earth orbit. In other words, greater efforts will have to be devoted to discovering methods for ensuring that these systems continue to function while under attack rather than to developing the kind of sophisticated sensors that modern industrial robots are likely to require.[8]

Another area in which there will be a substantial divergence between the military products and those which could be useful in the civilian economy are the directed-energy weapons (DEW). Although other forms of x-ray lasers may have civil applications, the space-based x-ray laser powered by a nuclear explosion has no conceivable use on earth. Aside from this, what the DEW laser/ particle beam research will be focused upon is the ability to make such devices very powerful. Whether this will quickly and automatically lead to devices that have the right combination of other, economically desirable, properties—such as small size, high energy efficiency, ease of use, and low acquisition and maintenance costs—may be seriously questioned. Most of the SDI laser/particle beam funds will ultimately be spent on developing and testing huge and more powerful devices, not on developing technologies of potential use to industry.

Finally, the area that may have the most promise for civilian application is the one that is receiving the smallest amount of funding at this point: Systems Analysis and Battle Management (SABM). This area poses some impressive conceptual and practical difficulties. The methods developed here—including new types of artificial intelligence software and hardware for real-time processing, and the advances that can be made in the theory and practice of controlling large systems—will have many important implications for manufacturing technologies (and perhaps for corporate and economic planning). However, this area is already recognized as being of such paramount economic significance that the $100 million provided by SDI does not represent an enormous increase over what private corporations such as General Motors or Fujitsu are already investing in this field.

In sum, secrecy and the large fraction of SDI funds that will be spent on DT&E of esoteric military devices make SDI distinctly inefficient and unpromising as a support program for civilian R&D. In the initial stages, useful spillovers may be expected to come mainly from the research component of the budget. While reliable figures are not available, it is probably safe to say that not too much of SDI qualifies as basic research or even applied research. It is probably also safe to say that as the program progresses, the research component will decline as more attention is devoted to the elaborate testing of advanced weapons systems.

Conclusions

Delivering a balanced judgment on the civilian benefits of large military R&D programs in the U.S. economy is an extremely difficult exercise. Much of this chapter has been devoted to suggesting that the benefits, while real, have been of uncertain magnitude and have been heavily concentrated in a few sectors directly related to weapons development; that these benefits, moreover, may have been generated far more by government-procurement policies than by R&D expenditures themselves, and that the latter without the former would have provided very small benefits; and that, at least in some of the most important cases, such as aircraft and semiconductors, these benefits may now be much lower than they were twenty or thirty years ago.

In order to maintain some perspective on these issues, it is essential to remind ourselves that these benefits, whatever their size, have been purchased at an immense cost—$32 billion in 1984 alone. It ought to be axiomatic that such costs should be incurred in the pursuit of national security and that they require justification in security terms. To be sure, we may still ask the question, Granted that these expenditures were undertaken out of security considerations, what economic benefits did they nevertheless generate? But then the issue is not just whether the economic benefits were large. In absolute terms, they were certainly large. But if one is examining military R&D in terms of civilian economic benefits, the question is whether they were large relative to the huge magnitude of resources committed to military R&D. In other words, what was the rate of return on these resources, and how might that rate of return compare to alternative economic uses to which they might otherwise have been devoted? The postwar experience of the Japanese economy suggests that it is not beyond the ingenuity of advanced capitalist societies to discover alternative ways of organizing their technological capabilities which yield far higher rates of return than military R&D.[9] Furthermore, I suspect it is no coincidence that throughout most of the postwar years, a substantially higher percentage of total R&D expenditures in Japan has been financed by private industry than has been the case in the United States.[10]

There is a final, and related, issue that needs to be made explicit. The costs to the economy may be expressed in terms of dollars expended on military R&D. But there are other aspects to that cost that need to be identified even if, as in so many other cases, quantification is difficult. The huge demand for engineering and scientific personnel in aerospace and telecommunications has raised the cost of performing R&D in other sectors. Other sectors of the economy, more strongly oriented toward consumer markets, have found themselves competing with the "deep pockets" of the military for skilled manpower, and confronting higher costs for attracting such manpower. In this respect, large military R&D programs must have brought about a substantial increase in costs and a reduction in the amount of resources committed to nonmilitary purposes.

This distorting effect has also extended back into the higher educational system, where federal funds (Department of Defense and NASA) have constituted a large fraction of all research support in engineering. Such support has rendered more attractive those disciplines oriented toward other civilian sectors, which have not been so closely linked with industries enjoying military largesse.

Such distortion of incentives in education and in the allocation of highly qualified manpower may have had a significant effect in slowing the rate of productivity growth and in contributing to declining international competitiveness, which has plagued the U.S. economy in recent years. The possibility needs to be seriously entertained that large-scale military R&D programs do not offer a solution to these intractable economic problems; rather, they may have constituted a serious part of the problem itself.

Notes

1. Of course, one result of the widened range of methods of federal subsidization is that it is not as easy as it once was to draw a sharp boundary line between "public" and "private." How, for example, should a "government-owned, contractor-operated" research center be classified?

2. Even though, as we saw earlier, only 3.2 percent of federal defense R&D in 1982 was for basic research, that was 3.2 percent of a very large number, and basic research supported by military agencies has been a significant component of federally supported basic research. The Office of Naval Research has been a supporter of basic research for forty years, and the Defense Advanced Research Projects Agency (DARPA) has played a crucial role in the early stages of research programs that eventually had direct and substantial civilian applications. DARPA is currently a major source and financial support in artificial intelligence research. It has long been deeply involved in research on computer technology and played a decisive role in the emergence of time-sharing.

3. See the recent report by the National Research Council, *The Role of the Department of Defense in Supporting Manufacturing Technology Development* (Washington: National Academy Press, 1986), especially chapter 2. According to this report, "Seldom can contractors attribute lack of success in a competition . . . to lack of manufacturing excellence. In such an environment, suppliers focus on designing new products with new performance features, not on improving production efficiencies.

"Once contracts are awarded, moreover, the conventional commercial pressures to improve efficiency do not prevail. On the contrary, there are significant disincentives for making process improvements. Reducing the cost of manufacturing lowers the base on which profits are calculated. Short-term procurement contracts permit the government to capture the full savings from process improvements during the negotiation for each new increment of acquisition" (p. 11).

4. Richard C. Levin, "The Semiconductor Industry," chapter 2, in Richard R. Nelson, ed., *Government and Technical Progress: A Cross-Industry Analysis* (New York: Pergamon Press, 1982), p. 58. The subsequent discussion of semiconductors draws upon this useful source.

5. "By his own account, Gordon Teal . . . turned his attention to the growth of single-crystal silicon in 1951 because silicon offered the potential for fabrication of transistors capable of meeting high-temperature performance specifications for military equipment. A conscious aim of the management of Texas Instruments when it hired Teal in late 1952 was to be the first to make a silicon transistor available to the military. . . . The breakthrough in silicon secured for TI its position as the largest merchant supplier of semiconductor devices." Levin, "The Semiconductor Industry," p. 61. Similarly for the integrated circuit: "Kilby's . . . own account of his invention makes clear that TI had the military clearly, indeed exclusively, in mind during the course of early R&D work on the integrated circuit." Id., p. 62.

6. W. Edward Steinmueller, "U.S. and Japanese Integrated Circuit Industries: Industry Structure and Government Policies," Center for Economic Policy Research, Stanford University, January 16, 1986, unpublished manuscript, p. 66.

7. These issues are discussed in Leslie Brueckner with Michael Borrus, *Assessing the Commercial Impact of the VHSIC Program,* Berkeley Roundtable on the International Economy Working Paper, December 1984, pp. 56-68.

8. Senate Hearings, *Department of Defense Appropriations, Fiscal Year 1986,* S. Hrg. 99-217, Pt. 2 (Washington, D.C.: G.P.O., 1986), p. 55.

9. Of course, it is also true that the Japanese derived substantial commercial benefits from U.S. military R&D spending—in classic free-rider fashion. On a number of occasions, the Japanese identified certain generic technologies in the early stages of their development in the U.S. defense sector and redirected them toward civilian applications. This was their successful strategy, for example, in numerically controlled machine tools and semiconductors.

10. At the same time, of course, the *absolute level* of company-funded R&D has been much higher in the United States than in Japan.

10

SDI, the Soviets, and the Prospects for Arms Control

John P. Holdren

The issues raised by the Strategic Defense Initiative run the gamut from the orbital mechanics of "constellations" of killer satellites to the dynamics of the nuclear arms race, the politics of the NATO alliance, and the role of military research and development in industrial and economic policy. While I must confess to a physicist's fascination with the quantitative arcana on the technological end of this spectrum—as illustrated in the chapter by Gregory H. Canavan in this book—I am afraid that the endless debates about these technical details obscure the larger conceptual issues more often than they illuminate them. Indeed, these excursions into power-aperture products, slew rates, and adaptive optics sometimes seem designed to persuade those lacking a Ph.D. in physics or engineering that they are not entitled to an opinion about SDI and should leave the whole issue to the "experts." This phenomenon is perhaps part of what Paul Barrett had in mind when he titled an article about SDI in the *Washington Monthly* "The Revenge of the Nerds."[1]

I do not mean to say here, of course, that the technical dimensions of SDI issues can be ignored. It is important to develop an understanding of what is technically feasible and what is not, and of what the feasible approaches to the problem—if any—might cost in dollars and cents. But the toughest questions—how far and how rapidly to expand work on strategic defense from calculation and small-scale experiment toward component testing and prototype construction, and, more fundamentally, whether pursuing a more "defense-oriented" nuclear strategy than our present one is sensible at all—depend on much more than the feasibility of particular kill mechanisms or the cost-exchange ratios associated with postulated chains of defensive measures, countermeasures, and counter-countermeasures; answering them also requires our best judgment concerning the overall impact of vigorous pursuit of strategic defenses on the perceptions and reactions of our allies and adversaries, on the character of the nuclear- and conventional-arms competitions in the short term and the long, and (not unrelated, and certainly most importantly) on the probability of nuclear war.

This chapter is concerned mainly with a subset of these broader questions, namely, (a) the perceptions about and reactions to SDI by the Soviets and (b) the potential influence of the programmed continuation and possible extension of SDI, and corresponding Soviet activities, on the prospects for maintaining existing arms-control agreements and negotiating new ones. The analysis is organized into three main sections: an opening discussion of the goals and prospects of SDI, in which it is argued that the *new* elements in the program are precisely the disturbing elements; a section on Soviet reactions, in which an attempt is made to assess the genuineness of and basis for official and unofficial Soviet pronouncements on SDI; and a concluding section in which the implications of the preceding points for the prospects for arms control are briefly indicated.

What Is New About SDI Is What Is Disturbing About It

A logical starting point for an inquiry into the meaning of the uproar generated by SDI (in the United States and among U.S. allies as well as among the Soviets) is to ask what is *new* about SDI. What are the "initiatives" in the Strategic Defense Initiative?

Certainly, the idea of defenses against strategic nuclear weapons is nothing new. Indeed, as chapter 2, by Herbert F. York, points out in considerable detail,[2] research on defenses against ballistic missiles has gone on in both the United States and the USSR since the 1950s, not to mention the on-and-off deployment of the Safeguard antiballistic missile (ABM) system by the United States at a missile field in North Dakota in the 1970s, the (so far) permanent deployment by the USSR of an ABM system around Moscow starting in the 1960s, and the heavy investments of the USSR in deployed air defenses against U.S. strategic bombers.

There are, nonetheless, some new elements and emphases in the Strategic Defense Initiative, and these account for much of the reaction SDI has elicited, both pro and con. The main new elements/emphases are four:

1. An emphasis on *space-based weapons and components* (and not merely sensors but, most importantly, speed-of-light directed-energy weapons), which, it is claimed, make it attractive to attack ballistic missiles in the early phases of their flight trajectory (boost phase and immediate post-boost phase).[3]

2. A *programmed rapid expansion of research and development funding* for missile defense: from the pre-SDI levels of about $1 billion per year, to the FY 1987 request in excess of $5 billion, to projected figures for FY 1991-FY 1992 in excess of $10 billion per year. This greatly expanded level of

activities is intended to permit a national decision in the early 1990s about whether to push forward toward actual deployment of a missile-defense system.[4]

3. A prescription, within the previously described program of expanded R&D activities, for specific tests by 1988 or 1989 that will be interpreted by the USSR and by most analysts in the United States as a *violation of the Antiballistic Missile Treaty,* specifically its prohibition of testing "ABM systems or components which are sea-based, air-based, space-based, or mobile land-based" (Article V).

4. An explicit, publicly declared presidential rationale for the program, establishing its *goal to be a defense of the territories and populations of the United States and its allies effective enough to render nuclear weapons "impotent and obsolete,"* permitting the present state of deterrence by the prospect of mutual assured destruction (MAD) to be replaced by defense that assures mutual survival.[5]

Let us turn to the concerns that these novel features of the SDI have aroused.

Space Basing

SDI's emphasis on space-based weapons and components is troubling in several respects. First, it threatens to greatly accelerate, extend qualitatively, and expand quantitatively the militarization of space. Near-Earth space, out to the 36,000-kilometer altitude of synchronous-orbit satellites, is already the locus of a good many military satellites, the functions of which include wartime reconnaissance and targeting as well as peacetime intelligence gathering, treaty verification, and early warning of attacks.[6] These functions inevitably invite an interest on the part of each side in being able to attack the satellites of the other, and this antisatellite (ASAT) issue exists irrespective of developments in ballistic missile defense (BMD).[7] But the deployment in space of actual weapons as well as sensors seems certain to lead to a huge increase in the level, complexity, and cost of military operations in space, opening up new horizons in the arms race, assuring continued expansion of military budgets without apparent limit, and greatly complicating (if not entirely ruling out) the kinds of U.S.-Soviet cooperation on peaceful research and exploration in space that many have viewed as a possible key to the reduction of tensions between the two societies in the long term.

A second and at least equally troubling dimension of SDI's emphasis on space-based weapons and components is the influence of space-based missile defenses on crisis stability. Given the reasonable assumption, examined more closely later, that deployment of space-based missile defenses by the United

States will be followed (albeit, perhaps, with a five- to ten-year lag time) by similar deployments by the USSR, it is necessary to inquire into the characteristics of a situation in which both sides possess such defenses along with offensive arsenals as formidable as today's or perhaps more so. Unfortunately, the very characteristics that make it possible for space-based weapons (especially, but not only, directed-energy weapons) to attack ballistic missiles in the early phases of their trajectory—namely, long-range, high-accuracy, quick-kill capability, and the ability to engage many targets in a short time—make these weapons highly effective for attacking directly the defensive weapons of the other side. Indeed, every type of space-based "defensive" weapon so far described seems likely to be even *more* effective against the adversary's own defenses than against his ballistic missiles.[8]

For this and other reasons, any missile defense that is even partly space-based will be more effective as an *adjunct* to a first strike (where it would be used first for suppressing the defenses of the other side and then for defense against the retaliatory blow by the adversary's surviving offensive forces) than as a *defense* against a first strike. Thus the existence of space-based defenses on both sides will increase the relative advantage of "shooting first," seriously aggravating crisis instability (which arises from perceived incentives for national leaders, if a crisis reaches the point where a nuclear exchange seems conceivable, to try to reduce the damage to one's own society by firing before being fired upon).

This problem of increased preemptive pressures resulting from space-based defenses would be compounded by the hair-trigger dynamics that these defenses bring about. Any system with the mission of attacking enemy missiles in the boost phase must be activated essentially instantly upon warning that those missiles are being launched.[9] Similarly, the nearly instantaneous defense-suppression capability of the adversary's "defensive" systems makes it necessary to try to destroy those systems at the first sign that they are being activated, lest they destroy one's own defenses before these can be used. The problems of developing the needed capacity to respond virtually instantaneously to signs of attack—without at the same time creating an unacceptable chance of triggering nuclear war by mistake—are overwhelming. Certainly, there will be no time for the exercise of human judgment (except what has been preprogrammed into the computers) once a signal has been received indicating that the enemy has launched his missiles or is activating his defenses. As more than one analyst of this matter has observed, the irony is that what will be made impotent and obsolete by pursuit of such strategic defenses is not nuclear weapons but the president himself—along with his Soviet counterpart.

Rapid Expansion

SDI's programmed rapid expansion of R&D activities on ballistic missile defense has generated a variety of additional concerns, perhaps most importantly the fear (as Edward Teller himself once expressed it in another context) that a "crash program" is more likely to lead in the end to a crash than to a program.

More specifically, there is concern in the United States and among its allies that the SDI budget, as it moves toward $5 billion per year, $10 billion per year, and more, will distort first military R&D priorities and then even procurement, siphoning money away from programs of greater practicality and relevance to real military needs. Few active U.S. military officers or officials in the Department of Defense are willing to voice such concerns publicly, but they have been widely expressed in private in the United States and publicly by Europeans.[10]

There is also concern that there are not enough sensible SDI R&D projects to absorb the expanding funding that has been programmed. Most independent analysts and a good many insiders argue that the things the United States ought to be doing in research on ballistic missile defense could be done for between $1.5 billion and $2.5 billion per year,[11] less than the $3 billion being spent in FY 1986 and much less than the $5.4 billion requested for FY 1987. (These last figures include SDI spending in the Department of Energy (DOE) as well as in the Department of Defense; the DOE component, often omitted from official and unofficial tabulations, was about $0.3 billion in FY 1986 and $0.6 billion in the FY 1987 request.) Of course, the work on SDI will expand to consume whatever funds become available; but what this means is that much money will be wasted on wholly unproductive and even preposterous projects. Can anyone seriously believe, for example, that SDI money now being spent on the design of fast-pulsed, orbiting *fusion* reactors (no misprint—fusion, not fission) as power sources for space weapons is a sound investment?

Meanwhile, many facets of nonmilitary R&D as well as more sensible military R&D efforts are critically and increasingly short of funds. Support of nonmilitary R&D has fallen from 52 percent of all federal R&D support in FY 1980 to 32 percent in the FY 1987 request,[12] and SDI is now a significant driving force behind this continuing trend. Among the victims of the R&D funding squeeze have been energy research (including fusion, fission, fossil, and renewable energy supplies, and conservation); research on resources and environment; health research; and nonmilitary space research. Long-term adverse impacts on economic productivity/competitiveness and other dimensions of national well-being are possible—to which SDI proponents respond, "Let them eat spinoff."[13]

Potential Violation of the ABM Treaty

Official pronouncements from the White House and the Department of Defense continue to insist that SDI is being and will continue to be carried out in full compliance with the ABM Treaty, even though (purportedly) the Soviets are themselves violating it.[14] These official pronouncements go on to indicate that before any decision is made to go beyond the presently defined SDI program in ways that would necessitate abrogation or renegotiation of the ABM Treaty, there will be full consultation with our allies and with the Soviets. (It is asserted at the same time that we do not propose to give the USSR a "veto" over the future direction of our program.)

These assurances have failed to diminish very much the widespread concern about the threats posed by SDI to the ABM Treaty, for at least two reasons. First, official descriptions of what is already part of the SDI program indicate that the United States proposes to test, by 1988 or 1989, technology certain to be considered by the Soviets (as well as by many analysts in the West) as air-based or space-based components of an ABM system, the testing of which is explicitly prohibited by Article V of the ABM Treaty. (Article V, Part 1, reads in full: "Each Party undertakes not to develop, test, or deploy ABM systems or components which are sea-based, air-based, space-based, or mobile land-based.") The most widely discussed example of this class of problems is the Airborne Optical System (also called the Airborne Optical Adjunct), initially scheduled to be tested as early as 1987 but now delayed by a year or more. The administration's contention that this system will not be a "component" but rather a "subcomponent" of an ABM system (the latter term being one that does not appear anywhere in the ABM Treaty) displays a flair for the sort of creative reinterpretation of treaty boundaries of which Americans have so often accused the Soviets in the past.

Even more seriously, then National Security Advisor Robert MacFarlane announced in 1985 a radical reinterpretation of the ABM Treaty's provisions governing ABM systems based on "new physical principles" (to be contrasted with ABM interceptor missiles, ABM launchers, and ABM radars as envisioned in 1972). This remarkable interpretation holds that Article V, Part 1, of the Treaty just quoted does not actually restrict systems employing, for example, beam weapons and tracking systems based on infrared detectors. The justification for this view is said to be Agreed Statement D, appended to the Treaty:

> In order to insure fulfillment of the obligation not to deploy ABM systems and their components except as provided in Article III of the Treaty, the Parties agree that in the event ABM systems based on other physical principles and including components capable of substituting for ABM interceptor missiles, ABM launchers, or ABM radars are created in the future, specific limitations on such systems and their components would be subject to discussion in accordance with Article XIII and agreement in accordance with Article XIV of the Treaty.[15]

But the wording of Agreed Statement D, the negotiating record, and the record of the ratification hearings in the U.S. Senate all make clear that Agreed

Statement D is intended to strengthen Article III's restrictions on what sort of ABM system may be deployed at the two fixed sites (later reduced to one) permitted to each side, *not* to loosen Article V's restrictions on mobile systems.[16]

Since the original reinterpretation by MacFarlane, Secretary of State George Shultz and Arms Control Advisor Paul Nitze have confirmed the administration's view that this new "less restrictive" interpretation of the ABM Treaty is justified. In an apparent attempt to dampen the resulting uproar, however, they have added that the United States nonetheless will continue to comply with the original "more restrictive" interpretation for the time being. This latter pronouncement offers scant consolation to supporters of the treaty, of course: it is only logical to suppose that "the time being" will end at the moment the United States is ready to test an SDI component that would violate the usual ("restrictive") interpretation of Article V.

If the United States persists in its reinterpretation and acts accordingly, the total collapse of the ABM Treaty becomes a likelihood, if not a certainty. Given the central role of the treaty in the web of arms-control agreements that today provide at least a modicum of restraint on the nuclear arms competition, the growing possibility of its collapse is understandably the cause of great concern. The linkages between the ABM Treaty and arms-control prospects more generally are treated in more detail later.

The Presidential Vision

The presidential vision of an escape from dependence on deterrence by the threat of mutual destruction is superficially appealing. Who would *not* prefer mutual survival, if it were available? Unfortunately, the condition of mutual assured destruction is not a doctrine that has been chosen deliberately and thus can be deliberately renounced. It is a result of the characteristics of modern nuclear arsenals—the enormous power of individual nuclear weapons, the huge numbers of them that exist, and the tremendous diversity of delivery systems available to bring them to their targets. Wishing for an escape from the mutual vulnerability created by the nature of these arsenals is understandable, but wishing cannot bring it about; neither will the expenditure of tens or hundreds of billions of dollars, if the escape is simply not there to be bought.

Nearly all technical authorities, including most of those who are working on SDI with the taxpayers' money, acknowledge the impracticability of the president's goal of population defense: the degree of perfection required of the defense, given that a single penetrating thermonuclear warhead can destroy the heart of any city, is simply out of reach. All that SDI might be able to achieve is a partial defense of strategic nuclear forces and other military targets—which are much harder to destroy and hence easier to defend than cities and people.

SDI proponents who embrace the goal of partial defense of military forces consider it a way to strengthen deterrence, not to escape from it. By continuing to insist that this is *not* what SDI is about, President Reagan and Secretary of Defense Caspar Weinberger put themselves in the awkward position of appearing either technically naive or politically dishonest. (Secretary Weinberger's FY 1987 Report to the Congress, for example, contains the statement that "the defense that might evolve from the research program will not be intended to defend our strategic weapons systems."[17]) Certainly there is ample political reason to misrepresent the goal of SDI, given that the U.S. Congress and the public are much less likely to support a program to defend nuclear weapons than one to defend people.

The lack of congressional and public enthusiasm for defenses of nuclear weapons is well warranted. Such defenses are not necessary except under a highly exaggerated conception of Soviet first-strike capabilities; and, if they were necessary, they could be successful only against a constrained offense (meaning that arms control would be required as an adjunct). Such defenses would not, in any case, require the space-based, directed-energy weapons emphasized in SDI; they could be provided by off-the-shelf technology employing simple kinetic-energy weapons for short-range defense of hardened missile silos and command centers. Protection of land-based retaliatory weapons could be provided most quickly and cheaply of all, moreover, by arms control alone—reducing, by agreement, the ratios of counterforce warheads on each side to vulnerable weapons on the other, and dispensing with the costs, risks, and uncertainties of deploying defenses.

By ignoring these realities and holding out the hope of a comprehensive technological fix for the nuclear danger, the president and his associates are diverting attention from important and tractable approaches to the problem, both technological and political. Most importantly, and perhaps not entirely coincidentally, they are undermining Western public support for arms control by offering people the appealing prospect that a defensive shield will make the complex and difficult process of negotiations superfluous. Without the public support for arms control that is being thus eroded, agreements seem unlikely even assuming that the Soviets are willing.

Why Have the Soviets Made Such a Fuss About SDI?

Many Westerners, including those who share some or all of the concerns just described, nevertheless have been moved to wonder aloud and in print why the Soviet reaction to SDI has been so intense. After all, the Soviets have devoted vastly more resources than has the United States to air defense; they maintain the one operational site permitted by the ABM Treaty, whereas that of the United States was dismantled a decade ago; and the size of their research program on directed-energy weapons (presumably for ABM as well as antisatellite applications) is generally regarded to be larger than our own, if not necessarily more productive.[18] How dare they then be so shrill in their condemnations of SDI?

Even the most studied and professional assessments of Soviet behavior and rhetoric cannot be fully persuasive—it is even harder to know what is in the heads of the Soviet leadership than to know what is in the heads of our own, and the latter task is not always easy. My own qualifications for the job, moreover, are not even those of a professional Sovietologist; I am simply a part-time professional defense analyst and amateur Soviet-watcher with fairly frequent opportunities to talk with informed Soviets. Based on use of those opportunities over the past few years and on picking the brains of professional Sovietologists, however, I think I have gained a reasonably coherent if not unassailable picture of what is behind the Soviet reactions to SDI.

First of all, while it may be true that the Soviets are never quite as alarmed and surprised by our actions as they would like us to think they are, there are at least five good reasons to think that much of their alarm in the current case is genuine:[19]

1. The Soviet leadership seems basically satisfied with—or at least re-signed to—a condition of effective equivalence in strategic nuclear forces (meaning offsetting advantages and disadvantages in different categories of weapons, with no net usable advantage to either side overall). Soviet leaders would prefer to maintain this form of parity relatively cheaply rather than relatively expensively, and they see the potential loss of the ABM Treaty as likely to open up an unlimited and fantastically expensive arms race.

2. The Soviets respect and fear American technological prowess, and they regard SDI as an invitation to an expensive, head-to-head technological competition in an arena where U.S. advantages in sensors, high-speed computing, pointing and tracking, and so on give the United States a formidable edge. This and point (1) are especially compelling in light of the Soviets' acknowledged recognition that they must give higher priority to modernizing the nonmilitary sectors of their economy over the next decade and more—and hence lower priority to the military.

3. The Soviet leadership resents SDI's thrust at the very heart of the USSR's strategic power—the land-based ICBMs that contain some 70 percent of her strategic warheads and represent the only category of intercontinental-range forces in which the USSR is not markedly inferior to the United States. (The space-based systems that are the centerpiece of SDI apparently would be more effective against intercontinental ballistic missiles (ICBMs) than against

submarine-launched ballistic missiles (SLBMs) fired at relatively close range on depressed trajectories. Most of the weapons being explored under SDI would have little or no capability against strategic bombers and cruise missiles.) Some Soviets may even regard SDI as (in part) yet another attempt by the United States to force the USSR to reconfigure its strategic forces in line with U.S. preferences—that is, away from land-based ICBMs.

4. The Soviets seem genuinely alarmed by the prospect of diminished crisis stability and reduced reaction times in the event that boost-phase and other space-based defenses are deployed (as discussed earlier). Reduced reaction times and concomitant pressure to delegate and/or automate launch authorization are particularly sensitive issues for Soviet leaders, who traditionally have been reluctant to delegate authority over nuclear launch and who have been mistrustful of automation. (The latter syndrome is sometimes attributed to the inferiority of Soviet electronic hardware, although the performance of U.S. computers and other automated systems would seem to give little cause for complacency on the U.S. side, either.)

5. Soviet military analysts may be concerned that spinoff from SDI onto the conventional battlefield will devalue much of the huge Soviet arsenal of conventional weapons. To a considerable extent, improved sensors, "smart" weapons, and other upgrades in the capacity to acquire and use information about the battlefield already have devalued the heavy investment of Warsaw Pact forces in tanks and armored personnel carriers. Insofar as SDI-related research and development might accelerate this trend, it gives SDI the appearance of a two-pronged attack on *both* of the main currencies of Soviet military power: not only the ICBMs, but also conventional armor.

It can be argued—and often is—that anything the Soviets are against we should be in favor of, in which case these five points provide the best possible rationale for pushing full speed ahead with SDI. Both simple logic and the history of the nuclear arms race should give pause to proponents of this view, however: in a situation wherein technology, politics, and geography combine to necessitate pinning one's security in substantial part on restraint by one's adversary, trying to maximize the adversary's discomfort is a questionable strategy; and the history of the nuclear era can be read as the continuing generation of increasing mutual insecurity through the pursuit of individual advantage.[20] Of the five Soviet concerns just listed, the only one that provides even a minimally plausible rationale for trying to make their fear into a reality is the fifth—the neutralization of certain Soviet advantages in conventional forces by the use of SDI-related technologies on the battlefield. If that makes sense, however, it makes even more sense to pursue these applications directly rather than as spinoff from an SDI program that has no sound rationale of its own.

Beyond these concerns, Soviet spokesmen routinely insist that SDI is part of a systematic U.S. attempt to reestablish the strategic nuclear superiority once enjoyed by the United States, and, more specifically, that in combination with such "counterforce" weapons as the Pershing II, the MX, and the D-5 (Trident II), the United States is seeking a preemptive first-strike capability against the USSR.[21] These claims are vigorously denied not only by the Reagan administration but also by many analysts in the middle of the road and to the left of center in the American defense debate. It is not in the "American character," it is said, to seek superiority or to strike first. Is it possible, none-theless, that the Soviets actually believe these accusations?

Alas, it is all too possible that many Soviet leaders and analysts at least genuinely fear—even if they are not completely convinced—that the United States is pursuing superiority and would like a first-strike capability, if not to execute such a strike then at least to intimidate the Soviets with the prospect. In the first place, just as worst-case analysts in the West comb the voluminous Soviet military literature to find (selected) evidence of the most belligerent attitudes and blood-chilling war plans, so it may be supposed that Soviet worst-case analysts have found ample grist for their mill in the writings of the likes of Colin Gray and even in such mainstream documents as the 1980 Republican platform on which Ronald Reagan was first elected (which prom-ises to restore American military superiority over the USSR). Even if the Soviets believe that the American people themselves have little interest in regaining superiority and even less interest in paying for it, they may well conclude, from the Reagan administration's systematic misrepresentation of the East-West military balance while arguing for increased defense spending,[22] that the administration is striving for superiority while trying to persuade the public it must pay to catch up.

The historical evidence on the degree of restraint imposed by the Amer-ican character, moreover, is complex and mixed. We did not mount a nuclear attack on the USSR when we had a nuclear monopoly, but it is far from clear that we would not have done so if their provocations in that period had been greater; and we did, after all, use nuclear weapons against Japan. Whatever one may think about the American character, moreover, it is impossible for Soviet leaders (or anyone else) to suppose that the actions of a few key decision makers under unprecedented pressures could be predicted on such a basis. Soviet thinking about what the United States might do is necessarily shaped at least as much by U.S. capabilities as by their judgments about the American national character (as is true of *U.S.* thinking about what the *USSR* might do).

Surely the most troublesome point for the Soviets, in pondering whether the United States really seeks nuclear superiority, is that NATO's official pos-ture of first use of nuclear weapons "if necessary" requires that our initiation of nuclear-weapons use—and our willingness to escalate from battlefield to theater and strategic nuclear weapons—be credible. That is why a crisis in confidence in the U.S. nuclear guarantee to our allies was caused by (belated) recognition in the mid-1970s of the USSR's achievement of strategic parity, and it is why many NATO defense specialists considered the deployment of Pershing II and ground-launched cruise missiles (GLCMs) in Europe essential—that is, to increase the credibility of the U.S. option/intention to escalate.[23] Why shouldn't the Soviets suppose, in these circumstances, that the United States wants strategic defense as a way to restore nuclear superiority and hence credibility that it would use nuclear weapons to defend its allies?

The foregoing is not to argue, or course, that the Soviets' motivations in pursuing their own strategic defense programs should seem any more benign to the United States than U.S. motivations do to them. Presumably they would prefer Soviet strategic superiority if they could have it, and are most determined in any case that U.S. superiority not be restored. I should think they have seen their own strategic defense programs as providing some small chance of achieving strategic superiority over the United States; an essential hedge against the United States achieving strategic superiority over them; and a fringe benefit in the form of a possibly significant degree of protection against the less capable French, British, and Chinese strategic forces. If the choice is mutual restraint or all-out competition in defensive weaponry, however, it seems reasonably clear that the Soviets are now opting for mutual restraint.

Implications for Arms Control

I believe that the Soviets are now ready to strike a major deal that would cut off significant areas of competition in the nuclear arms race—not, of course, because they have had a sudden attack of altruism but because they recognize that neither their military nor their economic self-interest is served by continuing competition in these areas. Such a deal would rule out or strongly constrain some of the most dangerous aspects of an expanding military competition in space and would reduce offensive strategic forces, emphasizing (if done sensibly) the ratios of counterforce warheads to vulnerable targets on the other side. If recent Soviet proposals in Geneva and in the press are any indication, the deal also could include limits on shorter-range nuclear and conventional forces as well. A bargain of this sort would be strongly in the interests of the United States as well as the USSR.

Retaining the ABM Treaty is essential to the prospects of achieving this major arms-control bargain. As noted earlier, the administration's "less restrictive" interpretation of that treaty is a farce—inconsistent with the wording of the treaty, the interpretations in the negotiating record, the interpretations in the ratification process, and the interpretations of every post-1972 administration, including this one, until late 1985. Continued observance of the straightforward ("restrictive") interpretation of the ABM Treaty would rule out pursuing those parts of SDI which involve testing air-based and space-based components of ABM systems, but it would not rule out continued research on strategic defense short of such testing. The Soviet leadership probably never meant as any more than bluster its early insistence that all SDI "research" would have to be stopped for arms control to go forward, and in any case it is not holding to that absurd position now; it clearly is prepared to settle for continued adherence to the ABM Treaty as the only limitation of research.

Hanging on to the ABM Treaty into the 1990s and beyond will require more than reaffirmation of the existing document, however. A variety of inter-connections between ASAT and ABM technologies and incentives make it impossible to constrain either ASAT or ABM in the long run without con-straining both. In the absence of limits on ASAT activity, ABM Treaty prohibi-tions on testing ABM components could be at least partly circumvented by using ASAT tests as a cover; any space-based or pop-up ABM system would be likely to have formidable ASAT capabilities, as would some kinds of ground-based ABM systems; and the existence of space-based ABM systems would inevitably stimulate efforts in ASAT capabilities for attacking the space-based ABM components. An ASAT agreement is therefore essential to augment the ABM Treaty. Sensible approaches to this problem exist and are adequately verifiable.[24]

If, on the other hand, the ABM Treaty collapses—whether by radical reinterpretation, abrogation, or the accumulated effects of piecemeal erosion on both sides—the unratified but still substantially observed SALT II limits will quickly follow it into oblivion, ripping the lid from offensive forces while both sides pursue the quickest, surest insurance against the undermining of their deterrents by the defenses of the other side.[25] (President Reagan's decision in November 1986 to exceed the SALT II numerical limits may have been a bargaining tactic designed to help elicit a replacement agreement that actually would lower those limits; but, at least equally likely, it could represent a genuine "preemptive attack" on offensive limitations, which, should they be abolished, would seem to invalidate the argument that we must retain the ABM Treaty in order to preserve them).

Given the sort of offense-defense arms race likely to follow the loss of both the ABM Treaty and the SALT II limits, even the venerable (1963) Partial Test Ban probably would not long survive the pressures to test defen-sive and antidefensive use of nuclear weapons in the atmosphere and in space. Testing (or basing) of nuclear weapons in space also would mean the end of the Outer Space Treaty of 1967. The effects of all of this on the nonproliferation regime, including the Non-Proliferation Treaty (NPT) of 1968, can only be guessed but are unlikely to be benign. The NPT, after all, is considered by most of the 120-plus non-weapons-state signatories to be a bargain in which they refrain from acquiring nuclear weapons in exchange for "negotiations in good faith on effective measures relating to cessation of the nuclear arms race at an early date" (Article VI) by the superpowers. The massive offense-defense arms race in prospect if the ABM Treaty and the SALT II limits disappear will be viewed, with justification, as making a mockery of this NPT commitment.

Issues concerning Soviet compliance with existing arms-control agreements are being blown out of proportion by the Reagan administration and should not be allowed to serve as an excuse for U.S. breakout from the ABM Treaty or from other agreements.[26] Both sides have tried to stretch treaty language and loopholes to suit their needs in various instances. The U.S. phased-array early-warning radars under construction at Thule, Greenland, and Fylingdales, Scotland, for example, are just as clearly in technical violation of the ABM Treaty as the Soviet radar at Krasnoyarsk. (The USSR has claimed that the ABM Treaty's loophole allowing large phased-array radars for space-tracking purposes covers Krasnoyarsk; the United States has asserted a right— not stated in the treaty—to "modernize" mechanically steered radars deployed before the treaty was signed by replacing them with large phased-array radars— in locations where the treaty forbids large phased-array radars to be.)

The most frequently cited complaints about Soviet compliance with the unratified SALT II Treaty involve encryption of telemetry in missile tests and the contention that the Soviet SS-25 ICBM is a forbidden second "new type" rather than a permitted upgrade of the SS-13, as the Soviets claim. Both issues are inherently ambiguous:

1. Encryption of missile-test telemetry is permitted by SALT II unless it interferes with verification of compliance with the treaty's provisions (which relate mainly to numbers of launchers, numbers of warheads, and throwweight of new or modified missiles). The United States has refused to tell the Soviets just how their (partial) encryption is interfering with U.S. ability to verify Soviet compliance with the treaty, on the grounds that doing so would reveal too much about U.S. surveillance capabilities. Thus the Soviets are able to claim, with some justification, that the United States has not demonstrated a violation on their part.

2. The SS-25 meets most of the treaty's criteria for being considered an "upgrade" of the SS-13, but the United States contends that the SS-25's throwweight exceeds, by more than the permitted 5 percent, that of the SS-13.[27] There are ambiguities in the definition and measurement of throwweight, however, and these are particularly troublesome in the case of experimental launches, as opposed to tests of operational missiles. The U.S. government has not revealed enough of its evidence on the SS-25/SS-13 throwweight issue to make a convincing case. The track record of U.S.-government assertions about Soviet compliance in other cases has not been so good that one can take this one on faith.[28]

Most importantly, the putative violations of SALT II are peripheral to the most significant and unambiguous provisions of the agreement, which are the numerical limits on launchers and warheads. These have continued to be observed by both sides, with the Soviets having dismantled more than a thousand ICBM launchers and ten missile submarines since 1974 to stay within the SALT I and SALT II limits, while the United States has dismantled fifty ICBM launchers and at least seven missile submarines to do so. (The Reagan administration announced in mid-1986 that two more U.S. missile subs were being dismantled for military and economic reasons rather than for reasons of compliance with SALT II limits, but the effect was to keep the United States in compliance until November 1986.)

In the cases of the ABM Treaty, the SALT treaties, and other arms-control agreements, the damage done by the loophole stretching and ambiguity exploitation on both sides so far is neither significant militarily nor beyond being patched up in the Standing Consultative Commission[29]—given only that both sides *want* to maintain and strengthen the arms-control regime. Both sides should very much want to do so. To give up the whole framework and approach of arms control in the expectation that SDI will somehow render arms control superfluous would surely rank as the surpassing blunder of the nuclear age.

Notes

1. Paul Barrett, "Star Wars: Revenge of the Nerds," *Washington Monthly,* Vol. 17, No. 12, January, 1986, pp. 50-52.

2. See also Alexander Flax, "Ballistic Missile Defense: Concepts and History," in F. Long, D. Hafner, and J. Boutwell, eds., *Weapons in Space* (New York: Norton, 1985), pp. 33-52.

3. See Sydney D. Drell, Philip J. Farley, and David Holloway, *The Reagan Strategic Defense Initiative: A Technical, Political, and Arms Control Assessment* (Cambridge, Mass.: Ballinger, 1985); and Office of Technology Assessment of the U.S. Congress, *Ballistic Missile Defense Technologies* (Washington, D.C.: Government Printing Office, June, 1985).

4. See Richard D. Delauer, "Statement on the President's Strategic Defense Initiative" (before the Subcommittee on Research and Development of the Committee on Armed Services, U.S. House of Representatives, 98th Congress, 1 March 1984), Washington, D.C.: U.S. Department of Defense (reprinted as Appendix C in Drell et al., *The Reagan Strategic Defense Initiative*); and Thomas K. Longstreth, John E. Pike, and John B. Rhinelander, *The Impact of U.S. and Soviet Ballistic Missile Defense Programs on the ABM Treaty* (Washington, D.C.: National Campaign to Save the ABM Treaty, March, 1985).

5. Ronald Reagan, speech on defense spending and defensive technology, March 23, 1983. *Weekly Compilation of Presidential Documents,* Vol. 19, No. 12, pp. 423-66 (reprinted in part as Appendix A in Drell et al., *The Reagan Strategic Defense Initiative.*)

6. Herbert F. York, "Nuclear Deterrence and the Military Uses of Space," in Long, et al., *Weapons in Space,* pp. 17-32, and Paul Stares, "U.S. and Soviet Military Space Programs: A comparative Assessment," in id., pp. 127-46.

7. Kurt Gottfried and Richard Ned Lebow, "Anti-Satellite Weapons: Weighing the Risks," in Long et al., *Weapons in Space,* pp. 147-70; and Ashton B. Carter, "The Relationship of ASAT and BMD Systems," in id., pp. 171-89.

8. Richard L. Garwin, "Space Defense—The Impossible Dream," *NATO's Sixteen Nations* (Moench Publications), Vol. 31, No. 2 (April 1986), pp. 22-25.

9. Hans A. Bethe and Richard L. Garwin, "Appendix A: New BMD Technologies," in Long et al., *Weapons in Space,* pp. 331-68.

10. Barnard Jackson, "The Roles of Strategic and Theatre Nuclear Forces in NATO Strategy: Part I," in *Power and Policy: Doctrine, the Alliance and Arms Control,* Adelphi Papers 205 (London: International Institute for Strategic Studies, Spring 1986), pp. 47-56.

11. Sydney D. Drell, Thomas H. Johnson, John A. Ernest, Philip J. Farley, John S. Foster, Jr., Richard L. Garwin, Sidney N. Graybeal, John W. Lewis, Wolfgang K.H. Panofsky, Theodore A. Postol, Condoleeza Rice, Melvin A. Ruderman, and George C. Smith, "Strategic Missile Defense: Necessities, Prospects, and Dangers in the Near Term," Special Report of the Center for International Security and Arms Control (Stanford: Stanford University, April 1985).

12. Office of Management and Budget, *Historical Tables, Budget of the U.S. Government* (Washington, D.C.: Government Printing Office, February 5, 1986).

13. For a general discussion of this issue, see chapter 9 in this book, by Nathan Rosenberg; John Tirman, ed., *The Militarization of High Technology* (Cambridge, Mass.: Ballinger, 1984); and John P. Holdren and F. Bailey Green, "Military Spending, the SDI, and Government Support of Research and Development: Effects on the Economy and the Health of American Science," Federation of American Scientists, Public Interest Report, Vol. 39, No. 7 (September 1986).

14. Caspar W. Weinberger, *FY1987 Annual Report of the Secretary of Defense to the Congress* (Washington, D.C.: Government Printing Office, February 5, 1986).

15. United States Arms Control and Disarmament Agency, *Arms Control and Disarmament Agreements* (Washington, D.C.: Government Printing Office, 1982), p. 143.

16. Abram Chayes, Antonia Handler Chayes, Eliot Spitzer, "Space Weapons: The Legal Context," in Long et al., *Weapons in Space,* pp. 193-218.

17. Weinberger, *FY1987 Annual Report,* p. 287.

18. See Reagan, speech on defense spending, March 23, 1983; and John Pike, "Assessing the Soviet ABM Program," in E.P. Thompson, ed., *Star Wars* (London: Penguin, 1985), pp. 50-67.

19. See David Holloway, "The Strategic Defense Initiative and the Soviet Union," in Long et al., *Weapons in Space,* pp. 257-78; and Seweryn Bialer and Joan Afferica, "The Genesis of Gorbachev's World," *Foreign Affairs,* Vol. 64, No. 3, 1986, pp. 605-44.

20. John P. Holdren, "The Dynamics of the Nuclear Arms Race: History, Status, Prospects," chapter 2 in Avner Cohen and Steven Lee, eds., *Nuclear Weapons and the Future of Humanity* (Totowa, N.J.: Rowman and Allanheld, 1985), pp. 41-83.

21. Committee of Soviet Scientists for Peace Against the Nuclear Threat, *Space Strike Arms and International Security* (Moscow: Novosty Press Agency Publishing House, October 1985), p. 66.

22. See Holdren, "The Dynamics of the Nuclear Arms Race"; id., "Why Does Reagan Say America Is Behind?" *Christian Science Monitor,* April 12, 1985, p. 23; and

Tom Gervasi, *The Myth of Soviet Military Supremacy* (New York: Harper and Row, 1986).

23. McGeorge Bundy, George F. Kennan, Robert S. McNamara, and Gerald Smith, "Nuclear Weapons and the Atlantic Alliance," *Foreign Affairs,* Vol. 60, No. 4 (Spring 1982), pp. 753-68; and Richard Burt, "NATO and Nuclear Deterrence," in Marsha Olive and Jeffrey Porro, eds., *Nuclear Weapons in Europe* (Lexington, Mass.: Lexington Books, 1983), pp. 109-19.

24. See Gottfried and Lebow, "Anti-Satellite Weapons," and Michael M. May, "Safeguarding Our Military Space Systems," *Science,* Vol. 232, (April 18, 1986), pp. 336-40.

25. McGeorge Bundy, George F. Kennan, Robert S. McNamara, and Gerald Smith, "The President's Choice: Star Wars or Arms Control," *Foreign Affairs,* Vol. 63, No. 2, Winter 1984/85, pp. 264-78.

26. For the administration's point of view, see U.S. Department of Defense, *Soviet Military Power* (Washington, D.C.: Government Printing Office, 1986) and U.S. Arms Control and Disarmament Agency (ACDA), *Soviet Noncompliance* (Washington, D.C.: ACDA, February 1, 1986). For counterarguments, see Gervasi, *The Myth of Soviet Military Supremacy*; John E. Pike and Jonathan Rich, "Charges of Treaty Violations: Much Less Than Meets the Eye," *F.A.S. Public Interest Report,* Vol. 37, No. 3 (March 1984); and Phillip R. Trimble, "Soviet Violations of Arms Control Agreements: A Legal Perspective," Los Angeles Center for International and Strategic Affairs, Working Paper No. 53 (November 1985).

27. U.S. ACDA, *Soviet Noncompliance.*

28. See Gervasi, *The Myth of Soviet Military Supremacy,* and Pike and Rich, "Charges of Treaty Violations."

29. See Trimble, "Soviet Violations of Arms Control Agreements."

Index

Conference Participants

Harold Agnew, GA Technologies

George E. Brown, Jr., member of the House of Representatives (Democrat)

Robert Buchheim, former U.S. Representative to the Standing Consultative Commission

Gregory H. Canavan, Los Alamos National Laboratory

John Cartwright, M.P., member of the House of Commons (SDP), United Kingdom

Steve Cohen, University of California, Berkeley

Ernst-Otto Czempiel, University of Frankfurt, F.R.G.

Richard DeLauer, Orion Group Ltd.

James Digby, California Seminar

Maurice Eisenstein, Rand Corporation

David Elliott, Science Applications International Corporation

Guenther Frommel, Nixdorf Computer Center Corporation

Allen Greb, Institute on Global Conflict and Cooperation, University of California

Achim Von Heinitz, Stiftung Wissenschaft und Politik, Ebenhausen, Federal Republic of Germany

Francois Heisbourg, Thomson International, Paris

Brett Henry, Institute on Global Conflict and Cooperation, University of California

John P. Holdren, University of California, Berkeley

Cecil I. Hudson, Jr., Titan Systems, Inc.

Lothar Ibrugger, member of the Bundestag (SPD), Federal Republic of Germany

Michael Intriligator, Center for International and Strategic Affairs, University of California, Los Angeles

Bhupendra Jasani, Stockholm International Peace Research Institute, Sweden

Frank Jenkins, Center for National Security Negotiations, Science Applications International Corporation

Gunter Joetze, Consulate General of the Federal Republic of Germany, Los Angeles

Gerald W. Johnson, TRW, Inc.

Harry Kreisler, Institute of International Studies, University of California, Berkeley

Sanford Lakoff, University of California, San Diego

Stephen Larrabee, Institute for East-West Security Studies, New York

Pierre Lellouche, Institut Français des Relations Internationales, Paris

Steven Maaranen, Los Alamos National Laboratory

Michael May, Lawrence Livermore National Laboratory

Giancarlo Monterisi, RAI (Radiotelevisione Italia), Rome

Michael Moodie, Special Assistant to the U.S. Ambassador, NATO

Benoit Morel, Center for International Security and Arms Control, Stanford University

Harold Mueller, Center for European Policy Studies, Brussels

Peter Schulze, Friedrich Ebert Stiftung, Bonn, Federal Republic of Germany

James Skelly, Institute on Global Conflict and Cooperation, University of California

Alan Sweedler, San Diego State University

Trevor Taylor, North Straffordshire Polytechnic, Stoke-on-Trent, United Kingdom

John C. Toomay, Major General (Ret.), U.S. Air Force

Brigitte Traupe, member of the Bundestag (SPD), Federal Republic of Germany

Randy Willoughby, Institute on Global Conflict and Cooperation, University of California

Roy Woodruff, Lawrence Livermore National Laboratory

Herbert F. York, Institute on Global Conflict and Cooperation, University of California

David S. Yost, Naval Postgraduate School, Monterey

About the Authors

Gregory H. Canavan is assistant physics division leader at the Los Alamos National Laboratory. A graduate of the Air Force Academy, he has served in the Departments of Energy and Defense. In 1983 he was a member of the Defensive Technologies Study Team, appointed by President Reagan to examine the feasibility of strategic defense, and has since written a series of papers on the subject.

Ernst-Otto Czempiel is professor of international relations at the University of Frankfurt and director of the Peace Research Institute, Frankfurt. He has written numerous books on German and U.S. foreign relations, the most recent being *Friedensstrategien: Systemwandel durch Internationale Organisationen, Demokratisierung und Wirtschaft* (1986).

François Heisbourg is director of the International Institute for Strategic Studies in London. He was previously a vice president of the French electronics firm Thomson. He is a graduate of the Ecole Nationale d'Administration in Paris. As a member of the French diplomatic corps, he served as international security adviser to the minister of defense from 1981 to 1984. He has written numerous articles on European defense issues and is the coauthor of *La Puce, les Hommes et la Bombe* (1986).

John P. Holdren is professor of energy and resources at the University of California, Berkeley; chairman of the Federation of American Scientists; and a member of the Executive Committee of the International Pugwash Conferences on Science and World Affairs. He has written extensively on various aspects of nuclear technology and public policy.

Sanford Lakoff is professor of political science at the University of California, San Diego. He has written extensively on science and politics and is coauthor of *Science and the Nation* (1960) and *Energy and American Values* (1982), and editor of *Knowledge and Power* (1964) and *Science and Ethical Responsibility* (1980).

Pierre Lellouche is associate director of the *Institut Français des Relations Internationales* (IFRI) and a consultant for *Le Point* and *Newsweek*. He is also a consultant to the French government and to a number of international institutions. He holds a master's degree and a doctorate from Harvard Law School as well as degrees in law and political science from Paris University and the Institut d'Etudes Politiques. He has written extensively on Western security issues. His most recent publications are *L'Avenir de la Guerre* (1985) and *La SDI et la Securité de l'Europe* (ed.), IFRI (1986).

Nathan Rosenberg is professor of economics at Stanford University. He directed the Stanford Program on Public Policy from 1979 to 1983 and chaired the Program on Values, Technology and Society from 1976 to 1978. Most recently, he coauthored *How the West Grew Rich* (1986) and coedited *International Technology Transfer: Concepts, Measures, and Comparisons* (1985).

Trevor Taylor is principal lecturer in international relations at the North Staffordshire Polytechnic in England. He received his Ph.D. from the London School of Economics. His most recent publication is *European Defense Cooperation* (1984).

Randy Willoughby is a Ph.D. candidate at the University of California, Berkeley, a research associate at the Institute on Global Conflict and Cooperation at the University of California, and lecturer at the University of San Diego.

Herbert F. York is professor of physics at the University of California, San Diego, and director of the University of California Institute on Global Conflict and Cooperation. He was the first director of defense research and engineering in the U.S. Department of Defense (1958-1961) and U.S. representative in the Comprehensive Test Ban negotiations from 1979 to 1981. He is the author of *Race to Oblivion: A Participant's View of the Arms Race* (1970) and *The Advisors: Oppenheimer, Teller, and the Superbomb* (1976).

David S. Yost is associate professor in the Department of National Security Affairs at the Naval Postgraduate School. He has been in Washington, D.C., since 1984, both as a special assistant in the Department of Defense and as a Fellow at the Woodrow Wilson International Center for Scholars. He has contributed to numerous volumes on the subject of European defense and is the author of *France's Deterrent Posture and Security in Europe,* Adelphi Papers 194 and 195 (Winter 1984/85).